Praise from

(Selected excerpts here. See full end(

M000285347

Looking for inspiration and guidance to plant churches and make multiplying disciples? *Stubborn Perseverance* is the book for you!

Ted Esler, President of Missio Nexus

Stubborn Perseverance isn't just a manual, it's a record of the inner workings of a real church-planting movement that invites readers to join the exciting adventure of launching such movements.

David Garrison, Executive Director of Global Gates, *A Wind in the House of Islam*

Stubborn Perseverance is one of the most practical resources yet for those called to ignite disciple-making movements.

Steve Richardson, President of Pioneers-USA

Stubborn Perseverance employs masterful characters, with whom we can all identify, to lead us to a clear understanding of how movement principles advance the gospel in real-world situations.

Doug Sullivan, Regional Leader for The Navigators

Stubborn Perseverance brings alive the key elements of launching a movement and helps one understand what it "looks like" to become a disciple-maker who makes disciple-makers. Every critical element for launching movements is well illustrated here.

Kent Parks, President of Act Beyond

Stubborn Perseverance offers the best hope for countering fear, anger and hatred that escalate Islamic radicalism. Follow this Spirit-led approach that applies principles for us to become be part of the so-elusive solution!

Mark Siljander, Ambassador, former U.S. Congressman, President of Bridges to Common Ground, *A Deadly Misunderstanding*

There is a great need for resources like this to equip fishers of men!

Victor Choudhrie, church-planting movement (cpm) leader in India, *Greet the Church in your House*

Stubborn Perseverance infuses a ton of foundational learning into a real-life chronicle of value to practitioners everywhere.

Doug Lucas, President of Team Expansion and Editor of Brigada

Are you among the thousands striving to launch a church-planting movement but lacking spectacular fruit? You'll find *Stubborn Perseverance* deeply encouraging. It is honest. The numbers are not unrealistic. And the stories are real. So take heart, you are not alone. And there is hope!

Floyd McClung, All Nations, *The Father Heart of God*, *Follow*

People cannot do what they cannot imagine. Many cannot imagine that kingdom movements can happen. *Stubborn Perseverance* will not only help them imagine with faith, but also implement! This book is a great gift to the global Body of Christ.

Stan Parks, movement trainer, VP Global Strategies for Act Beyond

Stubborn Perseverance can be applied with good results in many settings, not just with Muslims. The characters show flexibility in their approach to winning people to Christ. If you've ever thought "a movement can't happen here," read this book!

Bob French, missionary trainer with WorldTeam

Stubborn Perseverance tells a story that models the principles it teaches, then brings understanding alive through small group discussion. Anyone pursuing evangelism and church-planting movements needs this book!

Al Vom Steeg, Senior International Director, International Leadership Institute

The use of fiction in *Stubborn Perseverance* is truly a creative way to provide training in best practices for establishing movements.

Kevin Greeson, cpm trainer, *The Camel Method*

Stubborn Perseverance illustrates how multiplicative ministry integrates in a true-to-life situation. It is helpful for anyone desiring to help launch a Kingdom movement, especially those serving among Muslims.

Curtis Sergeant, cpm trainer, Founder of MetaCamp

The principles in *Stubborn Perseverance*, if lived out, will transform your sphere of influence. This paradigm shift will prove invaluable to many!

Neil Gamble, cpm trainer, *These Signs Shall Follow*

The experiences in *Stubborn Perseverance* are similar to our own. The material is ideal for our weekly meetings and monthly Roundtables. This is the perfect guide-book for continuing our journey.

Steven Steinhaus, cpm trainer for Muslim unreached people groups

Stubborn Perseverance reads like a journal rather than a manual. The journey it takes you on requires stubborn perseverance, but when you arrive you'll be surrounded by multiplying communities of Jesus followers. If that's where you long to go, read this book.

Steve Addison, movements.net, *Pioneering Movements: Leadership that Multiplies Disciples and Churches*

Church Planters: Do not overlook this gem! No matter how experienced you are, *Stubborn Perseverance* will stretch you, open new vistas, and give you a fresh appreciation of the scope and variety of church-planting movements. A rare combination of serious scholarship and fun fiction!

George Patterson, *Come Quickly Dawn, Obedience-Oriented Education*

If only we had these insights half a century ago we would have been prepared to see God do then what he is doing today. If this book sings to your heart, you may by an apostle in the making.

Galen Currah, cpm trainer, consultant for People of YES!, *Start Churches Now!*

Stubborn Perseverance is outstanding. It brings to life the principles of church-planting movements in a most remarkable way.

Felicity Dale, *An Army of Ordinary People*

Stubborn Perseverance is helpful for all practitioners ministering among Muslims. The story-telling utilizes a time-proven method of sharing Christ. I particularly appreciated how the believers interact with common objections raised by Muslims.

Phil Parshall, *Bridges to Islam: A Christian Perspective on Folk Islam*

Stubborn Perseverance is now my #1 training tool for church-planting movements! The story both explains and illustrates the essential steps of multiplying disciples to launch such a movement.

John Becker, Director of Fruitful Practices Research, director of Ministries for AIM

Stubborn Perseverance is both a readable story and a useful training tool, vividly portraying application of CPM principles by ordinary believers.

L.D. Waterman, cpm encourager and resource with Act Beyond

This book is an accessible guide for catalyzing movements among Muslim peoples. Complete. Practical. Engaging. Inspiring.

Jayson Georges, *The 3D Gospel* and HonorShame.com

A very practical and useful tool for those endeavoring to minister to Muslims. *Stubborn Perseverance* presents an effectual way of communicating the gospel with basic discipleship.

Dave Stevens, adjunct professor at Trinity Evangelical Divinity School

This is not fiction! I have seen thousands of Muslims follow Jesus through the principles illustrated so vibrantly in *Stubborn Perseverance*. This story will fill you with hope and enthusiasm.

Dave Hunt, V.P. for Disciple-Making Movements, Cityteam, Int.

If you long to see Muslims come to Christ and churches among the unreached, *Stubborn Perseverance* is for you. I'm going to have our whole staff read this roadmap for success.

Tom Doyle, Vice President and Middle East Director for e3 Partners, *Dreams and Visions—Is Jesus Awakening the Muslim World?*

Stubborn Perseverance brilliantly presents the often opaque interplay of culture, personality, spiritual engagement, and divine intervention that accompanies church multiplication within unreached people groups.

Bruce Sidebotham, Director and Founder of OpRev.org and ATFP.org

Stubborn Perseverance illustrates the Acts model of relational community, God-centeredness under the direction of the Holy Spirit, and the importance of prayer and spiritual warfare in the midst of persecution.

Linda Bemis, Prayer Director for International Orality Network

Stubborn Perseverance is a creative allegory, brilliantly weaving Disciple-Making Movement principles into a compelling story. Instructive and engaging at the same time!

Marv Newell, Senior Vice-President for Missio Nexus

Stubborn Perseverance is an engaging way to "teach" principles of promoting movements to Christ. It is a promising tool for small groups to read, discuss, and then apply in their context.

Jonathan Lewis, Go Global Network

What a treasure trove of practical help for anyone reaching out to Muslims or seeking to plant churches among the unreached. Read and apply this book, and watch God work!

Steve Shadrach, Executive Director, Center for Mission Mobilization

Stubborn Perseverance is an excellent guide for those seeking God for a church-planting movement. It teaches how to begin movements, how to disciple new leaders, and then how to "get out of the way" so others can repeat the process without outside interference.

Keith Carey, Editor for the *Global Prayer Digest*

Stubborn Perseverance depicts three couples in community, engaging their Muslim neighbors in following Jesus. Let's learn from this valuable model and put it into practice in our own communities!

Nate Scholz, Hub Community Network Facilitator,
Coffee & Orange Blossoms: 7 Years & 15 Days in Tyre, Lebanon

What an amazing read! The narrative helped me see the principles of disciple-making/church-planting movements, and how ordinary believers can pursue these in their daily lives.

Brent Lindquist, Link Care Center

Simple to understand, but application requires Christ's empowering presence. And that is what we see. The narrative drew me in and challenged me. Buy, read, and discuss in a small group!

Dick Nelson, Global Outreach Director (retired), Fellowship Bible Church

Anyone taking the Gospel across cultures (or across the street) would do well to apply *Stubborn Perseverance*. It clarifies vividly what a church-planting movement can look like, illustrating proven tools to move past theory—a refreshing and needed book!

Levi, Global Outreach Director, Fellowship Bible Church

I thought I'd be slow working through the book as I was busy with training and the harvest (four Chinese students baptized last night). But I couldn't stop reading it! SO practical! *Stubborn Perseverance* helped me visualize the disciple-making process like nothing else I've read.

Carole, discipler with Every Nation Ministries

WOW! *Stubborn Perseverance* is fully practical, not only for reaching Muslims, but anyone who doesn't know the true gospel. I'm applying these principles with middle-class Americans and Hindus, and God is moving and working! A must read for anyone wanting to reach the lost!

Beth, volunteer youth worker and homemaker

Stubborn Perseverance is chock full of field-tested insight and fascinating cultural tidbits. Stubbornly persevere in applying these principles and, by God's grace, He will use you to help launch a people movement to Christ.

Chris Lipp, Missions Pastor, McKinney Church

Stubborn Perseverance shows what applying CPM principles looks like. Every believer can benefit, as we are all called to make disciples. I look forward to seeing God move as I apply this among refugees in my city.

Lauren, Physicians Assistant and volunteer with refugees

Stubborn Perseverance helped me see how Discovery Bible Study can encourage Holy Spirit-led instruction, conviction and obedience even prior to salvation, and equipped me for more effective prayer.

Debbie W, sender, supporter, intercessor

Other movement materials left me confused and overwhelmed. They sounded good in principle, but I had no idea how to proceed on my own or explain the concepts to others. This book solves all of that.

Don Vincent, correctional officer pursuing a movement in a prison

Stubborn Perseverance

Study Edition

BY

JAMES NYMAN

Robby Butler, editor

Forewords by
David Watson
Jerry Trousdale

**How to launch
cascading movements to Christ,
among Muslims *and* others
(a true-to-life CPM story)**

"But the seed on good soil stands for those
with a noble and good heart,
who hear the word, retain it, and
by **persevering** produce a crop"

(Luke 8:15, NIV).

Stubborn Perseverance

Study Edition

BY

James Nyman

HOW TO LAUNCH A CHURCH-PLANTING KINGDOM MOVEMENT THROUGH DISCOVERY BIBLE STUDIES

For additional resources, quantity discounts, and promotional pricing, visit **StubbornPerseverance.com**

Except as noted:

Qur'an quotations are generally from the *Sahih International* translation, as found at **Quran.com**

Bible quotations are generally from the *English Standard Version (ESV)*, as found at **BlueLetterBible.org**

Published in collaboration with
Mission Network
17110 Brook Ct.
Mount Vernon, WA 98274
theMissionNetwork.org

Dedication

This book is dedicated to my wonderful wife. She has been a constant source of joy, an indomitable source of support, and an inexhaustible source of inspiration. We have partnered together in ministering, alongside the men and women whose stories are told in this book.

This book is also dedicated to my two children, the joy and pride of my life. They are everything a father could want.

Finally, this book is dedicated to my dear Indonesian friends and colleagues. They are my heroes. This book contains their stories.

Acknowledgments

This book would not have come into being without the help of many people—my national and expatriate colleagues who lived many of the realities on which this story is based, and the circle of friends and family who offered encouragement and feedback along the way.

Erin D gave detailed feedback at a key point in this book's early development. Fellow missionaries and mission strategists LD Waterman, Roger Dixon, David Garrison, Stan Parks, Kevin Greeson and Jonathan Ammon all gave helpful early feedback. Many others helped with editing and consulting including Don Vincent, Michael M, Elaine C, Debbie W, Martha McCandless, Kathy A. Allen, Brent Lindquist, Toni A, Lauren Gage, Curtis Sergeant, Jayson Georges, and Keith Carey. Werner Mischke also gave invaluable help in incorporating honor/shame awareness, and in formatting this book.

I especially want to thank Robby Butler for recognizing the potential of my early manuscript and investing countless hours in polishing this book into what it has become. His skill in editing and missiological understanding were a tremendous help in clarifying and refining the principles I have sought to convey.

Contents

APPENDICES

GLOSSARY

Foreword by David Watson

I first met the author and his wife at an underground training event in 2003. This highly dedicated missionary couple had given their lives to the peoples of Indonesia, yet were willing to risk losing access to the country they loved to attend my training. For five days we walked together through the biblical basis and processes of the church-planting movement I had led.

There was no way for me to know how to train local peoples all over the world, so my hope was the audience would adapt the approach in a culturally acceptable format for their context. Basically I said, "Here is the material. You will have to make it work in your context." But this was a horrible way to train, even though the audience was primarily Western.

Globally, my ministry has trained more than 60,000 people since 1997. But most gave up on the process because they were looking for a quick and easy way to reach people for Christ. This approach requires years of hard work, holding fast to the principles that outsiders must diligently train local leaders at all levels, and God will teach those seeking Him through His Word.

When I met this couple I had seen more than 20,000 churches started in my own ministry, but there were no success stories from Indonesia. Yet, the author and his wife were willing to try pursuing a movement there.

Many of us in Kingdom work have seen the value of story-based discovery Bible studies to help both oral and literate learners discover and share the gospel. *Stubborn Perseverance* shows how this proven method can help any believer, new or old, quickly grasp and pass on the core values of disciple-making and church-planting movements. This is unique!

Faisal's story will lead you on a learning adventure to experience the truths of Scripture in a simple, reproducible pattern for training others in church-planting movement principles and processes. Don't worry about getting so caught up in the story you forget to note the core principles. Questions following each chapter will help you identify the key lessons.

Have fun with this book! Study it with fellow laborers. Adapt it to your context. Dramatize the material for visual and oral learners. Apply it by conducting your own "Person of Peace" searches and then reading, discussing and retelling the Bible stories and studies.

Use *Stubborn Perseverance* also as a reference. Chapter headings will help you find answers to your questions, and the appendices are a storehouse of information.

Enjoy the story. Learn the lessons. Pass on what you learn to others. Launching a church-planting movement is not easy, but it will be the most enjoyable hard work you ever do.

Blessings!

David L. Watson, Co-author of
Contagious Disciple Making: Leading Other on a Journey of Discovery

Foreword by Jerry Trousdale

Much of our world is fixated on dealing with Islam. Responses range from bitter hostility to paralyzing fear. Tragically, none of the typical responses reflect Christian values, nor the reality of what God is already doing among Muslims today.

As I documented in *Miraculous Movements*, the Spirit of God is at work in many countries, creating unprecedented receptivity among Muslims to the Gospel of the Kingdom. In thousands of Muslim communities, where Kingdom values and principles shape Christians' response to Islam, God is drawing and transforming Muslims into passionate, grace-filled Christ Followers.

Now is the time for believers to seek God for compassion for Muslims who find themselves victimized by the inhumanity and horror in their communities. This is God's *kairos* moment for His people to embrace a counter-intuitive response of love and compassion in the face of rage and hostility.

Stubborn Perseverance will help anyone, male or female, wanting to partner with God and others in seeking disciple-making movements, especially among Muslims. It is really two books in one: a true-to-life narrative of how hundreds of thousands of Muslims have come to Christ, plus fifty pages of appendices providing detailed guidance for reproducing disciples, with a portion focused on reaching Muslims.

This book will help disciplers anywhere, and will be of extra value to those equipping Muslim Background Christ Followers for obedience-based disciple-making. It is a great complement to other recent resources on Kingdom of God movements among Muslims.

Jerry Trousdale, Director of International Ministries for Cityteam
Miraculous Movements: How Hundreds of Thousands of Muslims Are Falling in Love With Jesus and *The Kingdom Unleashed: How Ordinary People Launch Disciple-Making Movements Around the World*

Note to the Reader

This book uses the vehicle of story to demonstrate church-planting movement (CPM) principles in context, presenting various motivations that lead people to Christ, illustrating discipleship issues new believers face, showing how groups come to function as house churches, and describing a model for how local leaders are developed.

At this writing researchers are tracking about one hundred fifty CPMs around the world using one or both of two CPM models:[1] 1. Discovery, also called Disciple-Making Movements (DMMs), for which Discovery Bible Study (DBS) is central, and 2. Training For Trainers (T4T). Following a Harvest Cycle based on the Shanks' *Four Fields* (Appendix B), *Stubborn Perseverance* illustrates one integration of the Discovery approach with core elements of T4T.

While this story unfolds in a Muslim context, and several chapters give special focus to Islam, the principles can be applied in a variety of contexts, including among Hindus, Buddhists, and animists, and even nominal Christians. Many traditional churches are applying these principles to reach the unchurched and to reproduce small groups and lay leaders. This approach appeals especially to millennials, who hunger for authentic community, self discovery, and social activism.

This story can be read alone, but the greatest kingdom benefit will likely come through reading, discussing, and applying this material with others. And for this book's future value to you as a manual and reference, I encourage you to *highlight* key points in this book *as the Holy Spirit emphasizes them to you.*

The characters and circumstances in this book are all based on real people and experiences, from our own ministry or the ministries of fellow missionaries or Indonesian believers. This story is about people:

---

[1] MissionFrontiers.org/pdfs/32-35_Smith_KingdomKernels.pdf

- leaders battling discouragement, pettiness, and spiritual warfare;
- Muslims drawn to follow Jesus through dreams, healings, a vibrant personal witness, and bridging verses in the Qur'an; and
- new believers casting off old patterns and living as new creations.

This story illustrates how God heals the deepest hurts, restores broken interpersonal relationships, and transforms individuals and families. It reveals the brutality of persecution, the potential for victory in the midst of suffering, and the power of forgiveness.

This is the story of three couples who study the Scriptures and conclude God has led them to pursue a church-planting movement (CPM) among the Sayang—a fictional Indonesian Muslim unreached people group (Sayang means "beloved" in Indonesian)—and who together stubbornly persevere to see that movement mature.

Faisal and Fatima lead the team. They are joined by Yusuf and Nur, and Nasrudin and Amina. Each of them engages and disciples someone, and most of these in turn disciple someone else.

May the Holy Spirit use their stories to inspire and guide you to adapt the biblical principles illustrated here for your own context.

The chart below is for your reference, to help with the foreign names of the characters. Arrows indicate who shared with whom.

Faisal (teacher)	→ **Ahmad** (teacher)	→ **Hasan** (doctor)
Fatima (Faisal's wife)	→ **Inne** (caterer)	→ **Eka** (student)
Yusuf (taxi driver)	→ **Haji Ishmael** (imam)	→ **Sharif** (headmaster)
Nur (Yusuf's wife)	→ **Aysha** (unhappy wife)	→ **Wati** (bedridden)
Nasrudin (honey seller)	→ **Abdullah** (radical Muslim)	→ **Umar** (alcoholic)
	Titin (Abdullah's wife)	
	Saleh (Abdullah's best friend)	
Amina (Nasrudin's wife, nurse)		→ **Lily** (patient)

The frequency of certain foreign words in this story made the standard italicizing of all such words distracting. Therefore only the first occurrence is italicized and explained in a footnote. The glossary also explains these and other uncommon terms.

Each chapter ends with discussion questions to facilitate both individual reflection and small group discussion toward application of the CPM principles presented.

1

Casting Vision for a
Church-Planting Movement (CPM)[2]

Faisal and Fatima build a CPM team.

Faisal carefully placed his backpack between the handlebars and seat, then strapped it in place. Sitting on the motorcycle, he gently rocked it back and forth, making sure it was properly balanced. As a teacher, he sometimes carried books to class, so he knew the importance of getting the load right.

Like most Sayang people, Faisal had a medium build and olive skin. He was clean shaven and bald, with short black hair on the sides. His eyes were warm and friendly, and his cheerful, welcoming smile revealed coffee-stained teeth.

Faisal looked fondly at Fatima. She also was in her mid-30s, with wavy, shoulder-length hair and a small mole on her right cheek. "I'm really looking forward to this time with our friends."

"Me, too," she replied, wrestling with her own backpack. At Faisal's signal she mounted the bike behind him and wrapped her arms around his waist.

Their first stop was the house of their friends, Yusuf and Nur. They were ready with their own motorcycle. Yusuf, a slender man

---

[2] A rapidly reproducing movement, as in the book of Acts, in which obedient disciples, churches, and servant leaders all reproduce, to transform lives, relationships, and communities throughout a specific people group. Appendix A provides a list of Critical Elements of CPM.

with a firm handshake, had short cropped hair and crooked teeth. Nur, slightly overweight, had plump cheeks and sympathetic eyes. Her straight hair, parted on the side, hung to her shoulders. As a taxi driver Yusuf knew all the shortcuts, so he led the way as the two couples rode to meet Nasrudin and Amina at a convenient intersection.

Nasrudin had stocky shoulders, a thick mustache, and strong calloused hands. He sold honey for a living, but today he'd loaded his motorcycle with camping gear instead of honey bottles. His wife Amina was petite. Despite streaks of gray hair, her fashionable haircut and stylish glasses made her look younger than her 40 years.

Since Faisal had researched the route ahead of time, he took the lead as the three couples headed out of town.

They passed an elementary school, and children walking to school in red and white uniforms. Soon they were on an open stretch of road lined on both sides with terraced rice fields. Near one rice paddy a man walked behind a pair of water buffalo, preparing the ground for new plantings. At another paddy, a group of women performed the backbreaking work of planting the new seedlings in straight rows.

Faisal thought about how his life had changed since he had attended a seminar about church-planting movements (CPMs). *I was so frustrated over my ineffectiveness in reaching my own people, and that seminar turned my world upside down! Studying how the Holy Spirit equipped and led the first century believers to reach their world has given my life new purpose and brought me new and deeper friendships. God,[3] I know it could get difficult, or even dangerous, but would you use us to initiate a movement among our own people?*

Faisal's CPM training had concluded with a challenge for all the participants to gather groups to study CPM principles in the *Taurat*

---

[3] Since this story is in English, the characters say "God" in place of "Allah" (the common local name for the sovereign, creator God). "Though Christians in the West typically associate the name Allah with Islam, it was, in fact, Christian in origin. Arab Muslims borrowed the name from Arab Christians who had been praying to Allah for centuries before Muhammad was born." *A Wind in the House of Islam: How God is drawing Muslims around the world to faith in Jesus Christ* by David Garrison (Monument CO: WIGtake Resources, 2014), p. 110. Even today, tens of millions of Arabic Christians refer to God as Allah.

and *Injil.*[4] Faisal and Fatima had brainstormed who to invite, then narrowed the list to ten couples. Six had agreed to participate, but after the third week only Yusuf and his wife Nur, and Nasrudin and his wife Amina, wanted to continue.

Pursuing a CPM had required a high commitment from each of them. Faisal had had to stop doing many good activities, including leading a mens ministry and weekly fishing with other believers. Most of his friends hadn't understood his new passion to reach their Muslim neighbors, so he was especially grateful to God for these partners.

Faisal was amazed at how quickly God had knit their hearts together around the CPM vision. He looked forward eagerly to their weekly meetings, delighting in a depth of friendship he had not previously known.

The road took them along the beach, where palm trees swayed gently in the breeze. Faisal watched a young man climb a coconut tree bare-footed. Reaching the top, he tossed coconuts down to his friend below. *Those coconuts will probably be sold to a nearby restaurant, overlooking the ocean, where customers will enjoy the milk.*

The road began to rise as they entered the forest, where towering trees blocked most of the sunlight, and the cool mountain air sent a chill up Faisal's spine. On the side of the road, monkeys gathered in the hope passing motorists would throw them food. *I don't have food for you today,* Faisal thought as they sped past.

As they continued climbing, the road began to wind. Suddenly, an oversized bus, traveling too fast, rounded the curve in Faisal's lane. As he swerved sharply, his wife tightened her grip around his stomach. Faisal barely avoided the bus, then checked his rear view mirror to make sure the other two couples had also gotten out of the way. *Thank you Father that everyone is safe.*

Yusuf had suggested they take an outing to strengthen their friendship and give them more time to digest what they were learning

---

4 *Taurat* and *Injil* are Muslim terms for the Old and New Testament. This group followed a discovery approach to discuss what the Bible says about God, prayer, evangelism, discipleship, church formation, leadership, and multiplication. For more information on this training, visit **beyond.org/events**, email **training@beyond.org**, or call 469–814–8222.

about church-planting movements. After discussing the options, they agreed on hiking to the top of a local volcano and camping there overnight. Surprisingly, none of them had ever done this before, even though they had all grown up in its shadow.

They arrived at the Ranger Station, paid the entry fee, and picked up a map. The ranger walked outside and pointed to the trailhead.

"Sir, would you mind taking a picture of us?" Nur asked. "We want before and after photos."

"No, problem," the ranger answered, taking the camera.

"Yusuf, hiking this mountain was a great idea," Faisal said. "I already feel better just from being out of the city and surrounded by God's creation!"

Everyone smiled and nodded.

"We should commit this time to the Lord," Faisal said. "Let's pray.

"*Bismillahi arrahmani arrahim*," [5] Faisal recited before continuing in Sayang, "Gracious Father, we thank You for the privilege of hiking this mountain. Help us worship You as we behold Your beautiful creation. Use this time to strengthen our friendships and deepen our understanding of what You have called us to do. In the name of *Isa Al Masih*.[6] Amen."

"Remember," Faisal said, "when we take breaks we're going to discuss the CPM principles we've been learning about in Scripture. Is everyone ready?"

"Ready!" Yusuf declared as the others nodded.

They shouldered their backpacks and began the hike.

The trail started off fairly level around the base of the mountain. The mid-morning sun beat down as they passed through a field. One by one they began pulling handkerchiefs from their pockets to mop sweat from their faces. Then the trail led down a steep ravine where Faisal helped Fatima over a large rock. Climbing out of the ravine, the trail became steeper, taking the hikers into a wooded section.

After hiking for more than an hour Nasrudin paused to catch his

---

[5] Arabic for "In the name of Allah, the most gracious and most merciful."
[6] Arabic for Jesus Christ.

breath. "Let's take a break. My backpack has doubled in weight," he said, flinging it to the ground. "And I'm ready for a snack."

They each found a rock or a tree to lean against and pulled out their water bottles. Amina opened a bag of fried *cassava* and passed it around.

Nur massaged her thighs. "I see I'm a bit out of shape. I'm glad we stopped."

"Me too. I know I'll be sore tomorrow." Fatima rolled her head from side to side. "I'm sure enjoying the beauty here."

Faisal took a long drink from his water bottle and wiped his mouth with the back of his hand. "Let's start our discussion. What motivates you to study CPM principles?"

"That's easy," Yusuf said. "I remember what you asked us the first time we met. 'If not you, who? If not now, when?' Those questions really pierced my heart. Who is going to tell our unsaved family and friends about God's grace and mercy? Nur and I have been comfortable letting our lives be our witness. Yet if we don't share verbally about Isa now, when will we do it? No one knows the day of his death."

"You also asked us," Nasrudin said, "'How many of our ethnic group, the Sayang, will hear the good news of Isa Al Masih today?' It struck me that, besides the six of us, I don't know of anyone else who is telling our people about Isa. That's just not right!" he added, pounding his fist.

"I am motivated by all Isa has done in my life," Amina said. "When I stop to think about all the wonderful blessings Isa has given me, I'm really quite speechless. He healed the wounds in my heart and provided me such a wonderful marriage with Nasrudin. How could I not share with others? I want them to enjoy the same joy and peace I experience."

"I agree with these motivations," Nur said. "But for me, there is another motive. From studying the Taurat and Injil I know hell is real, and Isa is the only way to heaven. I can't bear the thought of my family and friends going to hell. It is always risky to talk about Isa, but what if they never hear Isa died for them because I am quiet?

What if they die and go to hell because Yusuf and I are afraid of how they will respond to us? I must choose to risk suffering in this life so the people I love won't needlessly suffer in the next life. I need training to help me overcome my fears and know what to say."

Faisal waited, but no one spoke further.

"Those are all excellent motivations," Faisal said. "I long to see God do among our own people what He has done among so many others in history. Learning how God can use just a few unified people to bring great change has given my life new meaning and purpose. I feel fulfilled in ways I have never felt before."

Faisal stopped to rub his calves. "Well, we still have a lot of mountain to climb, and we'll need several more breaks before we reach the top. We'll have another discussion during our next break. Is everyone ready?"

Each retrieved their backpack, and Yusuf took a turn leading. The trail climbed steeply, so every fifteen to twenty minutes they stopped to catch their breath.

Faisal looked down the mountain. To the right, he could see rows and rows of domed canvas structures. Inside, he knew, strawberries flourished in the rich volcanic dirt. To the left, he could see a herd of cattle grazing. Their meat would end up on dinner tables in Japan, Australia and Europe. Pressing on, they entered a large grove of coffee trees. *Coffee grows best at higher altitudes*, he thought.

When they reached a meadow, Yusuf stopped so they could enjoy the view.

Nasrudin sat down. "This seems like a good place for lunch. It's been almost two hours since our last break."

Everyone joined him on the grass, and Amina handed out small cardboard boxes containing rice, a small piece of chicken, fried tofu, fried green beans, and hot sauce.

Nasrudin finished first, leaned against a tree, and pulled his hat over his eyes. Faisal, always ready to tease, plucked a long blade of grass and tickled Nasrudin's ear with it. Nasrudin, eyes still shut, tried to shoo away what he thought was a fly.

Everyone burst out laughing and Nasrudin quickly sat upright, removing his hat in irritation.

Faisal smiled mischievously. "Hey, you can't sleep! We have things to talk about."

Realizing he wasn't going to get any sleep, Nasrudin settled himself against a tree.

"In our first meeting," Faisal said, "I said we were going to study CPM principles in the Taurat and Injil. Does anyone remember the definition I gave for church-planting movements?"

"How could we forget?" Yusuf responded sarcastically. "You really drilled it into us! A CPM is 'a rapidly reproducing movement of disciples making new disciples, of leaders equipping new leaders, and of churches planting new indigenous churches, which transforms individuals, families, and communities by the power of the Holy Spirit within a population group—a people group, city, province, or nation.'"

"Good job!" Faisal said. "As we discovered, CPMs aren't new at all. The book of Acts records several CPMs,[7] and there have been many more throughout history. Our task is to study the Scriptures to glean the principles God has given, then align our ministry with those principles. Applying these is no guarantee a movement will happen. Only God starts a CPM. Even if a movement never happens, applying these principles is a great church planting strategy. However we are praying for a movement!

"We also observed I am not the teacher. The Holy Spirit is our teacher and we are all learners. We use simple, open-ended discovery questions to guide discussion of the Sayang translation of the Taurat and Injil so the Holy Spirit can highlight points He wants to emphasize. What do you remember about God from our first discovery study[8] in the Injil?"

Nur was the first to respond. "The idea most obvious to me is that everything is about God's glory, and we exist to bring praise and

---

[7] e.g., Acts 12:24, 13:1–14:28, 19:9–10

[8] Discovery Bible Study (DBS) is an inductive approach in which a leader asks questions which the Holy Spirit helps participants answer *from the text*, with no one person "teaching." General questions are asked about a passage, and the participants share insights as they surface.

honor to our wonderful heavenly Father. Something else I remember is that nothing is impossible for God. In CPMs we face many, many challenges, but CPMs are God's idea, not man's. Nothing will thwart Christ's commitment to build His Church." [9]

"What are the main points you remember from our study the following week?" Faisal asked.

"That week we studied about vision," Yusuf said. "We start with God's vision. It is God's plan to call people from every tribe, tongue, and nation to Himself.[10] Then, He calls us to be involved in this great task. But we can't do it alone, so God leads us to others who share the same vision. We join together as a team so that we can support and encourage one another. I feel a unity and closeness with you that I've never felt with other groups. Our CPM vision binds us together."

Each looked at the others, nodding in agreement.

"This is a good time to pause our conversation," Faisal concluded. "Shall we continue our hike?"

The mountain still rose above them as far as they could see. The excitement and enthusiasm of the morning ebbed away and was replaced by tired legs and aching shoulders. The group hiked on in silence, each lost in his or her own thoughts. Soon a cloud engulfed them, and the temperature dropped dramatically.

Late in the afternoon, they climbed a particularly steep stretch to the rim of the volcano. From there they gazed down into the caldera, which was filled with a lake edged by almost vertical walls. A wisp of smoke rose from a new cone in the center of the lake, indicating this volcano was still active. They flung their backpacks to the ground and began snapping pictures.

All of a sudden everyone realized how cold they were. There on the rim, unprotected by rocks or trees, the wind blew against their sweat-drenched shirts and the setting sun took its warmth with it.

Without a word, the men quickly pulled the tents from their backpacks and set them up to change into warmer clothing.

---

[9] Matt. 16:18

[10] Acts 11:14, 16:31; Rev. 5:9, 7:9

Faisal, Yusuf, and Nasrudin went in search of firewood as Fatima, Nur, and Amina arranged stones for a fire and set out mugs for the noodles. Soon the fire was blazing and dinner was cooking.

Everyone enjoyed a hearty portion of vegetable and noodle soup, and small chitchat about their ambitious climb that day. *It's amazing how hungry you get from hiking all day*, Faisal thought.

The sun cast gold, red, and orange rays across the evening sky as they finished eating. Nasrudin put more wood on the fire, while Amina refilled the pot. Then they rinsed their mugs and made tea.

Faisal waited until everyone was settled again around the fire.

"This seems like a good time to continue our CPM discussion.[11] Are you all settled?"

Everyone agreed.

"After learning about God's glory and His plan to call His children to partner together to reach unreached people groups, we studied prayer. What do you remember from that discussion?"

"I was struck with how diligent the first believers were in prayer," Amina said. "They often prayed for hours at a time."

"It was common for God to do miracles in response to their faith and prayers," Nasrudin added. "Like when the early Church prayed for Peter's release from prison and he was escorted out by angels! The first disciples often prayed for the sick, and many were healed."

"We also learned about spiritual warfare," Yusuf said. "The first disciples cast out demons, tore down spiritual strongholds, put on the full armor of God, and stood strong in Al Masih."

Yusuf pushed the ends of the firewood toward the center to reignite the dying flame. Here, far from the city lights, the stars shone brightly. Occasionally they spied a bat, seeking its nighttime meal of mosquitoes.

"We also observed that the early Church often fasted," Faisal said. "Does anyone have a question about fasting?"

---

[11] Discovery CPM training (such as Faisal received) also includes these lessons: *God Draws and Teaches*, *Becoming Like Jesus to Reach the Lost*, and *Becoming Like the People We Want to Reach*.

"Yes," Amina said. "When we fast, do we have to fast from food *and* water?"

"What do you think?" Faisal asked, consciously trying to facilitate rather than appear as the expert.

"I know Esther once called for a fast of food *and* water, but as a nurse I think it's good to drink water when you're fasting. Some people I know will also drink juice. From a health standpoint it seems better for pregnant and nursing women not to fast, as well as those who are sick."

"That's helpful. Any other questions?"

"How long should we fast?" Yusuf asked.

"Who would like to answer that question?"

"We could skip a meal, like breakfast or lunch," Nasrudin said. "Or get up early to eat breakfast before it's light and then eat dinner after it's dark. If we do a twenty-four hour fast we could eat dinner one night and then eat dinner the following night. If we fast twenty-four hours, I think it's important to drink water or juice." [12]

"Great comments!" Faisal said. "There isn't a set biblical pattern for how to fast, so let's each fast according to our own convictions. From what I've read about CPMs around the world, most pray and fast at least once a week. Can we make the same commitment?"

Everyone nodded.

"So, when do we start?" Faisal looked around the circle.

"I think we should start this coming week!" Nasrudin suggested.

"I agree," Fatima said. "And are we ready for prayer-walking?"

"What's prayer-walking?" Amina asked.

"Prayer is effective anywhere," Fatima said, "but many people gain additional insight into how to pray and reach the lost from walking and praying around neighborhoods, schools, government offices, business districts, entertainment areas, and religious sites."

"The phrase 'prayer-walking' isn't in the Taurat or Injil," Faisal added. "Though prayer is the focus of prayer-walking, sometimes

---

[12] Each team should establish their own practical application of the scriptural teaching on fasting based on local culture and health sensitivities.

God orchestrates 'divine appointments' so we can share the gospel with those He has prepared."

"Won't we attract attention?" Yusuf asked.

"We don't wave our hands or shout," Fatima said. "We walk casually and act like we are talking to each other, but we're really talking to God."

"Oh, that's good," Yusuf exclaimed. "I was feeling nervous!"

"Where should we go prayer-walking?" Faisal asked.

"We all know there are spiritual forces at the *mosque*," [13] Nur said. "And many people believe bathing in water from the well on the edge of town will bring blessings and protect them from evil spirits. I suggest we prayer-walk at both places."

"Okay, so here is an idea," Faisal said. "Since none of us work on Sunday, let's fast and go prayer-walking then. What do you think?"

Everyone agreed.

"I've brought pencils and paper for each of us," Faisal continued. "As a further application of this lesson, let's each make a list of fifteen family and friends who don't know Isa. Then let's hold each other accountable to pray daily for God to prepare their hearts to be receptive, and to prepare us to start spiritual conversations with them. Then as we learn different skills for talking with people we don't know, we'll also apply those skills to the people on our lists."

"That sounds good to me," Nasrudin said.

Soon everyone had a daily prayer list to keep in their Bible.

"We're all tired," Faisal said. "Fatima, please close us in prayer."

"Bismillahi arrahmani arrahim. God, most loving and most merciful, words cannot express how much we love You and how grateful we are for Your work in our lives. Thank You for Your glorious plan to redeem people from every tongue, tribe, and nation. Thank You for calling us together to partner with the Holy Spirit to share this wonderful treasure with our families and friends. Help us to follow the example of the early Church and be diligent in prayer. In the name of Isa, our divine King, we pray. Amen."

---

[13] Muslim place of worship.

Discuss and apply

1. Faisal had to stop doing good activities so he would have time to focus on starting a CPM. What activities do you need to stop doing to have time to help start or build a CPM?

2. Four reasons were given for sharing our faith. State these reasons in your own words.

3. How would you define CPM in your own words?

4. What were the main points shared about God?

5. What were the main points about vision?

6. What were the main points about prayer?

7. What did you learn about fasting? What are some different ways people fast?

8. What did you learn about prayer-walking?

9. State the five places to prayer-walk listed in this chapter. Where else could you prayer-walk?

10. Schedule a time to fast and go prayer-walking with a teammate.

11. List 15 unsaved family or friends, and commit to hold each other accountable to pray for them daily.

12. Share what you believe God wants you to do in the next 24–48 hours from what you learned in this chapter.

13. In twos or threes, share the name of one person from each of your prayer lists, and pray for God to begin convicting them of sin and opening their heart to the gospel.

2

Understanding Shema, Persons of Peace, and Oikos

The team discusses core elements of CPM strategy.

Faisal opened his eyes. It was starting to get light outside. He rolled over and touched the side of the tent, causing condensation inside the tent to rain on him. *That will help you wake up.* He wiped the water from his face and looked over at Fatima. She was awake too, but clearly didn't want to get out of her warm sleeping bag.

Faisal kissed her cheek. "I'll get a fire going," he whispered.

Fatima nodded appreciatively.

Unzipping the tent, Faisal saw trash scattered all over. *I should have figured monkeys would scavenge our trash for something to eat.*

The fire was soon started, and Yusuf, Nur, Nasrudin, and Amina were stirring in their tents. Faisal poured water into a pot for coffee and warmed his hands by the fire. He looked down at the placid waters of the lake in the caldera. He could just make out a bird flying low over the water. The jagged edges of the opposite rim made a striking silhouette against the cloudless, deep blue sky.

At this time in the city his neighborhood would be noisy, but here on top of the mountain all was quiet except for a bird calling in the distance. Faisal sighed. *I could stay here all day.*

Breakfast consisted of noodles, sweet coffee, and boiled eggs.

When everyone had finished, Faisal said, "Let's return to our CPM discussion before we break camp. The week we discussed evangelism, we found that the early Church practiced anyone, anywhere, any time evangelism.[14] In other words, they were ready anywhere and at any time to talk to anyone about the Good News. Now I want to introduce you to the first of six tools I learned for drawing others into a regular study in the Taurat and Injil."

Faisal took a sip of coffee. When he saw everyone was ready he said, "Turn to Deuteronomy 6:4–9. I need two volunteers to read this passage, and two to retell it in your own words."[15]

Amina and Nasrudin each read the passage aloud:

Hear, O Israel: The LORD our God, the LORD is one. You shall love the LORD your God with all your heart and with all your soul and with all your might. And these words that I command you today shall be on your heart. You shall teach them diligently to your children, and shall talk of them when you sit in your house, and when you walk by the way, and when you lie down, and when you rise. You shall bind them as a sign on your hand, and they shall be as frontlets between your eyes. You shall write them on the doorposts of your house and on your gates.

Yusuf and Fatima each summarized the passage.

"Thank you," Faisal said. "Now let's discuss what the people were commanded to do."

After several minutes of lively discussion, Faisal said, "Who can summarize what we have learned?"

"In Deuteronomy 6:4, the word 'hear' is *shema* in the original Hebrew," Yusuf said. "The full meaning of shema is actually 'hear and obey.' This passage teaches that we should show our love for God through our words *and* deeds. In 'shema living' we take every opportunity to demonstrate God's love and declare God's goodness through the many ways He works in our lives. We intentionally and naturally drop spiritual comments into our conversation. It's like Paul

---

[14] This phrase is from *Any3: Anyone, Anywhere, Any Time—Lead Muslims to Christ Now!* by Mike Shipman (Monument, CO: WIGTake Resources, 2013).

[15] Some groups have everyone retell the story, pairing up to do so where the size of the group makes this impractical otherwise.

wrote: 'Be wise in the way you act toward outsiders; make the most of every opportunity.'" [16]

"That's perfect! Who can suggest a shema statement?"

"I'm so thankful the Lord has given me two healthy children," Nasrudin said. "When they are old enough I'm going to bring them camping at this spot!"

"I don't know what would have happened in my marriage if the Lord had not helped us," Amina added softly.

"Great!" Faisal said. "Our goal is not to pressure or persuade people into following Isa, but to find those in whom God's Spirit is already at work, just as Philip did with the Ethiopian.[17] As we go about our routines this week, let's each try to share a shema statement every day. In other words, let's try to bring God into all of our conversations in a natural way. Can we do that?"

Everyone nodded.

"Shema statements are a natural way to start a conversation, or direct a conversation in a spiritual direction," Faisal continued, "but shema statements alone aren't sufficient to determine who will receive our message. Another way we can practice anyone, anywhere, any time evangelism is to be ready to share our personal salvation story.[18] This has three parts: Part One is our lives before we came to know Isa Al Masih. We share about our felt needs and our misunderstandings about God. In Part Two, we share how we came to follow Isa, step by step. In other words, we answer the question, 'What convinced us to become Isa's followers?' In Part Three, we explain how our lives have changed since we committed ourselves to Him. We share both the joys as well as the difficulties we have experienced."

"How long should we take to tell our story?" Nasrudin asked.

---

[16] Col 4:5–6

[17] Acts 8:27-39

[18] This is sometimes called a personal testimony. We call it a "personal salvation story" to emphasize the story God is weaving in our lives. Use of an expanded personal salvation story is illustrated in Chapter 6.

"When we are talking with someone we can adapt to the situation by shortening or lengthening our story, but in practicing each of us should be able to share the core of our story in three minutes.

"Let's divide now into a mens group and a womens group and share our personal salvation stories with one another. Please give feedback to each other to make our stories as effective as possible."

They stood and stretched as they moved into groups, their muscles aching from the previous day's hike. Then they went to work, sharing how they had come to know Al Masih, and giving each other feedback.

When they were done, Faisal challenged each of them to share their personal salvation story with at least one person during the coming week. Everyone agreed. Then they broke camp, and began their journey home.

Everyone had assumed the return trip would be a breeze, but they soon discovered hiking downhill used the same muscles, which were now sore and stiff. *At least our backpacks are lighter!* Faisal thought.

They stopped where they had eaten lunch the previous day, and Amina distributed their boxed lunches.

"We only skipped rice for two meals," Nasrudin quipped as he pressed the rice between his fingers, "but I can't believe how much I missed it. I guess the saying is true: 'If you haven't eaten rice, you haven't eaten.'"

When everyone was finished, Faisal spoke up cheerfully, ignoring the weariness of his muscles and trying to inspire the others. "It's time for another CPM discussion."

The others were all glad for a reason to rest a little longer.

"When we go out to share," Faisal continued, "we are actually looking for a certain type of person. Let's study Luke 10:1–11 in our mens and womens groups and write down what the disciples were supposed to do, as well as the characteristics of the person the disciples were to seek."

After this the Lord appointed seventy-two others and sent them on ahead of him, two by two, into every town and place where He himself was about to go. And He said to them, "The harvest is plentiful, but the laborers are few. Therefore pray earnestly to the Lord of the harvest to send out laborers into his harvest. Go your way; behold, I am sending you out as lambs in the midst of wolves. Carry no moneybag, no knapsack, no sandals, and greet no one on the road. Whatever house you enter, first say, 'Peace be to this house!' And if a son of peace is there, your peace will rest upon him. But if not, it will return to you. And remain in the same house, eating and drinking what they provide, for the laborer deserves his wages. Do not go from house to house. Whenever you enter a town and they receive you, eat what is set before you. Heal the sick in it and say to them, 'The kingdom of God has come near to you.' But whenever you enter a town and they do not receive you, go into its streets and say, 'Even the dust of your town that clings to our feet we wipe off against you. Nevertheless know this, that the kingdom of God has come near.'"

Faisal waited until the two groups finished writing.

"What were the disciples supposed to do?" he asked.

"Isa sent them out two by two," Amina said. "In other words, they always had partners."

"They weren't to let themselves get distracted along the way," Yusuf added. "They knew their assignment, and they were to stay focused on that."

"If they were received by a family," Nasrudin said, "they didn't move from house to house."

"They also preached the Good News of the kingdom and healed the sick," Fatima said. "This verse shows that God cares for all our needs. I have heard that preaching the Good News is ministering to their spiritual needs, while healing the sick is ministering to their physical needs. Perhaps we need to be willing to pray with the lost with greater expectancy that God will hear our prayers."

"Wow," Nur added thoughtfully, "that's really significant. It is also sobering to see that if they didn't find a man or woman of peace there, they left the village. They weren't responsible for the response, just for looking."

"And what characterized the people the disciples were seeking?" Faisal asked.

"They opened their household to the disciples and listened to their message," Nur said.

"Right," Faisal said. "The word 'household' is *oikos* in Greek. An oikos can be a family or a group of close friends. 'Person of peace,' or POP, is a term commonly used for the kind of person Isa sent the disciples to find. From Isa's parable about four kinds of soil this person is sometimes also called a 'fourth soil' person. This person isn't necessarily a peaceful person, but he or she is searching for peace, and willing to open his or her oikos to the messenger of peace. So why do you think it is better to study with an oikos than just an individual?"

"If an oikos comes to Al Masih," Nur said, "the members can support each other in times of persecution. But if only an individual comes to Al Masih, who will support him?"

"Excellent observations!" Faisal said. "In the New Testament the vast majority of recorded instances of people coming to faith in Al Masih involved groups rather than individuals.[19] For instance, the Samaritan woman, Matthew, Cornelius, Lydia, and the Philippian jailer. [20] It seems the norm in the New Testament is for whole groups or oikos to come to Al Masih together." [21]

"I can see how important that principle would be for the Sayang," said Nasrudin thoughtfully.

"This has been a great discussion," Faisal continued, "but we need to be going."

It didn't take long to reach the ranger's office, where they again asked the ranger to take a picture of them.

---

[19] Acts records thirty-two instances of salvation. In twenty-nine of these we see groups believing, and just three occasions in which individuals believe.

[20] Jn 4:4-42, Mt 9:9-13, Acts 10:1-48, 16:11-34

[21] In movements, churches form as Jesus enters pre-existing relational networks (among people living, working or playing together). Regardless of where they meet (homes, caves, under trees), such gatherings become "church" as the group learns together to follow and obey Jesus.

As they got ready, Faisal glanced at Yusuf. His hair was a mess, he was unshaven, his clothes were dirty, and he smelled of sweat and smoke.

"Good thing you and Nur are married," Faisal laughed, slapping Yusuf on the back. "Otherwise she wouldn't take you home!"

Resuming a more serious tone, Faisal said, "Before we leave, I'd like us to think about the similarities of hiking a mountain and reaching the Sayang people."

"Both require unconditional love," Yusuf said, looking at Faisal.

Faisal was puzzled. "I understand reaching the Sayang requires unconditional love, but what does unconditional love have to do with hiking a mountain?"

"I hung out with you for a day and half! That's unconditional love!" Yusuf burst out laughing.

Faisal smiled at the joke.

"In hiking this mountain," Nur said, "we had a clear goal, to reach the top. In the same way, we need a clear goal to reach the Sayang. Our goal is to plant healthy house fellowships that multiply and are led by their natural leaders."

"We also needed a map to reach the top," Amina agreed, "just as we need God's plan to reach the Sayang."

"It took perseverance for me to reach the top," Yusuf said. "It will take perseverance to plant house churches among the Sayang."

"Yes, perseverance; and preparation too." Nasrudin nodded appreciatively at Amina. "To hike this mountain we needed the great food Amina prepared, along with tents, flashlights, and warm clothes. To reach the Sayang, we need the kind of training we have been receiving in our weekly studies in the Taurat and Injil."

"Climbing this mountain was a lot easier with you guys," Amina said, smiling back at Nasrudin. "I needed the encouragement to keep going, and I enjoyed the journey more with all of you."

"Thanks, everyone," Faisal concluded. "Let's head home."

Discuss and apply

1. How did you obey what you concluded God wanted you to do from the previous chapter?

2. Do you practice anyone, anywhere, any time evangelism? If not, what hinders you?

3. What is a shema statement? Role play making five shema statements each. Covenant with a teammate to each share a shema statement every day until your next meeting.

4. Outline your personal salvation story and practice with each other until you can share it in three minutes. Include all three parts: a) your felt needs and misconceptions about God before coming to Christ, b) your process of coming to Christ or what convinced you to follow Christ, and c) Your joys and difficulties since following Christ. Covenant with a teammate to each tell your personal salvation story at least once a week.

5. What has been your experience when you try to talk about Jesus? What encourages you to share even when you feel awkward or fear rejection?

6. How does "trying to persuade people to follow Jesus" differ from "seeking to find those whom God's Spirit has already prepared"?

7. Discuss how taking another person with you to share would help build your own confidence and benefit them as well. Make specific plans to take someone with you for a POP search.

8. What were the disciples told to do in Luke 10:1-11?

9. How might a messenger of peace go about finding a POP?

10. What are the characteristics of a POP?

11. Define oikos.

12. What are the advantages of reaching an oikos in comparison to reaching individuals?

13. What similarities do you see between hiking a mountain and starting a CPM among an unreached people group?

14. Share what you believe God wants you to do in the next 24–48 hours from what you learned in this chapter.

15. Share prayer requests and pray for one another.

3

New Believers
as the Best Evangelists

The CPM team debriefs their experiences sharing the gospel

Faisal was sound asleep when the call to prayer sounded from his neighborhood mosque. He opened one eye. It was still dark. *It must be about 4:30*, he estimated. Just then a rooster crowed, as if to arouse everyone tempted to sleep through morning prayers.

He looked over at Fatima, who was still fast sleep. Faisal turned over and let out a deep breath, thinking how nice another hour of sleep would feel.

Then he remembered the commitment he had made with Yusuf and Nasrudin. They had promised each other to pray for their neighbors each morning when the call to prayer sounded. Such accountability gave Faisal the extra motivation he needed to get out of bed and pray.

He had always resisted such accountability as a burden, but he had finally recognized that accountability helped him do the things he wanted to do, like praying for Muslims early in the morning.

Faisal slipped out from between the sheets and knelt by the bed. "Father," he whispered, "when will my Muslim friends and neighbors learn about how much You love them? Please use me as your hands, feet, and mouth in this place, for the glory of Isa Al Masih. Amen."

* * *

"*Assalam wa'alikum.*" [22]

"*Wa alikum salam.*" [23]

Faisal rejoiced that evening as he looked around the room at his friends. Everyone sat on the floor in a circle and wore a brightly colored *sarong*.[24] The men wore *peci*[25] on their heads and sat cross-legged, while the women covered their heads with scarves and sat with their feet tucked under them. Before each couple a Taurat and Injil was perched on a wooden stand. This was their first meeting since hiking the volcano.

"I'd rather be meeting on the mountain," Faisal grinned. "How about you?"

Everyone nodded.

"As we have discussed, our pattern starts with everyone sharing something they are thankful for," Faisal continued. "Then we share something we are struggling with and pray for each other."

"Who would like to start?"

Animated discussion ensued, followed by prayer for one another.

"We committed to share our personal salvation story with someone this week," Faisal continued. "How did it go?"

The group fell uncharacteristically silent.

"Was it awkward to share your personal salvation story?" Faisal asked.

Nasrudin looked down at his hands. "I can usually talk to anyone about anything. But when I tried to share my salvation story I was suddenly at a loss for words."

"Me too," Yusuf shook his head sadly. "I kept thinking, 'what will they think of me?' I wanted to share my salvation story, but I was afraid of being rejected."

"I was afraid too," Amina admitted.

---

[22] Arabic for "peace be unto you" (the common greeting).

[23] Arabic for "and peace be unto you" (the common response).

[24] Indonesian for a one-piece cloth commonly worn around the waist.

[25] Indonesian for a traditional hat worn mostly by Muslim men.

"I went to the market yesterday," Nur said. "On my way back, I saw a woman carrying a heavy bag of vegetables on one arm and a baby in the other. I offered to help her with her vegetables. As we walked to her house I wanted to share my salvation story with her, but I didn't because I couldn't find a way to work it into the conversation." She shrugged her shoulders.

Yusuf suddenly clapped his hands and everyone jumped.

"Sorry, I was just killing a mosquito."

"Fatima and I went to the park to exercise," Faisal said. "Both of us shared our salvation stories with someone there. It was awkward for me, too, but it helped that I had planned in advance how I would begin. I started by saying, 'There is something that changed my life, could I share a short story with you?' My person said 'Yes,' so I went straight into my story. He listened politely but then didn't want to hear any more. He said he needed to get back to exercising. What other suggestions would help us move beyond the fear of rejection?"

"Knowing in advance how I'll start will give me confidence," Yusuf said. "But it will also help if I remember they aren't rejecting me. They are really rejecting Isa."

Just then the electricity went off, engulfing the room in darkness. Fatima jumped up and returned a few minutes later with candles. "I guess we are like those early disciples in more ways than one," she joked. "They didn't have electricity either!"

After the candles were lit Amina continued, "It helps me to think of myself as a doctor with medicine. The people I share with may not know it, but they are sick. They have an illness caused by sin, and I have the only medicine that will heal them."

Nur looked serious in the flickering candlelight. "I need to recall all Isa has done for me. I want others to experience the same joy and meaning in life I have. I also don't want people to go to hell."

"We can't be discouraged about sharing," Fatima exhorted. "Our job is to look for persons of peace, and God's job is to open hearts. All He expects of us is faithfulness."

"That's a good reminder," Faisal said. "Let's keep seeking opportunities to share our personal salvation stories with those on our prayer lists and with those we meet. Let's not give up.

"Now, please turn to Luke 8:26–39. I'd like two people to read these verses."

Amina and Yusuf each read the passage aloud.

"Now would someone state the passage in their own words?" Faisal asked.

"Isa cast out demons from a man who lived in a cemetery." Nur said. "When Isa was ready to leave, the man wanted to follow Him, but Isa said, 'Return to your home and describe what great things God has done for you.'"

"Does this shock you?" Faisal asked. "This man wanted to follow Isa, and Isa said 'no.' On top of that, Isa told him to share with his friends and family. Wouldn't you expect Isa to train the man first and then send him out?"

"Right!" Amina said. "What could this guy possibly share? He doesn't know anything about following Isa!"

"Actually, he knows a lot." Yusuf smiled, confident in his answer. "We've been learning how to share our personal salvation story. This man could share what Isa did in his life to set him free from bondage to evil spirits."

"Guess what," Faisal said. "That is exactly what he did. The next time Isa returned to that area, five thousand people gathered to hear Him, and He fed them all. This illustrates an important CPM principle: 'New believers are the best evangelists.'

"What do you think?"

"I agree," Nur said. "New believers are enthusiastic about their new faith, and they still have relationships with non-believers. The changes Al Masih has brought to their lives are still fresh, and they can easily tell everyone about what Isa did for them."

Outside a street vendor called, "Satay! Satay!" Faisal and his family often enjoyed these delicious chicken kebabs covered with a spicy peanut sauce, but tonight they had other interests.

"I think it is dangerous for new believers to be witnessing," Yusuf objected. "What if they are careless and share with the wrong person, who then stirs up trouble? That person could persecute the new believer, and the new believer could fall away from the faith."

"Yusuf makes a good point," Faisal said. "What do the rest of you think?"

"Well, there's always a risk," Fatima said. "But in my experience, suffering usually strengthens our faith. It causes us to evaluate whether our beliefs are worth suffering for. Furthermore, isn't there a risk we could be so cautious that we don't share at all? I agree we should exercise common sense, but let's be careful not to dampen the enthusiasm of new believers. Besides, observe what Isa did. He told the man He set free from demons to go tell everyone."

"I have another concern." Yusuf continued. "Suppose the new believer shares with someone who knows the Qur'an well and can articulate the Muslim faith. That person could ask a question that would cause the new believer to doubt his new faith. Do we want that to happen?"

"Of course not," Nasrudin said. "But if what we believe is Truth, then there is an answer to every question anyone could ask. Like the man in our story, the new believer only needs to know the truth of what happened in his own life. No one can take that away from him. And I think the questions he encounters should only strengthen his faith. If he doesn't know, he can ask one of us and we can find the answer together. The Truth can stand up to scrutiny. We shouldn't fear questions even from a genius. The Holy Spirit will help us."

"These are great points to consider," Faisal concluded. "Now, let's take some time to practice our personal salvation stories again with a partner."

When everyone was done, Fatima excused herself and returned with six cups of hot sweet tea and a plate full of fried plantains. The men slid to one corner and talked about fishing, while the women huddled together to discuss a problem one of their children was having at school.

Discuss and apply

1. How did you obey what you concluded God wanted you to do from the previous chapter?"

2. In your opinion, when is accountability positive or negative? What perspective does Faisal demonstrate toward accountability?

3. Do you agree with this statement: "New believers make the best evangelists"? Why or why not?

4. Review the definitions of shema, person of peace and oikos. Refer to the previous chapter if necessary.

5. Refer to your list of fifteen family and friends you are praying daily for. Role play telling your personal salvation story to one of them. Ask God to prepare that person to receive what you share. Plan to talk to that person this week.

6. Read the Critical Elements of CPM listed in Appendix A. What examples of these do you observe in this chapter?

7. If you haven't done prayer-walking and fasting, plan with a teammate to do so this week.

8. Share what you believe God wants you to do in the next 24–48 hours from what you learned in this chapter.

9. Faisal and his group start their meeting by asking what they are thankful for, then they share their struggles and pray for one another. This is one way of expressing care for one another. Take a few minutes now to do this with your team and pray for one another.

4

Engaging in Spiritual Warfare

Faisal discerns spiritual attack and leads the CPM team in responding.

The call to prayer came earlier this morning, or at least it seemed to. Faisal felt unusually tired and unmotivated, and was tempted to roll over and get some more sleep. Then he remembered Yusuf and Nasrudin were hearing that same call to prayer and would be hitting their knees on behalf of their Muslim friends. By sheer force of will, Faisal slipped from between the covers and knelt by his bed.

"O God, most loving and most merciful, we have tried to be faithful to Your calling, but it hasn't been easy. Pour out Your Spirit on these people for whom Al Masih died. Give them dreams and visions about Isa. Please use us, Your humble and fallible servants, to declare Your love among these people. In the name of Isa Al Masih, our divine Master. Amen."

This short prayer brought to the surface all of Faisal's feelings about the difficulties his team had experienced recently. He gazed at his sleeping wife and hesitated for a moment. Then he thought, *I need a long talk with God. I'm going for a walk.*

Slipping on long pants and sandals, Faisal headed outside. The sky overhead was clear and a few stars were still visible. He remembered from Psalm 147:4 that God has given all the stars names. He looked at the brightest star and wondered what its name is.

"O God, I know You are here, and I can come to You with my disappointments and frustrations. I know I can pour out my heart, and You will listen. My life hasn't been the same since I decided to follow You with all my being, but sometimes it's hard, God, really hard. Many times I don't understand what You are doing. Sometimes I feel tempted to quit. But I can't do that; You mean too much to me. All I want is to please You, but right now I don't think I can take much more. I'm spiritually dry, physically spent, and emotionally drained. I'm overwhelmed and hopeless, anxious and fearful, confused and depressed. I'm at the end of myself, and I don't know if I can keep going. I desperately need Your strength."

As he walked down the street, most of the houses were dark, their inhabitants still asleep. At the corner house, a dim light flickered in a kitchen window. Jawaria, his wife's friend, was preparing spring rolls to sell to the elementary school students who would walk past her house in a couple of hours.

"God, whom we call Father, my friends and I feel like giving up. Every day we are making shema statements. Two or three times a week we share the Good News, but so far we haven't found a single person who is open. It is so difficult to keep sharing day in and day out with no results. I know You understand, but somehow I feel better expressing my feelings to You."

Faisal paused at the local mosque. The *imam*[26] who had led the call to prayer this morning was still there, seated cross-legged facing Mecca. He wondered if the imam understood the Arabic he sang each morning, as very few Sayang actually comprehend Arabic.

Faisal counted four others, all men, who had come to pray in the mosque. *Muslims are allowed to pray at home*, he thought, *but doing so doesn't earn as much merit as praying in the mosque. I wonder how many actually wake up to pray in their homes.*

A sense of hopelessness came over him. *God, what will it take to break through to these precious people? When will they understand You take no pleasure in vain repetition?*[27]

---

[26] Islamic leader or teacher.

[27] Matt. 6:7

Faisal continued walking. The sun cast its golden rays across the eastern sky. He could make out rows of freshly planted rice seedlings. Along the edge of the rice fields, *moringa* trees were planted, their roots enriching the soil and their leaves providing nutrition to nursing mothers. He paused to behold the beauty of the sunrise.

"Lord, it seems like everything that could go wrong has gone wrong. I'm so discouraged and confused. I want to quit and run away. The price we are paying seems too high."

Faisal reviewed the recent events: Nasrudin's honey business had been slow, forcing him to work extra hours and miss a couple of meetings. And the river had risen and flooded Nasrudin and Amina's house, covering the floor in mud and ruining most of their wooden furniture.

Faisal was proud of how their group had responded, helping Nasrudin and Amina mop out the mud and collecting money to buy a used bed and a table to replace the damaged ones. They had responded sacrificially to meet Nasrudin and Amina's need, obeying Isa's command to love one another.[28]

But this victory had quickly turned to defeat when Yusuf advised Nasrudin to pay more attention to the weather and move his furniture to higher ground the next time it looked like the river might flood. Nasrudin had exploded with a string of profanity that had offended Yusuf, who then refused to speak to Nasrudin or even attend meetings if Nasrudin was going to be there. The unity they had worked so hard to develop had evaporated so quickly, and over something so insignificant.

Faisal had tried to reconcile the two, pleading with them to look at the situation from the other's point of view, pointing out their duty to go to their brother if they thought there was an offense.[29] But neither would be the first to apologize, and the more Faisal appealed the more hardened they became.

---

[28] John 13:34–35
[29] Matt. 5:23–24

And his own family hadn't been immune to problems. Fatima had been awakened with bad dreams over the past several nights. Their daughter, Sarah, had been accused at school of being a follower of Isa, and supposed friends had pushed her down and spit on her. Faisal was especially angry that the teachers had looked on and done nothing. He had protested to the headmaster, who had assured him this kind of behavior would not be tolerated again. But Faisal worried this was just an empty promise.

Then their son Iman[30] had come down with a fever. Faisal had taken him to the doctor, but the doctor couldn't tell what was wrong. He just gave Iman a fever medication and sent him home.

Finally, three days ago, Faisal had been driving his motorcycle when a dog ran in front of him. Unable to swerve, Faisal hit the dog and went flying over the handlebars, suffering abrasions on his right shoulder and thigh. Even now, it hurt to walk. His front wheel was slightly bent but he didn't have money to fix it.

Faisal turned and began walking home.

The neighborhood was now bustling. Women were busy sweeping the small yards in front of their houses. Children, dressed in their uniforms, were walking to school. Parents were heading to work. Sellers were loading horse-drawn carriages to haul their wares to the market.

As Faisal's house came into view, a sudden thought occurred to him: *Satan wants to discourage and sidetrack us through these challenges. We must not let him win!* Just that realization lifted his spirits. Each of the problems he and his team were experiencing had a natural explanation, but the fact they had all hit at the same time made him think that there was something more to this. He quickened his pace; he knew what he needed to do.

Faisal shared with Fatima his sense that they were experiencing spiritual warfare, and the two prayed together. Again Faisal went to Nasrudin, who finally admitted he had overreacted. Faisal quickly

---

30 Arabic for "faith."

conveyed Nasrudin's change of attitude to Yusuf and asked him to attend that night's CPM meeting.

It shouldn't have been necessary for me to serve as mediator, Faisal reflected, *because Nasrudin and Yusuf know that mature believers take initiative to reconcile with each other.*[31] *But they are still clinging to the Sayang habit of holding onto offenses.*

This whole ordeal reminded Faisal that old habits are deeply embedded. *The process of replacing old cultural patterns with new biblical ones isn't easy, requiring humility and teachability. Both men seem to be softening towards the other, but I'm still not sure either will attend our next meeting.*

* * *

Faisal and Fatima agreed that their group needed to spend extra time in fellowship that night. To improve the atmosphere, Fatima cooked Nasrudin and Yusuf's favorite snack, made from rice, shredded coconut, and brown sugar.

The time for their meeting came, but no one showed up.

Fifteen minutes passed. Still no one.

Finally, Nasrudin and Amina arrived thirty minutes late.

Fifteen minutes later Yusuf and Nur walked in.

No one apologized for being late, but Faisal was thankful everyone was there.

Tension filled the air as Faisal began. "Assalam wa'alikum."

"Wa alikum salam," the others replied half-heartedly.

"We are going to do something different this week," Faisal said. "Think of all that has happened to us these past few weeks: Nasrudin's honey business, the flood, the conflict between Nasrudin and Yusuf, Fatima's bad dreams, Sarah being abused at school, Iman's fever, and my accident. Do you think those things are just coincidence?

"Think about what we've been doing! We are faithfully sharing the Good News. Satan is angry and he's fighting back!

---

[31] Gal. 6:1

"Well, guess what? I'm not giving in. I'm going to take the fight right back to him. Would you join me in getting on our knees and interceding? Let's declare our victory in Al Masih and remind Satan of his sure defeat. Isa is building His Church and the gates of hell cannot prevail against Him. Let's sing a couple of worship songs and then go directly to prayer."

After they sang Faisal prayed, "O God, You are the sovereign God. You rule over heaven and earth. Isa became like us so He might render the devil powerless. In Isa's death He defeated the power of Satan, and in His resurrection He disarmed all the powers of darkness." [32]

"I praise You, O God," Nasrudin prayed, "that we have been crucified, buried, and raised with Al Masih, and we are seated with Him in the heavenly places." [33]

Yusuf prayed next, "Isa, You possess all authority in heaven and on earth. God has put everything, including all the powers of darkness, under Your feet." [34]

"Satan, you are a defeated foe," Fatima prayed. "We bind you in any way you would try to kill, steal, or destroy. We cancel every scheme and reject every plan you have crafted against us, except what God allows for our good and His glory. Amen." [35]

When they had finished praying, they all shook hands.

Nasrudin said to Yusuf, "I should never have lost control and said what I did. I was angry at what happened, and took it out on you. I'm very ashamed of my behavior. Will you forgive me?"

"Of course I'll forgive you, my brother. Will you forgive me for being insensitive in what I said, and for taking offense over something so trivial?"

"Certainly!"

Nasrudin and Yusuf embraced.

---

[32] Heb. 2:14, Col. 2:15

[33] Rom. 6:4–6, Eph. 2:5–7

[34] Matt. 28:18, 1 Cor. 15:25

[35] Matt. 12:29, 16:17–19, John 10:10, Rom. 8:28

"We clearly needed to spend some time together in prayer." Faisal commented. "Let's always remember we are in a spiritual battle. Satan will do all he can to divide us. If he can't drive us apart, he will try to tempt us into sexual immorality, pride, or materialism. If that doesn't work, he will try to discourage us or fill us with fear. He has many weapons. But it doesn't matter what he throws at us, we are victorious if we abide in Al Masih and stay united. We can't let offenses drive us apart. Do you agree?"

"Yes," everyone said in unison.

Fatima brought out the special snack she had prepared, and the group fellowshipped together long into the night as they savored the unity and closeness they again felt toward one another.

Discuss and apply

1. How did you obey what you concluded God wanted you to do from the previous chapter?"

2. How is your relationship with God? Can you pour out your heart to Him like Faisal did? If not, what hinders you?

3. Have you ever experienced spiritual warfare? Explain. If so, what helped you during that time?

4. Discuss with your teammates what you learned in this chapter about spiritual warfare praying.

5. Satan often tries to divide our teams. What principles are helpful to remember to guard the unity of your team?

6. What principles do you follow to resolve conflict with others?

7. How does this chapter help you to not be quickly offended or, if you have been offended, to quickly be reconciled?

8. Discuss with your teammates how you will each respond when you see conflict developing with your team. Express to one another your determination not to divide you.

9. In what practical ways can you serve your team members today?

10. Share what you believe God wants you to do in the next 24–48 hours from what you learned in this chapter.

11. Pray now with your team, and daily on your own, for God to keep you alert to the spiritual battle surrounding you and your team.

5

Finding Persons of Peace

The team learns key tools for finding POPs, and what to do next

When they met a week later, Faisal looked at his team with joy. "Let's review. We have studied CPMs over the last several months, and learned that God is glorified as He is worshipped among every people group.[36] To achieve this goal, God calls His people to work in teams to reach unreached people groups. We also observed the importance and practice of prayer in the early Church.

"Isa sent His disciples out to look for a person of peace, or POP. This POP introduced the disciple to their oikos. We observed in Acts that in most cases whole groups were reached, and not just individuals. We have discussed and practiced two tools: making shema statements and sharing our personal salvation stories. A third tool for finding a POP is asking people if they know someone who has had a dream from God. Even if they say 'No' to the question we may discover spiritual openness."

"I read," Fatima added, "that in some places a team has gone prayer-walking around an area, asking God to send dreams and visions there, and not long thereafter a person has had a dream about Isa and becomes the key to reaching the entire community." [37]

---

36 John 15:8

37 Asking about a dream is illustrated in Chapter 13. According to another CPM trainer, one team that went prayer-walking and then asked about "dreams from God" found that 20% responded positively.

"Yes," Faisal said. "We plead for God to give dreams and then ask people if they have had one. Let's pray in pairs for God to send dreams among the Sayang."

When they had finished praying Faisal continued, "A fourth tool I learned for finding POPs is talking to people until we discover a felt need, and then praying with that person on the spot. Most needs fall into three categories: sickness,[38] demonization,[39] or whatever people find overwhelming—like a personal or family crisis. We call this last category the 'storms of life.'[40]

"For each felt need we have a story about Isa which we tell before praying for that felt need. For sickness we use the story of Isa healing the paralytic in Luke 5:17–26. For demonization we tell the story of Isa casting out the demon from the man in the synagogue in Luke 4:31–37. And before praying for the 'storms of life' we tell Mark 4:35–41, about Isa calming the storm on the sea. We'll role play these stories and praying for felt needs in future meetings.

"A fifth tool for finding a POP is using verses about Isa in the Qur'an as a bridge to offer to discuss the Taurat and Injil.[41] A sixth tool is a gospel presentation called *Creation to Al Masih*,[42] summarizing the theme of sacrifice in the Taurat and how this was fulfilled in Isa's life. We will also practice these last two methods later.

"We have six different tools to find POPs, but one goal: to find those whom the Holy Spirit has prepared and invite them and their oikos to discuss prophet and Isa stories with us.

"Now we want to discuss what we do if someone responds to one of these methods." Faisal glanced around to see that everyone was tracking with him. "Many times we meet someone who is open, but how can we make certain he or she is a POP?"

---

[38] Offering prayer for healing is illustrated at the end of Chapter 19.

[39] Offering prayer against demonization is illustrated in Chapters 15–16.

[40] Offering prayer for "storms of life" is illustrated in Chapters 13 and 14.

[41] Use of the Qur'an in leading to the Bible is illustrated in Chapters 9–11, 21.

[42] Appendix C. Use of *Creation to Christ* is illustrated in Chapter 20.

Amina answered, "The only way I know is to ask the person if they will gather their oikos to discuss chronological stories in the Taurat and Injil[43] with us."[44]

The others nodded in agreement.

"Right. Now let's talk more about these stories," Faisal continued. "We have ten prophet stories, and fourteen Isa stories.[45] Why do we start with prophet stories?"

"This is how God chose to reveal Himself to His people to prepare them for His Son. These stories are especially relevant to our Muslim friends because they already know something about the prophets, and by starting there we can build on points of agreement rather than getting into arguments," Yusuf replied.

"Through these stories, they also observe the character of God," Nasrudin added. "God is all-knowing, so He knows all our sins. He is just, so He punishes us for these sins. He is loving and merciful, so He saves us from our sins. And through these stories, our friends observe that all the prophets offered sacrifices. Why? God's Word tells us, 'without the shedding of blood there is no forgiveness of sins.'"[46]

"Exactly," Faisal said. "Then we move directly to the Isa stories. They learn of His virgin birth, teaching, miracles, death and resurrection. For the first time, they must face the question Isa asked, 'Who do men say that I am?'

"Through these stories our friends discover what Peter himself did, that Isa is the Messiah, the Son of the living God.[47]

---

[43] Discussing Bible stories in chronological order increases retention and depth of understanding.

[44] Often it isn't clear if someone is a POP in the first meeting, so the CPM practitioner will build rapport and establish trust while guiding conversation to spiritual topics over weeks or months. The CPM practitioner may need to address objections (e.g. claims that the Injil hasn't been corrupted), identify a felt need as a bridge to the stories (e.g. a family problem), or create interest (e.g. point out inconsistencies in what the Muslim believes). Sometimes a person is not a POP when we first meet them, but a later crisis may cause them to start searching so that they contact the CPM practitioner ready to study. The CPM practitioner must be Spirit-led to know when to reduce time with one person who is not ready to focus on searching for others who are ready to study now.

[45] Appendix C.

[46] Heb. 9:22

[47] Matthew 16:13-16.

"In this life we face so many challenges," Faisal continued. "We want to obtain blessings and avoid calamity. Who can give me some examples?"

"We need God's help to pass a test, get a job, find a spouse, and have a child," Amina said. "And we need God's blessings on our crops, our businesses, and our families."

"We also want protection from sickness, curses, and accidents," Fatima added. "We fear the future, death, and evil spirits."

"And we long for protection, peace, and guidance," Nur said.

"These are all legitimate needs," Yusuf said, "and God meets each one through Isa Al Masih. So Isa is the key to eternal life, and the key to living abundantly in this life." [48]

"Yes! Then in the fourteenth Isa story, we invite people to surrender their lives to Isa as their Savior and Lord," Faisal said. "How is this approach different from other approaches?"

"This is a win-them-slow approach," Nur answered. "We build the foundation by exploring God's character and letting them discover the truth that without the shedding of blood there is no forgiveness of sins. Then we help them see the wonder and beauty of Isa and discover that the Son of God shed His blood on a wooden cross to provide cleansing for their sins."

"People who are not open will become bored and drop out," Nasrudin added. "This actually reduces the risk to us, because only those who persevere to the end are invited to follow Isa. This process also gives the oikos time to consider together exactly who Isa is, and count the cost of following Him."

"Wow!" Faisal said, "We really have learned a lot together.

"Now there are two essential yet difficult transitions to make if we are to establish healthy house fellowships that multiply and are led by oikos leaders.[49] In the first transition the outside leader encourages and attends meetings with the oikos. In the second transition the

---

[48] Formal Islam answers, "What happens when I die?" Folk Islam answers, "How do I live well in this life?" The prophet and Isa stories together demonstrate that God in Christ answers both.

[49] An "oikos leader" is a leader from within the household.

outside leader transfers leadership to the oikos leaders[50] and stops attending the meeting with the oikos.[51]

"What does that look like for us?" Faisal asked rhetorically. "We are outside leaders. We ask the POP to gather his or her oikos, and we attend several meetings. Then we identify the oikos leaders, equip them to lead, and stop attending the meetings ourselves."

"I don't understand," Nur said. "Who are the 'oikos leaders'?"

"Our goal," Faisal reiterated, "is to reach an oikos and equip some in the group to lead. You and I are outsiders because we aren't members of that particular oikos. Every oikos has natural leaders. We don't choose the leaders; we simply identify them. We call them oikos leaders."

"So once we identify oikos leaders," Nur continued, "how do we equip them?"

"Great question. Let's take a quick break and then discuss this." Faisal turned to Fatima. "Honey, would you bring out the snacks?"

Fatima returned with six mugs of coffee and a snack of sliced papaya and mango.

Yusuf added three large teaspoons of sugar to his coffee.

"I see you like a little coffee with your sugar," Faisal teased.

Yusuf just grinned as he stirred his coffee.

Faisal waited until everyone had been served. "Okay. Let's talk about how to equip oikos leaders. Really it is quite simple; in the presence of the group we affirm the leaders and their natural leadership abilities, and we let the group know these leaders will facilitate the group."

"But what if the oikos leaders aren't ready to lead?" Nasrudin asked with concern.

---

50 The Biblical pattern is multiple leaders. Where possible identify two or more leaders.

51 The outside leader may skip these transitions and equip the oikos leader directly if: 1) the outside leader's presence creates problems (such as suspicion in a hostile community), or 2) the outside leader already knows who the oikos leader is and senses God's leading to model with them privately rather than in front of the whole oikos. In such circumstances, the outside leader can simply practice the model with just the oikos leader. This is illustrated in Chapter 12 with Haji Ishmael and Sharif, and in Chapter 13 with Fatima and Inne.

"We assure the group that we will prepare the leaders for the next story prior to each meeting, and answer any questions he or she may have at that time."

"Isn't it risky for non-believers to study the Bible on their own?" Yusuf asked in disbelief.

"No," Faisal said, "the Holy Spirit is a very competent teacher.[52] These groups will read the text twice and retell it twice. In a group process they will correct each other if someone has misunderstood the text. Simple discovery questions focus on application rather than high theology. Also, there is high accountability between the outside leader and the oikos leaders. If the group begins going astray, the outside leader will know immediately. Finally, there are many stories of people picking up the Bible and coming to faith on their own."

Faisal glanced around the room. Everyone seemed skeptical, but willing to give it a try.

"Let's move to application now. Take out the list of fifteen family and friends you have been praying for daily. Let's divide into mens and womens groups, and discuss who you want to share with and what you will say to invite them to study with you. Role play sharing your personal salvation story with that person. Remember we want to share with everyone on our list until we find someone who wants to study with us." Faisal said.

Yusuf coughed. "Explain that again?"

Clearly all that sugar is affecting Yusuf's brain, Faisal laughed to himself. "You approach the first person on your list and share your personal salvation story. Conclude your story by offering to discuss chronological stories in the Taurat and Injil with him and his oikos. You can say something like, 'I've found some stories from the Taurat and Injil that have really changed my life. May I share them with you?' If the first person isn't open, go to the second person. If the second person isn't open, continue on to the third person. Share with each person on your list until you find someone who wants to discuss the prophet stories with you."

---

[52] John 6:45, 16:13

"What if no one on our list wants to discuss these stories with us?" Nasrudin asked.

"Then we need to approach people we don't know. We need to be determined. We need to pray, pray, pray and share, share, share until we find someone who wants to discuss the prophet stories with us." Faisal spoke with the passion of a preacher. "Remember that God has promised He will prepare people's hearts. Persons of peace are out there, wanting to be found. We need to knock on doors until one opens to us." Faisal paused to let his points sink in.

"In order to gain more confidence in sharing our personal salvation stories, Fatima and I would like to schedule separate times when we can go as men and as women to look for persons of peace."

They agreed on a time.

"Amina, would you close our time together in prayer?"

Discuss and apply

1. How did you obey what you concluded God wanted you to do from the previous chapter?"

2. Faisal gave a brief overview of CPM methodology studied thus far (God's glory, prayer, partners, shema, person of peace, and oikos). Explain this process in your own words.

3. We have now introduced six ways to find a POP:
   - making shema statements,
   - sharing your personal salvation story,
   - asking if they know someone who has had a dream from God,
   - offering prayer for healing, demonization, and "storms of life" (with a Bible story showing Jesus' power),
   - using verses in the Qur'an as a bridge to the Bible, and
   - sharing a *Creation to Christ* gospel presentation.

   Share what the response has been when you have used each of these tools. Which of these are you not trying consistently?

4. Discuss what you would say to ask someone if they know someone who has had a dream from God?

5. State in your own words the purpose of the prophet stories and the Jesus stories.

6. How does a win-them-slow approach reduce the risks, to you and others, of bringing Muslims to Christ?

7. State in your own words the two transitions Faisal described. Why are these difficult, and why are they important?

8. If you have not already done so, write down fifteen family and friends who don't know Jesus. Practice with a partner how you will introduce and share your personal salvation story with one of them, and how you will conclude to invite them to discuss chronological Bible stories with you.

9. Share what you believe God wants you to do in the next 24–48 hours from what you learned in this chapter.

10. Pray with your team now for the people on your list, and then daily on your own.

6

Sharing a Personal Salvation Story

Faisal shares his testimony with his old friend Ahmad (teacher)

Faisal had invited Ahmad to meet him at a local coffee shop. From childhood playmates who pretended to be seafaring marauders to college roommates, Ahmad had been his closest friend growing up. *I wonder what he will think about my decision to follow Isa Al Masih*, thought Faisal as he arrived at the coffee shop. Ahmad was already seated at a table. He was darker than most Sayang. His hair and mustache were thick and his sideburns bushy. He was generally friendly, yet more reserved than Faisal.

"Assalam wa'alikum."

"Wa alikum salam."

Ahmad stood to give Faisal a warm hug and a slap on the back.

Faisal liked this coffee shop because it served only locally grown coffee raised in the mountains outside their town. The waitress brought a menu and two bowls of water for them to wash their hands, along with a notepad to write down their order. Soon she also brought sugar and their coffees to the table.

Faisal took a deep breath and tried to calm his nerves. Ahmad was the next name on his list of fifteen names, and he had been praying for Ahmad every day for a week. He had just texted Yusuf and Nasrudin, asking them to pray for this meeting, so he couldn't back out now. *Why is this so hard?*

Trying to sound normal, Faisal began, "Ahmad, you and I have known each other a long time."

"Yeah. That's for sure." Ahmad grinned. "We grew up in the same village, and played soccer in the field behind my house when we were finished taking care of the sheep. We climbed coconut trees when we were thirsty, and we went fishing every chance we got. We even got circumcised at the same time, remember?"

"How could I forget? We were so excited. We were only seven but we got to wear our traditional clothing and ride on the back of that wooden horse. Everyone was singing and dancing, and we were loving all that attention. But then they did the actual circumcision! Never in my life have I felt such pain!"

Both men laughed and crossed their legs. Ahmad was clearly enjoying this walk down memory lane. "We both decided to attend teachers college in the capital. I think we were too afraid to go to the big city alone."

Ahmad pulled a cigarette from his breast pocket and offered it to Faisal. Faisal had smoked since he was twelve years old, but he had quit about a year after becoming a follower of Isa, when he realized he was wasting money on himself that would be better spent on milk for his growing children. However he accepted the cigarette, figuring it might help create a more relaxed atmosphere.

Ahmad took a deep drag on his cigarette and exhaled slowly. "We rented a house with other guys from our village. We all used to hate when it was your turn to cook. You made the worst fried rice ever!" Ahmad laughed at his own joke.

"After we graduated, we got hired at schools in different districts. I'm glad we have both transferred back to this area. We may be at different schools, but it's nice to see you from time to time."

"I feel the same way."

Sharing with Ahmad is going to be more difficult than I had imagined. I enjoy Ahmad and want to remain friends. What I am about to share could change our friendship forever. But I've got to do it.

"Something has happened in my life I want to share with you," Faisal stammered and glanced at the wall over Ahmad's shoulder. *I've rehearsed this introduction with Yusuf and Nasrudin, so why does my voice sound so tentative? I am about to share the most important news in the whole world, news that Ahmad needs to hear. It isn't an exaggeration to say this news is a matter of life and death. I must speak with confidence and enthusiasm. After all, this really is good news!*

"As you know, we started Muslim instruction at the mosque when we were six years old. The imam said I was his most diligent student. I memorized verses from the Holy Qur'an, faithfully said my prayers, and fasted during Ramadan;[53] but if I'm honest I always felt empty in my heart, as if I was searching for more."

Ahmad nodded as if he understood and sipped his coffee. He held the coffee in his mouth for a moment before swallowing to savor the rich blend of coffee and sugar.

"You recall that, when I was eleven years old, my older brother got deathly sick. My father took him to the imam who prayed for him, but he didn't get well. Then my father took him to the local shaman. Instead of getting better, my brother got sicker. I prayed desperately that my brother would be healed, but then he died. I was filled with grief, disappointment, and confusion."

Ahmad reached across the table and gently squeezed Faisal's arm. "I remember when that happened. I wanted to say something to comfort you, but I didn't know what to say."

"Then someone in our village became possessed by an evil spirit. Sometimes I would hear him yelling, and that made me afraid I too would be possessed. Growing up I had so many fears: fear of death, evil spirits, the future. I felt alone and confused. One night I went for a walk. I looked up into a night sky filled with stars and a full moon, and said in my heart, 'God, are you there? Why did you create me? What is my purpose in this life? How can I find meaning and peace? How can I overcome these fears?' But the more questions I asked, the more confused and hopeless I became."

"I've had some of those fears too."

---

53 The Muslim holy month of daily community fasting from dawn to sunset.

"As you know, I fell in love with Fatima when we were at teachers college. To me, she was the most beautiful woman in the world, and we got along great. We got married and had our first child. I thought there could never be a more beautiful child. Fatima began giving more attention to our baby and I felt neglected. Since our baby slept with us, we didn't have our usual intimate times, plus Fatima was always tired. Frequently I got angry at her, and said things I'm ashamed to admit."

Ahmad shook his head. "I can relate to that."

"When I first started teaching, my salary was very low, and I had a wife and child to support. A friend and I decided to start a small business. He said he had an uncle in Jakarta who would send us high quality T-shirts we could sell. Supposedly this uncle wanted to help his nephew so he didn't require full payment for the shirts when they were delivered, but he did ask for a down payment so he would know we were serious. I borrowed money from everyone I could, took all the money Fatima and I had, which wasn't much, and gave it to my friend.

"The next day, he disappeared and I haven't seen him since. I can't tell you how ashamed I felt around the people I had borrowed from, and how guilty and foolish I felt in squandering what little money Fatima and I had saved. I was so angry at my 'friend.' I hated him and wanted revenge. If we had met, I'm sure I would have killed him on the spot. My anger, shame, and guilt gave me an ulcer and made me even more irritable. As a result Fatima and I argued constantly. I was a slave to my feelings. I wanted to be free but I didn't know how."

Ahmad leaned forward, captivated by Faisal's story.

"It wasn't long afterwards I saw a film about Isa Al Masih on the Internet. I was amazed that Isa could speak our language. The film explained that Isa was born of a virgin, lived a sinless life, healed the sick, and raised the dead. I remembered from our Muslim classes that the Qur'an taught the same thing, and I felt a deep longing to know more about Isa.

"As it happened another teacher at my school was a follower of Isa Al Masih. I noticed he worked hard, never complained, and was always cheerful. Finally I got up the courage to ask if he had an Injil. He said 'Yes,' and agreed to loan it to me. I began reading the Injil, and felt such peace and joy whenever I read it. Even Fatima noticed how different I was."

Ahmad frowned. He leaned back and crossed his arms.

"One day I was walking past this teacher's house and heard the most beautiful music. The songs were praising God in our Sayang musical style and language. I stood there, mesmerized.

"A few days later, I decided to pour out my heart to this teacher. I told him the whole story about how my supposed friend had deceived me and taken all my money. I confessed that I hated him, and couldn't stop being bitter and disappointed. This man listened patiently until I finished. He seemed to really empathize with me. Then he said, 'The only way you can be free from this bitterness is through forgiveness, but humanly this is impossible.' I could see my bitterness was wrecking my health and ruining my relationship with Fatima, so I asked him, 'How can I forgive this man?'

"He told me the story of how God created Adam and Eve, and placed them in Paradise, a place called Eden. They were naked, but didn't feel any shame. Unfortunately, they disobeyed God. When they sinned, their eyes were opened and they realized they were naked. God clothed them with animal skins and then drove them out of Paradise.

"'You may be wondering why He used animal skins,' he said. 'The answer is found in the Injil, which says, "Without the shedding of blood there is no forgiveness of sins." God shed an animal's blood to cover Adam and Eve's nakedness.' This teacher then explained that all the prophets offered blood sacrifices because that is what God demanded for their sins. 'Why a blood sacrifice?' he asked? A verse in the Taurat says the life of the creature is in the blood.[54] It is for this reason we sacrifice a sheep or goat during Id Al-Adha just like Abraham did. The shedding of blood reveals the seriousness of our sin, and the cost of restoring our relationship with God.'

---

[54] Lev. 17:11

"This teacher also reminded me how important blood is in our culture. For instance, before we plant or harvest a crop, we sacrifice a chicken. Before we go on a long trip or build a house we sacrifice a chicken. Furthermore, if someone is killed in one village, people from that village will murder someone from the killer's village. Why? Eye for eye, tooth for tooth and blood for blood."

Ahmad nodded to affirm the importance of blood in their culture. The waitress offered more coffee, and both politely declined.

"This teacher then told me only one prophet never offered a sacrifice, because *that* prophet *became* the sacrifice. As the Qur'an and 'before books' teach, Isa Al Masih never committed a sin, so His blood alone is holy. Isa Al Masih shed His blood on a wooden cross so that we might receive forgiveness of sins.

"This teacher concluded by telling me if I confessed my sins and asked Isa to forgive me, He would. And He would give me the power to forgive the man who deceived me.

"I prayed a simple prayer asking Isa to forgive me, and I gave my life to Him. It is impossible to describe all that Isa has done in my life since then. I am no longer bitter or angry. Instead I have peace, joy, and meaning in life. I no longer fear death, evil spirits, or the future. And Fatima and I now enjoy a deeper, closer marriage.

"As my close friend, Ahmad, I wanted you to know what had happened to me. What do you think?"

"To be honest I'm really not sure. I had no idea those things had happened to you. You have given me a lot to think about. I'm glad you told me. But it's getting late; I should be heading home."

Faisal looked intently at his friend. "There is one more thing I'd like to ask you. Following Isa has radically changed my life for the better, and I want that for you too. I have downloaded some stories about the prophets in Sayang from the Internet. These stories come from the Taurat, Zabur, and Injil, and they have transformed my life. Could I share one of them with you and Hajar to see if you like them?"

Ahmad hesitated.

"I won't pressure you to believe these stories. I would just like to come over and share a story about Adam.[55] If you like it, I've got other stories. If not, no worries. We'll be friends like always."

Ahmad put out his cigarette. "I guess that would be okay."

"When would be a good time for me to come over?"

"Tomorrow is alright, I guess. Let's be done before magrib.[56] I'll definitely want to go pray after we meet."

"Who else will be there?"

"Hajar and my sister Siti, who lives with us and goes to the same teachers college we did. My son, Rahmat, will also be there."

"That sounds like a great group. See you tomorrow. Assalam wa'alikum." Faisal stood and patted his friend on the back.

Ahmad looked puzzled and hesitated, then replied softly, "Wa alikum salam."

After Ahmad left, Faisal quickly texted Fatima and his friends. "You'll never believe what just happened!"

---

[55] As this book is being published, the author is experimenting with "hook" stories—biblical stories involving felt needs like worry, stress, and fear which serve as a bridge for inviting others to study the prophets stories. See **StubbornPerseverance.com**

[56] Arabic for the fourth daily prayer of Muslims, around sunset.

Discuss and apply

1. How did you obey what you concluded God wanted you to do from the previous chapter?"

2. Can you relate to Faisal's fears about sharing his personal salvation story with his friend Ahmad? How do you overcome your fears?

3. How did Faisal introduce his personal salvation story?

4. A personal salvation story should have three parts: a) the felt needs you had before coming to Christ, b) the process of coming to Christ, and c) how your life has changed since coming to Christ. Look back at Faisal's story and find examples of each part.

5. What did Faisal say to offer the stories to Ahmad?

6. How did Faisal encourage Ahmad to invite his oikos?

7. Practice your personal salvation story with each other. Keep it under three minutes.

8. Share what you believe God wants you to do in the next 24–48 hours from what you learned in this chapter.

9. Share prayer requests with your team and pray for one another.

7

Introducing the First Prophet Story

Faisal leads Ahmad's family through the story of Adam and Eve

Faisal texted his CPM friends: "I'm heading to meet with Ahmad and his family. Please pray."

He parked his motorcycle next to Ahmad's and called out the customary greeting through the open front door.

"Assalam wa'alikum."

Ahmad appeared and extended his hand hesitantly. "Wa alikum salam."

To Faisal, Ahmad seemed neither warm nor distant, as if he hadn't quite made up his mind about what Faisal had shared, and was hesitant about discussing the story of Adam and Eve with him.

Ahmad ushered Faisal through the visitor's room and into the family room. Ahmad pointed to an old sagging couch for Faisal to sit on. Ahmad took his seat in a wooden chair next to the couch. No other furniture was in the room except a new large flat-screen TV that blared from the wall opposite the couch. An old calendar with a beautiful mountain scene decorated one wall.

Ahmad's wife Hajar brought in a chair from the kitchen, and his sister and son brought in chairs from the visitor's room. All eyes turned to Faisal. He glanced at the TV. Ahmad, taking the cue, got up and turned it off.

Faisal looked around the room and smiled warmly at each person. Turning to Hajar, Faisal remarked about how good it had been to visit with Ahmad at the coffee shop the day before. "It's been a long time since I laughed that hard. Ahmad recalls quite a few embarrassing tales about me!"

Hajar returned the compliment politely, yet with little emotion. "Ahmad enjoyed himself too."

Faisal sensed they wanted to be done with the small talk, so he began. "Yesterday when we met, I told Ahmad I had found some stories about the prophets in Sayang on the Internet. These stories have really helped my family and me, so I asked Ahmad if I could share them with you.

"Before we start, I think it is good to express something we are thankful for. I'll start and then we'll go around the room. I'm thankful God gave me a good friend like Ahmad. I have so many memories of us growing up together, and I'm sure I wouldn't have finished teachers college if Ahmad hadn't been there."

Ahmad spoke next. "I'm thankful for a friend like you too, Faisal. I'm glad we could meet yesterday. Your life has such purpose and peace. It makes me wonder if I have been searching for something, and didn't even know it."

Hajar took a turn. "I'm thankful Ahmad has a job in the city now. He used to leave early Monday morning to go to the village to teach, and then return home Saturday afternoon after school got out. With Rahmat almost a teenager, he needs his father around more."

"I'm thankful to be healthy again," said Siti, Ahmad's sister. "For two weeks I was sick with malaria."

Rahmat acted very shy and didn't want to speak.

"I have another question for us," Faisal said. "What are some challenges or struggles you are facing right now? Since I've had time to prepare I'll go first again. I hit a dog and fell off my motorcycle a few weeks ago. I'm pretty much healed, but my shoulder is still sore."

Precedent had been set, so Ahmad went next. "One of the teachers at my school is out on maternity leave. Since we teach the same grade, now I have to teach her class too."

"This is actually my mom's house," Hajar said. "She's visiting my sister right now, but next week she'll be back. This house has only three bedrooms, so when she's gone Ahmad and I use her bedroom and Siti and Rahmat have their own rooms. But when Mom comes back, Ahmad will move into Rahmat's room and I'll move into Siti's room. We would like to move into our own house but right now we don't have enough money."

Siti said she had fallen behind in her school work while she was sick. "It's been hard catching up."

Rahmat mentioned that he was nervous because he had to take the national tests soon at school.

Faisal pulled out the piece of paper he had brought along. "This story comes from the Taurat, but I find it is easiest to print the story out front and back on a piece of paper. Ahmad, would you read the story?"

Ahmad took the piece of paper and read the story of creation and Adam and Eve's fall from honor into sin and shame.[57]

"Thanks, Ahmad. The story is long, and it has a lot of details. Hajar would you mind reading the story again?"

Ahmad quickly interjected, "Actually Hajar doesn't read well. She only finished third grade. Let Siti read it."

Faisal's heart sank for embarrassing Hajar. *Why didn't I think to ask one of the students to read the text?* "Oh, I'm sorry. No problem. Here Siti, please read the story."

"Thanks, Siti," Faisal said. "In my family we take turns retelling the story. It helps us remember the story, and brings it alive. Hajar, would you like to give it a try?"

"I'll try as long as the others help me out," she said shyly. Hajar slowly recounted the story, chuckling as she imagined a snake speaking to Adam and Eve.

"Excellent. Who else would like to try?"

"I guess I could." Siti told the story with great animation, putting her palms together against her cheek and tilting her head as God made Adam go to sleep, and then lowering her voice to make it sound authoritative when God called out to Adam and Eve.

---

[57] Appendix C lists the chronological Bible stories referenced in this book.

"You're a good story teller, Siti! Now I have three questions for us to consider. First, what do we learn about God from this story?"

"God is all powerful. He created heaven and earth."

"He's also all-knowing because He knew Adam and Eve had eaten from the Kholdi[58] tree."

A gecko made a clicking sound behind a curtain, but no one paid any attention.

"We know God is just because He punished Adam, Eve, and the serpent. Yet we see He is also merciful because He didn't destroy Adam and Eve, and He provided animal skins for them."

"Good answers!" Faisal was pleased to see the Holy Spirit leading everyone to discover truth for themselves.

"Now for the second question. How can we apply this story to our personal lives?"

"If you meet a talking snake, run!" Ahmad quipped.

Hajar was more thoughtful. "For me, it is a reminder that there is nothing hidden from God's sight."

After a few more comments Faisal continued. "Here is the third question: How can we apply this story to help someone else? It is important not only to obey God's Word for our own benefit, but also to apply it to help others."

"I'm not sure if this is the right answer, but this would be a good story for my friend who is facing temptation right now."

As their discussion wound to a conclusion, Faisal said, "This has been a very enjoyable time, but I should be heading home. I have another story, about Noah. Would you like to hear it next week?"

Ahmad smiled as he stood up. "Sure, why not? Halfway through today's story I felt goosebumps and remembered my mom telling me that goosebumps happen when a demon is nearby. 'But wait a minute!' I thought. 'I don't feel fearful, I feel peaceful. Maybe that means this story is true!'"

"I believe it is.

Is there anyone else you'd like to invite next time?"

---

[58] The Qur'anic name for the tree of the knowledge of good and evil.

Hajar nodded. "My mom will be here. Can she come?"

"Well, of course!"

As Faisal turned toward the door, Ahmad touched him on the arm. "Before you rush off, Hajar has baked some cake, and boxed it up for you to take home to your family."

Discuss and apply

1. How did you obey what you concluded God wanted you to do from the previous chapter?"

2. Why do you think they read the story twice?

3. Why is it important to retell the story twice?

4. Why is it important to stress obedience?

5. Do you think it was awkward for Faisal to meet with the family? What did he do to give himself courage?

6. How did Faisal trust the Holy Spirit to lead the discussion?

7. If you haven't shared chronological Bible stories with anyone, what obstacles do you face in starting?

8. Whom can you invite to discuss chronological Bible stories with you? What is their oikos? What can you say to invite them? When will you invite them?

9. Review the Critical Elements of CPM listed in Appendix A. What examples of these principles do you observe in this chapter?

10. Share what you believe God wants you to do in the next 24–48 hours from what you learned in this chapter.

11. Pray specifically with your team for opportunities to discuss chronological Bible stories with non-believers.

8

Training Others to Facilitate Discovery Groups

Faisal equips Ahmad to lead, and Ahmad talks with Hasan (doctor)

Faisal rejoiced inside as he looked around at Ahmad's family.

They had just concluded their fourth discovery group meeting,[59] and all the awkwardness of the first meeting had evaporated.

They had enjoyed energetic discussions and laughed often through the stories of Noah, Abraham and Lot, and Abraham and Ishmael.

When Rahmat played the part of Noah and acted out herding the animals into the ark, everyone laughed because he had trouble getting a stubborn elephant into the ark.

Faisal was impressed by their insights, and how they had applied the stories to their lives. Now it was time for a transition.

"Next week we'll have a new leader," Faisal announced.

"Who?" everyone asked, surprised.

"Ahmad. Ahmad will lead us next week."

Faisal smiled mischievously at Ahmad, who looked back in shock. "Don't worry. I'm going to equip Ahmad privately to lead you. I'll be here too, but Ahmad will facilitate our next meeting."

Everyone seemed doubtful, but no one protested.

After a snack and talking about the weather, Faisal set a time when he and Ahmad could meet, then excused himself to go home.

---

[59] A "discovery group meeting" is an oikos containing at least some non-believers, gathered to discuss chronological Bible stories.

* * *

Faisal met Ahmad at the same coffee shop where they had first met. "I know you are skeptical that you can lead the group, but I'm going to coach you through it. We use this same pattern every time we meet:

1. What are you thankful for?
2. What are your struggles?
3. How did you apply the last story?
4. Read the new story aloud two or three times.
5. Have two people retell the story in their own words.
6. What did you learn about God?
7. How can you apply these verses to your life?
8. How can you apply these verses to help someone else?

"Isn't this simple?"

Ahmad nodded.

"This pattern is important. Instead of telling people what the Taurat and Injil say, we ask questions that open the door for God to speak to them. Using these simple questions we can quickly learn to facilitate studies. Discovery questions like these keep lessons grounded in God's Word rather than human opinion. And insights that people discover for themselves stay with them much longer than those they hear from others."

Faisal handed the next story to Ahmad. "This is about Abraham offering his son. Now, you facilitate our discussion."

Ahmad raised his eyebrows as if to ask, "Are you sure?"

Faisal just smiled.

Ahmad slowly picked up the paper. "So Faisal, what are you thankful for?"

Ahmad continued facilitating the remaining questions.

"Great job!" Faisal said after their discussion. "I knew you could do it. This pattern is really simple. Do you think you can do this with your family?"

"I'm not sure, but I'll give it a try."

"I'll be there to help you, but I'm going to let you facilitate."

* * *

At Ahmad's suggestion they met again at the same coffee shop. It was convenient for both of them, and there was a booth that offered some privacy. They both ordered coffee.

"How did you feel the meeting with your family went?"

Ahmad's face lit up. "I think it went great. It felt good to lead my family spiritually. Thanks for being there to support me."

"Hey, I was glad to. Now let's study the sixth prophet story so you'll be ready to facilitate it with your family. Only this time I'm not going to attend. You are ready to lead, and my presence would hinder the group from considering you their leader."

"But what if they ask me a question I can't answer?"

"Don't worry. Point them to the text and ask, 'What does the text say?' Besides, I'm going to meet with you after each meeting. You can ask me the question then and, if I don't know the answer, I'll find someone who does."

After role playing the sixth prophet story, Faisal asked, "What do you think of these stories?"

"They are fascinating. I never knew these details about the prophets. I love reading and discussing them with my family. Studying these stories has really brought my family closer together. And these stories are changing my life in other ways, as well."

"That's what happened in my family too. When we started studying these stories and discussing their application, we each began changing, and the time we spent brought us closer together as a family. You know, these stories are too good to keep to ourselves. Whom else could you share these stories with?"

"I don't know. I'm just a teacher. What do I know?"

"You know what God is doing in your life. Open your eyes! There are people around you who need God to change them too. Will you do that?"

"Okay. These are powerful stories. I'll be on the lookout for people who might benefit from discussing them."

* * *

Ahmad set his paintbrush down and wiped the sweat off his forehead with the back of his hand. The head imam had called the men of the neighborhood to come clean up the mosque. Everyone had an assignment. Some were cutting the grass while others were trimming shrubs. Still others, like himself, were painting the fence.

Ahmad noticed a man in his early fifties gulping down water and resting in the shade of a mango tree. He was very overweight, breathing hard, and perspiring profusely. Obviously, it had been a long time since he had last done manual labor. Although they had never met, Ahmad recognized him as the doctor who lived at the opposite end of his neighborhood.

Ahmad strolled over and introduced himself.

"I'm Ahmad."

"I'm Hasan." The doctor nodded at the sun. "It sure is hot."

Ahmad took a deep breath and sighed. "It really is!"

"When I was young I used to do this kind of work all the time. When I got home from school my dad made me help him make mud bricks. It was backbreaking work, but it taught me one thing: the value of working hard. I think I was able to complete medical school because I knew how to work diligently."

Ahmad nodded. "My dad made me cut grass for the cows we kept at home. Sometimes my hands ached from cutting all that grass, and my legs felt like rubber after I peddled my bike home with the bag full of grass. However, it taught me responsibility, and the importance of hard work."

"You know, I worry about the young generation. Take my kids, for example. We have air conditioning and a TV in every room, and they each have their own cell phone. They are constantly texting their friends and checking Facebook. Their greatest worry is not having the newest phone. When I was a kid, our greatest worry was not selling enough bricks to buy food."

The sun shone hot. Ahmad didn't mind taking a longer break, and he could see that Hasan wanted to talk.

"Honestly I can't blame my kids. I'm a bad example. As my medical practice became established I started buying more and more stuff. The more I had, the more I wanted. If a fellow doctor bought a car, I bought a nicer one. I don't know how I got here, but I've become very materialistic.

"And I spoil my kids. When they want a new motorcycle, they whine until it wears me down, and I buy a new one for them.

"Recently my daughter in high school bought some sexy clothes. I have told her repeatedly she can't leave the house looking like a tramp. But she just ignores me."

Hasan shook his head in disgust and kicked the ground. He looked up to see if there might be a mango to eat, but it wasn't the season yet.

"And my son! The other day I went into his room. He had left his computer on and I could see he had been looking at pictures of naked women. One night he came home really late and I smelled alcohol on his breath.

"And then there's my wife!" Hasan gestured with both hands. "All she can talk about is buying new clothes and jewelry and throwing big dinner parties.

"In medical school, I used to dream about how much money I would have, and all the things I could buy. Now I have all these things, but my life is empty. All my wife cares about is outward appearance and my kids are on the wrong path. Something needs to change."

Suddenly Ahmad remembered his promise to Faisal to be on the lookout for people who might need to hear these stories. Even standing in the shade he started to perspire, and his heart began to race. Yet, he knew it was the right thing to do.

"You know, I've been re-evaluating my life as well. Not long ago, a friend shared some stories about the prophets with me, and I've been sharing them with my family. They have really impacted our lives by helping us get on the right track. They help us focus on spiritual matters and away from material things. To be honest, they have turned my family around and brought us closer together. And being the spiritual leader of my family has given me honor, and has been very rewarding."

Hasan didn't say anything, but gazed off in the distance. Then he turned and looked at Ahmad. "How can I get these stories?"

"I'll come by your house tomorrow and bring the first story. It will take me about an hour to go through it with you and explain our discovery pattern. How does that sound?"

"Great! Come by my house about four in the afternoon. That's after I get home from the hospital, and before I start my private practice."

"Okay. We had better get back to work."

Discuss and apply

1. How did you obey what you concluded God wanted you to do from the previous chapter?"

2. The questions for each of the stories don't change. Take a minute to review those questions.

3. After four stories, Faisal trained Ahmad to facilitate subsequent stories with his family. Do you think Ahmad was ready? Why or why not?

4. Discuss what Faisal did to equip Ahmad to facilitate the stories and give him confidence.

5. What reasons did Faisal give for Ahmad to share the stories with others?

6. How had Dr. Hasan been a bad example, and why was he worried for his family?

7. What did Ahmad say to Dr. Hasan to make him interested in discussing the stories?

8. In this chapter Ahmad (still a Muslim) invites Hasan (also a Muslim) to discuss chronological Bible stories with him. This pattern is happening in CPMs all over the world. Why do you think a Muslim would invite another Muslim to discuss Bible stories, and why would a Muslim accept such an invitation?

9. Faisal tried to make the meetings with Ahmad's family lively and fun. If you are facilitating a discovery group, what can you do to make your group more fun?

10. Share what you believe God wants you to do in the next 24–48 hours from what you learned in this chapter.

11. Share prayer requests with your team and pray for one another.

9

Guiding Muslims from the Qur'an to Discover Jesus[60]

Yusuf asks Haji Ishmael (imam) about "Jesus verses" in the Qur'an

Yusuf looked in the mirror as he buttoned up his blue taxi driver uniform. As he headed outside, the mosque's loudspeaker informed the neighborhood an old man had died during the night. All men were expected to attend the burial at four that afternoon.

* * *

By the time Yusuf arrived at the home of the deceased, the body had already been washed and covered in a plain white cloth. He helped the other men lift the body onto a stretcher, then he joined the procession of men, all dressed in a traditional sarong and Muslim hat, to escort the body to the graveyard. The grave had already been dug. Three balls of dirt were placed at the bottom of the grave for the head, chin, and shoulder. The body was then lowered into the grave so that he lay on his right side, with his head pointed in the direction of Mecca. Each man picked up three fistfuls of dirt and dropped the dirt onto the body saying

---

[60] This chapter condenses to a single discussion what might in real life take several conversations. This chapter illustrates the *Camel Method*, an approach to seeking POPs that uses the Qur'an (3:40–55) as a bridge for talking about Jesus Christ. *The Camel: How Muslims Are Coming to Faith in Christ!* by Kevin Greeson (Richmond, VA: WIGTake Resources, 2007).

in Arabic, "To God we belong, and to God we return." With palms raised in prayer each man asked God to forgive the deceased for his sins.

Walking from the graveyard, Yusuf approached Haji[61] Ishmael, an elderly imam. "May I ask you about a passage in the Qur'an?"

"Sure, come back to my house with me."

Haji Ishmael was highly esteemed in this community because he had studied at the prestigious Al-Azhar University in Cairo. Upon graduation, he had returned to teach at the local Islamic University and was the head imam at the local mosque. As they walked slowly along the road Yusuf thought, *Ask anyone in our community who the best Muslim is, and they would undoubtedly name Haji Ishmael.*

When they arrived, Haji Ishmael led Yusuf into a room where they washed their face, ears, hands, and feet. They took a sip of water, swished it around their mouths, and spit it out. Then Haji Ishmael led Yusuf into a room he used for tutoring students in Arabic. A whiteboard stood in one corner covered with Arabic writing, and a woven mat covered the tile floor.

Yusuf sat cross-legged and leaned against one wall. Haji Ishmael sat down under a large picture of thousands of pilgrims crowded around the Kaaba at the mosque in Mecca.[62]

In front of Haji Ishmael was a wooden stand with a large, well-worn copy of the Qur'an. Yusuf noticed the mark on Haji Ishmael's forehead from repeatedly touching it to the ground during prayer.[63] Reverently, Haji Ishmael picked up the Qur'an, touched it to his forehead, kissed it, and then laid it again on the wooden stand.

With his white hair sticking out from under his white cap, and his long white beard and reading glasses, Haji Ishmael looks every bit the scholar.

---

[61] Muslim title of respect for a man who has made the pilgrimage to Mecca. (A woman who has made this pilgrimage is called *Hajja*.)

[62] The Kaaba is Islam's holiest site. Muslims believe Abraham and Ishmael built the Kaaba to house a black stone which fell from heaven. The Al Haram mosque built around the Kaaba is the holiest shrine in Islam. During the pilgrimage, pilgrims walk seven times around the Kaaba.

[63] Muslims touch their foreheads to the ground when they say their prayers. Over time this leaves a mark on their foreheads.

Haji Ishmael glanced up and waited for Yusuf's question.

"I read Ali Imran verses 42–55 this morning, and I was wondering if you could explain the meaning to me."

"I'll try." Haji Ishmael opened the Qur'an to the third chapter, read each verse in Arabic, read the Indonesian translation, then explained the meaning.

وَإِذْ قَالَتِ ٱلْمَلَـٰٓئِكَةُ يَـٰمَرْيَمُ إِنَّ ٱللَّهَ ٱصْطَفَىٰكِ وَطَهَّرَكِ وَٱصْطَفَىٰكِ
عَلَىٰ نِسَآءِ ٱلْعَـٰلَمِينَ ﴿٤٢﴾

Qur'an 3:42 And [mention] when the angels said, "O Mary, indeed Allah has chosen you and purified you and chosen you above the women of the worlds."

"Mary was chosen by God above all other women."

إِذْ قَالَتِ ٱلْمَلَـٰٓئِكَةُ يَـٰمَرْيَمُ إِنَّ ٱللَّهَ يُبَشِّرُكِ بِكَلِمَةٍ مِّنْهُ ٱسْمُهُ
ٱلْمَسِيحُ عِيسَى ٱبْنُ مَرْيَمَ وَجِيهًا فِى ٱلدُّنْيَا وَٱلْآخِرَةِ وَمِنَ ٱلْمُقَرَّبِينَ ﴿٤٥﴾

Qur'an 3:45 [And mention] when the angels said, "O Mary, indeed Allah gives you good tidings of a word from Him, whose name will be the Messiah, Jesus,[64] the son of Mary—distinguished in this world and the Hereafter and among those brought near [to Allah]."

"Isa is called *Kalimatullah*. He is distinguished in this world and in the next world."

"What does Kalimatullah mean?"

"The Word of God."

"Is any other prophet called Kalimatullah in the Qur'an?"

"No," Haji Ishmael replied matter-of-factly.

"Is the Arabic word for 'distinguished' used to describe any other prophet in the Qur'an?"

---

[64] Qur'an.com generally translates "Isa" as "Jesus."

"The word 'distinguished' is '*wajeeh*' in Arabic. Moses was wajeeh in this world, but according to the Qur'an only Isa is wajeeh in the next world."[65]

قَالَتْ رَبِّ أَنَّىٰ يَكُونُ لِي وَلَدٌ وَلَمْ يَمْسَسْنِي بَشَرٌ قَالَ كَذَٰلِكِ ٱللَّهُ يَخْلُقُ مَا يَشَاءُ إِذَا قَضَىٰ أَمْرًا فَإِنَّمَا يَقُولُ لَهُ كُن فَيَكُونُ ﴿٤٧﴾

Qur'an 3:47 She said, "My Lord, how will I have a child when no man has touched me?" [The angel] said, "Such is Allah; He creates what He wills. When He decrees a matter, He only says to it, 'Be,' and it is."

"Isa was born of a virgin. No one else was ever born of a virgin. This makes Isa different from every other person. Nothing is impossible for God."

وَرَسُولًا إِلَىٰ بَنِي إِسْرَٰءِيلَ أَنِّي قَدْ جِئْتُكُم بِآيَةٍ مِّن رَّبِّكُمْ أَنِّي أَخْلُقُ لَكُم مِّنَ ٱلطِّينِ كَهَيْئَةِ ٱلطَّيْرِ فَأَنفُخُ فِيهِ فَيَكُونُ طَيْرًا بِإِذْنِ ٱللَّهِ وَأُبْرِئُ ٱلْأَكْمَهَ وَٱلْأَبْرَصَ وَأُحْيِ ٱلْمَوْتَىٰ بِإِذْنِ ٱللَّهِ وَأُنَبِّئُكُم بِمَا تَأْكُلُونَ وَمَا تَدَّخِرُونَ فِي بُيُوتِكُمْ إِنَّ فِي ذَٰلِكَ لَآيَةً لَّكُمْ إِن كُنتُم مُّؤْمِنِينَ ﴿٤٩﴾

Qur'an 3:49 And [make him] a messenger to the Children of Israel, [who will say], "Indeed I have come to you with a sign from your Lord in that I design for you from clay [that which is] like the form of a bird, then I breathe into it and it becomes a bird by permission of Allah. And I cure the blind and the leper, and I give life to the dead—by permission of Allah. And I inform you of what you eat and what you store in your houses. Indeed in that is a sign for you, if you are believers."

"Isa has power to heal the blind and leper, and raise the dead."

---

65 Ron George, *Newer Paths in Muslim-Christian Understanding*, 2007.

"What other prophet healed the blind and the leper, and raised the dead?"

"Isa was the only one."

$$وَمُصَدِّقًا لِمَا بَيْنَ يَدَيَّ مِنَ التَّوْرَاةِ وَلِأُحِلَّ لَكُم بَعْضَ الَّذِي حُرِّمَ عَلَيْكُمْ وَجِئْتُكُم بِآيَةٍ مِّن رَّبِّكُمْ فَاتَّقُوا اللَّهَ وَأَطِيعُونِ ۝$$

Qur'an 3:50 And [I have come] confirming what was before me of the Torah and to make lawful for you some of what was forbidden to you. And I have come to you with a sign from your Lord, so fear Allah and obey me.

"Isa is a sign from God. There are very grave consequences for the person who neglects God's signs. It says elsewhere in the Qur'an that that person will live in hell forever.[66] This verse also says we are commanded by God to obey Isa."

$$إِذْ قَالَ اللَّهُ يَا عِيسَىٰ إِنِّي مُتَوَفِّيكَ وَرَافِعُكَ إِلَيَّ وَمُطَهِّرُكَ مِنَ الَّذِينَ كَفَرُوا وَجَاعِلُ الَّذِينَ اتَّبَعُوكَ فَوْقَ الَّذِينَ كَفَرُوا إِلَىٰ يَوْمِ الْقِيَامَةِ ثُمَّ إِلَيَّ مَرْجِعُكُمْ فَأَحْكُمُ بَيْنَكُمْ فِيمَا كُنتُمْ فِيهِ تَخْتَلِفُونَ ۝$$

Qur'an 3:55 Thus, GOD said, "O Jesus, I am terminating your life, raising you to Me, and ridding you of the disbelievers. I will exalt those who follow you above those who disbelieve, till the Day of Resurrection. Then to Me is the ultimate destiny of all of you, then I will judge among you regarding your disputes." [67]

"God raised Isa to Himself."

"Does this mean Isa is alive right now, with God in heaven?"

---

[66] Qur'an 19:21, 7:9, 7:36, 7:40

[67] *Quran: The Final Testament*, translated by Rashad Khalifa (Universal Unity, 2001).

"It does."

"So Isa knows the way to heaven because He is already there?"

Haji Ishmael scratched his head. "I've never been asked that before. Yes, it is logical that Isa knows the way to heaven. Do you have any more questions?"

"Yes. Would you also explain Maryam 19."

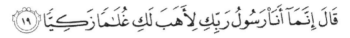

Qur'an 19:19 He said [to Maryam], "I am only the messenger of your Lord to give you [news of] a pure boy."

"What does the word 'pure' mean in Arabic?"

Haji Ishmael put his finger on the verse and read it slowly to himself, "The word in Arabic is *zakiy,* which means 'sinless.'"

"If I have understood you correctly, this verse teaches that *Maryam* was given a sinless boy."

"Yes."

"Is any other person in the Qur'an described as 'zakiy?'"

"No, only Isa." [68]

"Is Muhammad (pbuh)[69] described as 'zakiy?'"

Haji Ishmael thought a moment, then turned to Al Fath.

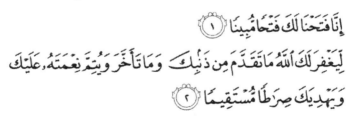

Qur'an 48:1–2 Indeed, We have given you, [O Muhammad], a clear conquest That Allah may forgive for you what preceded of your sin and what will follow and complete His favor upon you and guide you to a straight path.

---

[68] Ali Mansour, *The Secrets of the Blessed Feast Id Al-Adha,* electronic copy, 1996, English translation, 1997. Revised and corrected, 2005, p. 9.

[69] Devout Muslims generally say "peace be upon him" after mentioning Muhammad. In writing this is abbreviated in English "pbuh," or in translated Arabic as "SAW," for *salle alaa hu alaihi wa sallim.*

"As you can see, God forgave Muhammad (pbuh) his sin."

"Thank you, Haji Ishmael. That helps me understand what the Qur'an says about Isa. He really is quite remarkable—born of a virgin, sinless, able to heal the sick and raise the dead, distinguished in this life and the next life, and raised up by God so He is in heaven right now."

"Yes, that's right," Haji Ishmael said thoughtfully.

"It surprises me that the Qur'an commands us to obey Isa."

"Why should that surprise you? Isa is a holy prophet of God."

"Have you ever read the Injil?"

"No! Why should I?" Haji Ishmael seemed slightly offended.

"The Qur'an says we are supposed to obey Isa, but how can we obey Him if we don't know His commands? Doesn't the Injil tell us His commands?"

"Yes, the Injil contains the commands of Isa, but it has been corrupted by Jews and Christians. It has been lost. All the truth of the Injil has been incorporated into the Qur'an. It is enough to read the Qur'an," Haji Ishmael said authoritatively.

Yusuf stood. "You've given me a lot to think about. Thank you again for your time and insight."

Haji Ishmael stood and extended his right hand. Yusuf took it gently, then kissed the back of Haji Ishmael's hand as a token of respect. "I should go home now."

Discuss and apply

1. How did you obey what you concluded God wanted you to do from the previous chapter?"

2. Role play reading and discussing Qur'an 3:42–55 with one person as Yusuf and the other as Haji Ishmael.

3. If you have experience in ministering to Muslims, what other verses from the Qur'an have you found useful as a bridge to sharing about Jesus Christ?

4. Mention Muslim leaders in your community with whom you might try this approach.

5. What could you say to invite a Muslim leader to explain Qur'an 3:42–55 to you? Keep in mind that you are not there to teach him. You want to draw out the truth by asking questions.

6. Share what you believe God wants you to do in the next 24–48 hours from what you learned in this chapter.

7. Share prayer requests with your team and pray for one another.

10

Leading Muslims from the Qur'an to the Bible[70]

Haji Ishmael discovers that the Qur'an affirms the accuracy of the Bible

Yusuf returned to Haji Ishmael's house and sat in the same position. Excited, yet nervous, he began, "Thank you again for your time last week."

Haji Ishmael nodded slightly, neither smiling nor frowning.

"I couldn't get out of my mind what you said last time about the Injil having been corrupted. So I did some research, and now I have more questions."

I wish all my students were this diligent, Haji Ishmael thought.

"Would you mind explaining a few more verses for me?"

Haji Ishmael nodded.

"The first is An-Nisa verse 136."

يَـٰٓأَيُّهَا ٱلَّذِينَ ءَامَنُوٓاْ ءَامِنُواْ بِٱللَّهِ وَرَسُولِهِۦ وَٱلۡكِتَـٰبِ ٱلَّذِى نَزَّلَ
عَلَىٰ رَسُولِهِۦ وَٱلۡكِتَـٰبِ ٱلَّذِىٓ أَنزَلَ مِن قَبۡلُ وَمَن يَكۡفُرۡ بِٱللَّهِ
وَمَلَـٰٓئِكَتِهِۦ وَكُتُبِهِۦ وَرُسُلِهِۦ وَٱلۡيَوۡمِ ٱلۡأٓخِرِ فَقَدۡ ضَلَّ ضَلَـٰلَۢا
بَعِيدًا ﴿١٣٦﴾

---

[70] This chapter condenses to a single conversation what might in real life take several conversations.

Qur'an 4:136 O you who believe! Believe in Allah, and His Messenger (Muhammad SAW[71]), and the Book (the Qur'an) which He has sent down to His Messenger, and the Scripture which He sent down to those before (him), and whosoever disbelieves in Allah, His Angels, His Books, His Messengers, and the Last Day, then indeed he has strayed far away.[72]

"It is imperative for all Muslims to believe in God, His messenger, the Qur'an, the previous Scriptures, angels, the prophets, and the final judgment. If you don't believe in these doctrines, you have wandered far from God."

"What does it mean by the 'previous Scriptures'?"

"The Taurat, Zabur, and Injil."

"Why does God say 'believe in the previous Scriptures' if they have been corrupted? Shouldn't God have said, '*Don't* believe the previous Scriptures'?"

Haji Ishmael opened his mouth, but realized he had no answer. He had never thought of this before. *It doesn't make sense to believe in the previous books if they have been corrupted. Surely, God would warn man to not believe in the previous books if they had been altered.*

Yusuf continued, "Please explain Al-An'am 115"

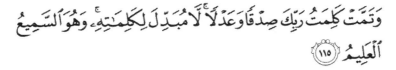

Qur'an 6:115 And the word of your Lord has been fulfilled in truth and in justice. None can alter His words, and He is the Hearing, the Knowing.

"There is no one who can alter God's words."

"What about God's words in the Taurat, Zabur, and Injil?"

Haji Ishmael immediately saw the ramifications of this question. *No one can change God's words. His words include the Taurat, Zabur, and Injil. Yet why do some people say the previous books have been corrupted?* These thoughts troubled Haji Ishmael, yet one thing he

---

71 *SAW* is an abbreviation of the Arabic equivalent of "Peace be upon him."

72 From the Muhsin Khan translation at **Qur'an.com**

knew—he must believe what the Qur'an said, and not opinions of man about what the Qur'an said.

"God is all-powerful. No one can oppose Him. He is infinitely superior to even the most powerful of men. God will rain down fierce judgment on anyone who tries to change, distort, or alter in any way His Holy Word as found in the Taurat, Zabur, and Injil." Haji Ishmael's voice rose with authority as if he were preaching a sermon.

"If we could continue, would you explain Al Ma'idah 48?"

وَأَنزَلْنَا إِلَيْكَ ٱلْكِتَبَ بِٱلْحَقِّ مُصَدِّقًا لِّمَا بَيْنَ يَدَيْهِ مِنَ ٱلْكِتَبِ وَمُهَيْمِنًا عَلَيْهِ فَٱحْكُم بَيْنَهُم بِمَآ أَنزَلَ ٱللَّهُ وَلَا تَتَّبِعْ أَهْوَآءَهُمْ عَمَّا جَآءَكَ مِنَ ٱلْحَقِّ لِكُلٍّ جَعَلْنَا مِنكُمْ شِرْعَةً وَمِنْهَاجًا وَلَوْ شَآءَ ٱللَّهُ لَجَعَلَكُمْ أُمَّةً وَاحِدَةً وَلَكِن لِّيَبْلُوَكُمْ فِى مَآ ءَاتَىٰكُمْ فَٱسْتَبِقُوا۟ ٱلْخَيْرَاتِ إِلَى ٱللَّهِ مَرْجِعُكُمْ جَمِيعًا فَيُنَبِّئُكُم بِمَا كُنتُمْ فِيهِ تَخْتَلِفُونَ ﴿٤٨﴾

Qur'an 5:48 And We have sent down to you (O Muhammad SAW) the Book (this Qur'an) in truth, confirming the Scripture that came before it.[73]

Haji Ishmael hesitated before explaining the verse. He read it several times to himself in Arabic, then said, "God sent the Qur'an to Muhammad (pbuh). The Qur'an confirms, or validates, the Scriptures which came before it."

"Which Scriptures does this refer to?"

"This refers to the Taurat, Zabur, and Injil ...." Haji Ishmael pondered the implications.

"I have one more verse if you don't mind. Would you please read Yunus 94?"

---

[73] From the Muhsin Khan translation. Qur'an 6:92 makes the same point.

Haji Ishmael was clearly relieved to be rescued from his troubling thoughts. He read,

فَإِن كُنتَ فِى شَكٍّ مِّمَّآ أَنزَلْنَآ إِلَيْكَ فَسْـَلِ ٱلَّذِينَ يَقْرَءُونَ ٱلْكِتَٰبَ مِن قَبْلِكَ لَقَدْ جَآءَكَ ٱلْحَقُّ مِن رَّبِّكَ فَلَا تَكُونَنَّ مِنَ ٱلْمُمْتَرِينَ ٩٤

Qur'an 10:94 So if you are in doubt, [O Muhammad], about that which We have revealed to you, then ask those who have been reading the Scripture before you. The truth has certainly come to you from your Lord, so never be among the doubters.

"This verse tells us that if Muhammad (pbuh) had any doubts about the message God had revealed to him, he should ask the people who had the Scripture before him." Haji Ishmael was clearly comfortable in his role as teacher.

"Who were the people Muhammad (pbuh) was told to ask?"

"They were Christians and Jews."

"And what Scripture did the Christians and Jews have?"

"They had the Taurat, Zabur, and Injil," Haji Ishmael replied confidently.

"So if Muhammad (pbuh) had any doubts, he was supposed to ask the Christians and Jews of his day what the Taurat, Zabur, and Injil taught. These Christians and Jews must have had copies of the Taurat, Zabur, and Injil that had *not* been corrupted. Otherwise, why would Muhammad (pbuh) be commanded to talk to them if he had doubts?"

Haji Ishmael recoiled. He didn't like being challenged by this young, uneducated man. But Yusuf made a good point. *Why would Muhammad consult with Christians and Jews if the Taurat, Zabur, and Injil had been corrupted? That wouldn't make sense,* Haji Ishmael thought. *But this goes contrary to everything I've been taught. Even my teachers at Al-Azhar University said the Taurat, Zabur, and Injil had been corrupted. I never questioned any of my teachers.*

Lost in thought, Haji Ishmael looked down at the Qur'an in front of him, his brow furrowed. The room was silent except for the ticking of the clock on the wall. Finally Haji Ishmael muttered, "This is very interesting."

"So that I'm clear, is it true that there is no verse in the Qur'an which says the Taurat, Zabur, and Injil have been corrupted?"

"I would like to research that question before I give you my answer. Come back next week."

* * *

"I have read the Qur'an cover to cover, checked the *Hadith*[74] and my commentaries, and talked to other imams. The Qur'an says in 3:78 and 4:46 the Jews misquoted the Scriptures, but it doesn't say the Scriptures were corrupted. There is a big difference between changing and misquoting. There is no verse in the Qur'an which says the Taurat, Zabur, and Injil have been corrupted."

"Earlier you said the Qur'an confirms what was given in the previous Scriptures, the Taurat, Zabur, and Injil?"

"Yes."

"And didn't you say that, if Muhammad (pbuh) had doubts about the message of the Qur'an, Yunus says he should ask the Jews and Christians to explain it to him from the Taurat, Zabur, and Injil?"[75]

"Yes."

"Haji Ishmael, you are very wise and educated. I appreciate you explaining to me what the Qur'an says about the earlier books.

"Whenever I have to wait as a taxi driver I like to read. I found some stories from the Taurat, Zabur, and Injil on the Internet. Would you like me to bring them to you?"

Haji Ishmael hesitated, not sure how to answer.

---

[74] Traditional commentaries on the Qur'an. These are often ascribed nearly as much authority by Muslims as the Qur'an itself.

[75] Appendix J contains a fuller discussion of Qur'anic evidence that the Old and New Testament have not been altered, changed, or corrupted.

"Wouldn't it be a good idea for a man of your education and learning, a man who is a leader in the mosque, to at least read the Taurat, Zabur, and Injil, even if you believe they have been corrupted? Wouldn't studying these books complete your education, and better equip you to answer questions about the holy books?"

Haji Ishmael thought, *When my teachers at Al-Azhar University said the Taurat, Zabur, and Injil had been corrupted I was curious about what they said. What harm could there be in reading these books now? It's not like I'm going to be led astray! I am the leader of the mosque. I should know what is in them. I can read them and satisfy myself that they have been corrupted.*

Finally he said, "Yes, you may bring stories from the Taurat, Zabur, and Injil. But not when others are here."

Yusuf again thanked Haji Ishmael and kissed the back of his hand. He left rejoicing, and immediately texted his friends to share his excitement at Haji Ishmael's positive response and to ask them to pray.

Discuss and apply

1. How did you obey what you concluded God wanted you to do from the previous chapter?"

2. How did Yusuf answer Haji Ishmael when he said the Taurat, Zabur, and Injil had been corrupted?

3. What else could you say if someone claims the Taurat, Zabur, and Injil have been corrupted?

4. What did Yusuf say to invite Haji Ishmael to study the stories with him? What would you say in a similar situation?

5. Role play reading and discussing the passages from the Qur'an in this chapter to answer the objection that the Bible has been corrupted.

6. Share what you believe God wants you to do in the next 24–48 hours from what you learned in this chapter.

7. Share prayer requests with your team and pray for one another.

11

Discussing Jesus as the Lamb Slain for Sins

Haji Ishmael discovers there is no forgiveness without shedding blood

Being a taxi driver had its advantages. Yusuf liked taking Nur to the market when he didn't have a customer. And waiting for passengers gave him time to study and pray.

He was glad business was slow today so he had extra time to pray and prepare for his upcoming meeting with Haji Ishmael. He found a tree and parked his taxi under it.

* * *

"Assalam wa'alikum," Yusuf called from Haji Ishmael's yard.

After a few minutes Haji Ishmael appeared, wearing the same sarong as before. "Wa alikum salam," he said softly.

"Is this a good time to continue our conversation?"

Haji Ishmael looked around nervously. Seeing no one, he invited Yusuf in.

Yusuf pulled a piece of paper from his pocket. "I brought a story from the Taurat with me."

The two sat in their usual places, but Haji Ishmael seemed tired. *I wonder if our conversation from last week upset him. I wonder if he is having trouble sleeping as a result.*

"This story is about creation, and Adam and Eve's fall from honor into sin and shame. Before we read the story, I wonder if we could each share something we are thankful for."

In discussing the story, Yusuf faithfully followed the eight-step pattern[76] he had received from Faisal.

"What do you think of this story?"

"It's very interesting."

"Who else should hear it?"

"Well, everyone."

"Does that include your wife and kids?"

"Yes, of course."

"When would be a good time to tell them?"

"I'll probably do it before we go to sleep tonight."

"I've read this and other stories with my family too, and they have really helped us."

Again Yusuf nodded politely and kissed the back of Haji Ishmael's hand. "Well, I should be going."

* * *

Several weeks later, Yusuf dropped off his passenger and glanced at his watch. He had just enough time to deliver the taxi to his partner for the next shift, go home for a shower, and change clothes before his next appointment with Haji Ishmael.

Haji Ishmael had been nervous and uptight when they discussed the first prophet story. But the more they studied, the more relaxed he had become. Haji Ishmael now smiled when Yusuf arrived.

"Assalam wa'alikum."

"Wa alikum salam."

Haji Ishmael welcomed Yusuf into his home.

After some small talk, they each shared what they were thankful for as well as their current struggles. Then they reviewed the previous week's story, especially how Haji Ishmael and his family had applied it.

Yusuf handed Haji Ishmael another paper with the passages for the ninth prophet study. "Please read Job 25:2–4 aloud twice, then explain it in your own words."

---

[76] See Chapter 8.

Dominion and fear are with God;
He makes peace in His high heaven.
Is there any number to His armies?
Upon whom does His light not arise?
How then can man be in the right before God?
How can he who is born of woman be pure?

"This is a good question, isn't it? How can a person be just, or clean before God?"

"Yes, this is the ultimate question. All men seek the answer to this question," Haji Ishmael commented philosophically.

"Would you mind also reading Hebrews 9:22?"

Indeed, under the law almost everything is purified with blood, and without the **shedding** of blood there is no forgiveness of sins.

"What does this mean?"

"It is very clear. There must be a shedding of blood for mankind to receive forgiveness of sin."

"Would you read the next verse, Leviticus 17:11?"

For the life of the flesh is in the blood, and I have given it for you on the altar to make atonement for your souls, for it is the blood that makes atonement by the life.

"In your own words, tell me why must we have the shedding of blood? Why not some other way to obtain forgiveness of sins?"

"This verse explains that the life and honor of all humanity is in the blood; therefore, only blood can make atonement. I lived in the Middle East for a number of years, and saw this truth illustrated many times. If a family is shamed, there must be a shedding of blood to restore the family's honor. This is called 'honor killing.' For example, if your sister has sex outside of marriage, she must be killed to restore the family's honor. If this is true when a person sins against another person, how much more serious when someone sins against God!"

"That is a great explanation. Now please read Genesis 3:21."

And the LORD God made for Adam and for his wife garments of skins and clothed them.

"Several weeks ago we discussed the story of Adam and Eve, and their fall into sin. We noticed after they sinned that they sewed together fig leaves to cover their nakedness. If they already had clothes, why did God make new clothes with animal skins for Adam and Eve?"

"I'm not sure."

"Could it be that God shed the blood of animals and then used their skins to cover Adam and Eve's shame?"

"That's probably right."

The two men continued their discussion, examining the blood sacrifices made by the prophets Noah, Abraham, Job, Moses, Aaron, David, and Solomon.[77]

"Let me summarize the common element in these stories," Yusuf said. "All the prophets offered animal sacrifices because there must be a shedding of blood for the forgiveness of sins."

"That's very concise."

Yusuf handed Haji Ishmael a piece of paper. "In the coming weeks, we will discuss stories about Isa Al Masih from the Injil. I printed out this list of verses from the Qur'an and the Injil about Isa so you can compare them."[78]

Yusuf said farewell and went home.

---

[77] Appendix C provides these references for the ninth Old Testament study.

[78] Appendix J provides this list.

Discuss and apply

1. How did you obey what you concluded God wanted you to do from the previous chapter?

2. Try as a group to recall and write out the eight points of the discovery study presented in Chapter 8, then check your answers.

3. Why do you think Yusuf stressed to Haji Ishmael that without the shedding of blood there is no forgiveness of sins?

4. Why did Yusuf say the shedding of blood is necessary for the forgiveness of sins (Lev. 17:11)?

5. What did Haji Ishmael say about the importance in the Middle East of shedding blood?

6. Why is it significant that when God drove Adam and Eve from the garden He made clothes for them from animal skins?

7. Share what you believe God wants you to do in the next 24–48 hours from what you learned in this chapter.

8. Share prayer requests with your team and pray for one another.

12

Addressing Felt Needs:
Emptiness and Fear of Death

Haji Ishmael and Sharif (headmaster) discuss needing a changed heart

"Assalam wa'alikum."

Haji Ishmael stepped onto the porch and greeted Sharif, a hand-some and well built man with a square face, meticulously groomed mustache, and hair dyed black to cover premature graying. His long sleeve shirt was carefully pressed and tucked into new khaki pants. Sharif had been chosen headmaster of the local high school over older candidates because he possessed the rare blend of a passionate pursuit of excellence with a genuine concern for others. He set high standards for himself and others, and had little tolerance for excuses.

"Wa alikum salam."

"Haji Ishmael, I have something on my heart that is troubling me. May I come in?"

"Of course." Haji Ishmael ushered Sharif inside.

"I have tried to be a good Muslim all my life. I faithfully say my prayers five times a day. I never miss Friday services. I fast during Ramadan. When others are eating and smoking in private, I never do. I read through the Qur'an every Ramadan and I even fast the six extra days after Ramadan.[79] I pay my alms in full and even give a little extra. I've made the pilgrimage to Mecca. I always attend the

---

[79] Especially devout Muslims follow Syawal, an extra six days of fasting after Ramadan.

funeral prayers for the deceased. If the imam needs help, I'm the first to volunteer. I try to be honest and to help others. But I feel like something is missing." Sharif's bottom lip began to quiver, and he seemed close to tears.

"I want to serve God and please Him, but He seems so distant. I pray, but I wonder if He hears, or even cares. Even when I fast I don't feel close to God. I lay awake at night and wonder why I was created, and what I'm supposed to do with my life. I'm terrified of death. What will happen to me when I die? Are my good works enough?"

Sharif glanced at Haji Ishmael, uncertain whether to continue. Haji Ishmael nodded encouragingly.

"In the past my religion teachers and imams have rebuked me for my questions. They said, 'Don't question what you read in the Qur'an. Just have faith.' Don't they know that when they refuse to answer my questions, they only increase my doubts? I have so many questions; I just want answers!" Sharif threw up his hands in frustration.

The words tumbled out as Sharif continued to release all his pent up frustration. "Besides, I look around at the Muslims I know and all I see are hypocrites. Even the officials who work for the Department of Religion steal money from people going on the pilgrimage. They are supposed to be the godliest people, and yet look how they act!

"I even know several men who have made the pilgrimage, and yet view pornography on their cell phones!

"We send our daughters to work as maids in Saudi Arabia, and what happens? They are insulted, beaten, and raped!"

"When I was at the university, I decided I wanted to become a headmaster. I wanted to change society for the good, and thought education would be the best way to do that.

From somewhere in the rafters a lizard called out "toe-kay."

"Now I work hard at my school. I try to motivate the teachers and students, but nothing seems to change. It's as if all my hard work is for nothing. I'm so discouraged. I don't know what to do."

Sharif suddenly felt vulnerable. He had never poured out his heart like this to anyone. *Does Haji Ishmael think I'm a fool? Will he reject or ridicule me for what I've said? I wish I had never come!*

Sharif clasped his hands together tightly and bowed his head, embarrassed by what he had just shared. He wished there were some way he could slip out of the house unnoticed.

To Sharif's surprise, Haji Ishmael placed his right hand on top of Sharif's hands. Sharif looked up into the old man's eyes and found them warm and inviting, not judgmental and harsh.

Looking over his glasses, Haji Ishmael said, "I want to tell you something I've never told anyone in my life."

Haji Ishmael took a deep breath. Sharing inner struggles was not common for the Sayang, and Islamic teachers never disclosed their doubts because others look to them to have all the answers.

"People look up to me as an Islamic scholar and leader of the mosque. They think I don't have any struggles. I can't be honest with them because they would not respect me. But inside, I'm just like you. When I pray and fast, I also feel empty. I wonder if God even notices me. I wonder if my best deeds satisfy the righteous demands of His holy character. I fear God's judgment when I die."

Sharif was speechless. *If Haji Ishmael doesn't have assurance of paradise after he dies, what about me? He is the epitome of the perfect Muslim. I am so far below him! What am I to do?*

"I know you are a good man. I know you care about your students, and work hard to give them a better life than the one you grew up with. I know you long to change society, but this is what I have found: To change society you must first change the individual. To change the individual you must change them on the inside. It's the only way."

Relief swept over Sharif, then confusion. *Haji Ishmael understands me. He doesn't think I'm some crazy lunatic. But he is supposed to help me. How can he do that if he is in the same situation as me?*

Haji Ishmael seemed to read Sharif's mind. "Recently I've been learning about how to change the heart. Wait here."

Haji Ishmael returned with his well-worn Qur'an. He touched it to his forehead and kissed it, then placed it on its wooden stand. He sat back down on the floor under the large picture of the pilgrims in Mecca, and opened the Qur'an to the passage he and Yusuf had first discussed, Ali Imran 42–55.[80] "Allow me to read these verses to you. They will explain who Isa Al Masih is."

When they concluded their discussion, Haji Ishmael instructed Sharif, "I want you to go home and gather your family together tonight. Turn off the TV so they won't be distracted, and share with them what I just shared with you.

Then come back tomorrow. I want to share with you some stories from the Taurat and Injil which you can then also share with your family."

---

[80] Qur'an 3:42–55

Discuss and apply

1. How did you obey what you concluded God wanted you to do from the previous chapter?

2. What questions, doubts, and frustrations did Sharif have?

3. What did Haji Ishmael share with Sharif that he had never shared with anyone else?

4. Have you ever shared with someone as openly as Sharif and Haji Ishmael shared with each other? Why not? Take turns now in your group for each person to share their own questions, doubts, and frustrations. Listen non-judgmentally, and commit to hold this sharing in confidence.

5. What did Haji Ishmael say was the key to changing a person?

6. Faisal set an example by facilitating the first four stories, then he equipped Ahmad to lead. Yusuf, on the other hand, never met Haji Ishmael's family. Instead he discussed the story with Haji Ishmael, and made sure Haji Ishmael understood the pattern so he could do the same thing with his family. Discuss the pros and cons of Faisal's approach vs. Yusuf's. Under what circumstances would one approach be better than the other?

7. Share what you believe God wants you to do in the next 24–48 hours from what you learned in this chapter.

8. Share prayer requests with your team and pray for one another.

13

Moving toward Jesus through Dreams and Acts of Kindness

Fatima and Inne (caterer) discuss dreams
and Jesus' power to calm storms

Fatima put the dirty clothes into an old paint bucket in the bathroom and filled it with water. She added a small amount of detergent, and pushed the clothes up and down several times to create suds. She took a shirt from the top of the bucket, and rubbed the fabric back and forth in her hands. Then she dipped the shirt back into the bucket and squeezed it several times. Finally she placed it in another bucket where she would rinse all the clothes later.

Fatima's life had gained a new sense of purpose since Faisal had begun sharing with her about CPMs. Fatima herself had talked to many, but no one had wanted to discuss a prophet story. So she determined to pray more fervently. She tried getting up at 4:30 with Faisal, but that didn't work for her. Then she realized she could pray during many of her daily activities. In fact, washing clothes became one of her best prayer times. She also decided to pray for people in the houses she passed as she walked to the market. Many times she knew the families, and would pray for them specifically. Other times, she didn't know them, or what to pray for, so she prayed that God would give them dreams and visions about Isa. And when others were resting, she would take out her prayer list and pray through the names.

Fatima also found it helpful to pray with others. Nur and Amina also wanted to improve their prayer lives, so they all agreed to meet three times a week for an hour of concerted prayer. Often it was difficult to coordinate their schedules, yet they persevered because they were convinced of the importance of prayer.

Fatima finished rinsing her clothes and hung them on a clothesline strung between two trees. As she walked to the market, she prayed, *O Lord, lead me to a person of peace.*

On the way, she saw her friend Inne hanging up her own laundry. Inne was slender and average in height. Her stylish hair was pulled back into a ponytail so she could do her work. Butterfly earrings dangled from her ears.

"I just finished hanging up my own laundry! Let me give you a hand," Fatima offered cheerfully. They chatted casually as they worked, then Fatima asked, "Inne, do you know anyone who has ever had a dream from God?"

Inne's eyes got big, and she almost dropped her clothes bucket. "As a matter of fact, I had a troubling dream last night; may I tell it to you?"

"Sure, but not here in the hot sun! Can we go inside?"

Fatima followed Inne inside and into the kitchen. Inne filled a pot with water, and set it on the stove. She took two cups from the shelf, set them on the table, and added two teaspoons of sugar to each cup. As they waited for the water to boil, Fatima said, "Tell me about your dream."

"Okay. I was at our neighborhood mosque, where we ritually wash our hands, feet, and face before praying. I cupped my hands and put them under the water from the faucet. When my hands were filled with water, I started to bring them up to wash my face. But suddenly a little girl was there who pushed my hands away.

"I thought, 'This is odd.' I cupped my hands again and tried to bring the water to my face, but again the little girl pushed my hands away. 'Why are you doing that?' I thought. I tried a third time, and again the little girl pushed my hands away. Only this time she took me by the hand and led me outside. She led me down the street until we came to a house. She led me inside, right up to a man wearing a long white robe. He had a beard, and his eyes were so kind. He extended his hands to me, and I woke up. Guess who the man was?"

"I already know."

"How could you?"

"Because, I too had a dream."

The water reached a boil, so Inne poured the water and dipped a tea bag into the cups until the water turned light brown. She handed a cup to Fatima. "Let's sit in the family room."

Fatima settled down on a couch. "The man in your dream was Isa Al Masih, wasn't it?"

Inne nodded in astonishment. "Yes! How did you know?"

"Several years ago I too had a dream. I was standing outside the gates of heaven in the midst of a great crowd. Isa Al Masih opened the gate and stepped outside. He motioned to everyone around me to enter. One by one they filed in until I was the only person remaining outside. Isa never looked at me. He just turned around, went through the gate, and shut it. Then I woke up."

"What did you do?" Inne sipped her tea.

"I knew Isa was warning me to not be left outside. I understood He was the gatekeeper, and if I wanted to go to heaven I had to enter through Him. I knew He was calling me to be His follower."

Inne sat for a moment in stunned silence, then whispered, "I keep seeing Isa's face in my mind. His expression is so warm and inviting, and His eyes are filled with love and acceptance."

Fatima put her cup down on the coffee table and placed her right hand over her heart. "I understand. I've experienced that love and acceptance from Isa. It's real. I believe He is calling you to be His follower too."

Inne's mind suddenly swirled with a hundred questions. She bowed her head slightly, and began rubbing her thumbs against her temples. *Why was I led out of the mosque and taken to Isa? Who is this Isa Al Masih? What does it mean to become His follower? Will I have to change my name, dress differently and start eating pork? Can I be Sayang and follow Isa? What will my husband think? If I become a follower of Isa who will bury me?*

Fatima leaned back on the couch and smiled knowingly at Inne.

"What do I do?" Inne asked.

"First of all, don't be afraid. I'm a follower of Isa. I can help you understand who Isa is, and you can decide if you want to become His follower too. I know some stories about Isa. Would you like to read them together?"

Inne was relieved to know that she didn't have to make a decision right away. *What harm could there be in reading some stories about Isa?* "Sure. Where did you get them?"

"These stories come from the Injil."

"The Injil? We can't read the Injil. It's been corrupted!"

"No, it hasn't. The Qur'an says we must believe in the previous Scriptures, the Taurat and Injil, and no one can change God's words. Do you think God would let someone change His words?"

"Well, I guess not," Inne said hesitantly.

"Let's look at the stories together. You can make up your mind later. Do you have time now?"

"My kids won't be home from school for another hour. I have time until then.

"Great!" Fatima said as she pulled a piece of paper from her pocket. "These stories are on the Internet. I always carry a printed copy with me." She handed the paper to Inne. "To understand who Isa is, we have to learn about the prophets who came before Him. Let's start with a story that helps us understand the need for a sacrifice.[81]

"When I discuss a story with someone I like to start with each of us sharing something we are thankful for, and then something we are

---

[81] Sometimes we encounter people eager to learn about Jesus. They may have had a dream about Him, watched the *Jesus Film*, been healed or delivered in Jesus' name, been intrigued by verses about Him in the Qur'an, or responded to a *Creation to Christ* presentation. For these we start with the sacrifice (ninth prophet) story so they will understand "without the shedding of blood there is no forgiveness of sins," before proceeding to the prophecy and Jesus stories.

struggling with. Then we read the story twice, and take turns retelling it. How does that sound?"

"Fine, I guess."

As they progressed through the eight steps, Fatima was impressed with Inne's insights from the story.

When they concluded, Fatima asked, "Inne, how did you like the story?"

"It was fascinating. It makes sense that without the shedding of blood there is no forgiveness of sins."

"Who else needs to hear this story?"

"It would be good for my family."

"Why don't you tell them then?"

"I couldn't do that. My husband would never let himself be taught by a woman!"

Fatima threw back her head and laughed. "I know exactly what you mean!" She held up both hands like a soccer player does after scoring a goal. Inne clapped Fatima's hands.

Fatima took the paper from Inne's hand. "Here's what you do. When your husband gets home tonight, tell him you found this interesting story, but you don't understand it. Ask him to explain it to you. Hand him the piece of paper and ask him to read it. Then ask him to read it again to help you understand. Next, ask him to retell it in everyday language because some of the words are hard to understand. Finally ask him the same questions I just asked you, and let him answer them. Do you think that would work?"

Inne smiled. "Definitely. My husband thinks he's smarter than me. He likes to explain things to 'simple me.'"

"Why don't you try tonight?"

* * *

Fatima was sitting on the floor, folding clothes and praying through her prayer list, when she heard a knock at the front door. As she stood and stretched, she realized she had been sitting for far too long. She entered the front room to find Inne standing there, her face beaming.

Inne handed her a box of food. "You know I am a caterer. I made a little extra for you."

Fatima lifted the cover and smelled chicken, vegetables, rice, and, of course, hot sauce. Inne was an excellent cook, and Fatima didn't mind these "extras" when they met.

Inne had taken the sacrifice study back to her family, and they had loved it. Inne and Fatima had then discussed the prophesies about Isa and the first Isa story. Inne had continued following Fatima's advice to gather her family and coach her husband to teach them these same stories.

Fatima settled on the couch and motioned for Inne to do the same. "Tell me how the story about Isa's birth went? I especially want to hear how everyone applied the story."

"That's wonderful," Fatima said after hearing their applications.

"Today's story is one of my favorites. Would you read Mark 4:35–41, then tell it in your own words?"

After reading the story aloud, Inne retold it. "Isa and His disciples were in a boat crossing a lake when a fierce storm suddenly crashed upon them. Strong winds and high waves threatened to capsize the boat. The disciples were terrified but Isa was asleep on a cushion. The disciples woke Isa and cried out, 'Do You not care that we are about to die?' Isa raised His arms and commanded the storm, 'Be still.' Immediately the winds ceased blowing, and the waters became calm. The disciples looked at each other and said, "Who is this man that even the wind and the sea obey Him?"

"You are a really good storyteller."

Inne nodded appreciatively.

"What do we learn about Isa from this story?"

"He has power over nature. He just spoke, and the wind and waves died down."

"Great. How can you apply this story to your own life?"

"I'm not really sure."

"Isa calmed a literal storm. I may not have wind and waves, but I have plenty of storms in my life that are just as real. I have children who are sick, bills to pay, problems with my in-laws. Need I go on? I have lots of storms right now! Sometimes, it feels like I'm sinking under the wind and waves. How about you?"

Inne nodded, processing this new idea. *What storms do I have in my life?* For a moment she was lost in thought. She bit down hard on her bottom lip and stared blankly at her hands folded in her lap. Tears began to fill her eyes, then they spilled out, rolling down her cheeks. Finally her shoulders began shaking, and like a dam bursting she wept uncontrollably.

Fatima slid next to Inne and slipped her arm around her shoulders. Inne collapsed like a little child in her arms.

Eventually Inne regained her composure, and Fatima pushed the hair from Inne's swollen eyes. "What is it, dear friend?"

"I'm so ashamed that sometimes I don't even want to leave the house. My husband and I have been trying to have a baby for three years, but I can't get pregnant. I see the stares of the neighbors, and feel their scorn. Someone even said God has cursed me. Whenever somebody has a baby, I burn with envy. And recently my husband began hinting he may take a second wife if I don't get pregnant soon." Inne burst into tears again.

Fatima got up, fetched a tissue roll, and handed it to Inne. "That is a huge storm. I would feel the same way if I were in your shoes. That is such a weight to carry around."

Inne nodded.

"Is there anything in today's story that comforts you?"

"I've never thought about not getting pregnant as a storm, but it really is. It's all I think about. Sometimes I feel like I'm drowning because the waves are sweeping over me."

"Yes, and Isa has power over the wind and the waves. Both the Qur'an[82] and the Injil say Isa is in heaven right now. He can see this storm you are experiencing. Do you know He cares very deeply for you?"

"I thought He was just a prophet."

---

[82] Qur'an 3:55

"He is a prophet, but He did things no other prophet did. When He walked this earth, He had power to calm the wind and the waves. Now in heaven, He still has power to calm our storms. I know because He has done so many times in my life."

This was all so new for Inne. She didn't want others to know how she struggled with not getting pregnant, but she felt safe and accepted by Fatima. She had never considered Isa in this way. Inne took a deep breath, and exhaled slowly. "I can't explain it, but this story does give me hope."

Fatima reached over and patted Inne on the hand. "I'm very honored that you would share such a private matter with me. My heart is very burdened for you. May I pray for you in Isa's name?"

Inne nodded.

"Bismillahi arrahmani arrahim, God most merciful and most gracious. Thank you that when Isa walked this earth He had power over the wind and the waves. Even now in heaven, we believe He still has power over the various storms we experience. Thank you that you care so much for Inne. You see every tear she has shed. I ask in faith in Isa's name that You grant a child to Inne and her husband. We believe nothing is impossible for You. In Isa's name, Amen."

Inne smiled appreciatively.

"These stories aren't just for you and your family. They are for others too. Who do you think you could share this story with?"

Inne thought for a moment. "I sell food to the college women who live in the house next to me. One of them, named Eka, buys the food from me and takes it to the others. I don't know much about her background except that she comes from a very poor family. When she comes by, she always seems worried."

"Why don't you tell her this story and see if she would like to discuss other stories with you?"

"I think I will."

Inne gave Fatima a big hug, then excused herself to go home.

Discuss and apply

1. How did you obey what you concluded God wanted you to do from the previous chapter?

2. Describe Fatima's practice of prayer. What can you do to improve your prayer life?

3. In what ways did Fatima show care and compassion to Inne?

4. Why did Fatima start with the ninth prophet story rather than with Adam? Discuss the pros and cons of starting with the first prophet story (Adam) or the ninth prophet story (on sacrifice, outlined in Appendix C). How will you decide where to start?

5. What does Fatima advise so that Inne can facilitate her husband leading them to discuss the same stories?

6. Is anyone you know experiencing a "storm" in their life? Role play sharing the story of Jesus calming the storm, and praying for each other. How you will start? What will you say to invite the other person to discuss the prophet stories with you after you share this story and pray for them?

7. What is Inne's "storm?" Do you know anyone like this? Role play how you can minister to them?

8. Who is Inne's oikos?

9. Share what you believe God wants you to do in the next 24–48 hours from what you learned in this chapter.

10. Close in prayer with your team, asking God to give dreams and visions to Muslims, and to open the hearts of those with whom you are each going to share this Jesus story.

14

Listening for Felt Needs

Eka (student) pours out her heart in response to Inne's caring questions

Inne heard a knock at the front door and found Eka standing in the open doorway, wearing a tight T-shirt and blue jeans. "Come in!" she said with motherly affection for her long-time customer. "I am almost done preparing the food. Come back to the kitchen with me while I finish up."

The kitchen was a simple room at the back of the house. Unlike the main part of the house, which was tiled, the floor of the kitchen was rough concrete. A few pots hung from nails on one wall. Against the opposite wall was a small table where Inne was preparing the food. A gas stove under a small window was in the corner. As they entered, Inne shooed a cat off the table and out the open door. Inne motioned with her hand for Eka to sit on a plastic stool next to the table. Inne picked up a cucumber to peel.

"How's school going? Are your classes difficult?" Inne asked.

"I'm taking accounting right now, but not doing very well. The professor offers tutoring, but I don't have money for the fees so I'm getting further and further behind. I'm in danger of failing the class and, if I do, I might have to drop out of school because my dad said he won't keep paying for college if I can't pass the courses."

"Oh, I'm so sorry to hear that. That must be tough."

"Yeah," Eka sighed, biting her fingernails and tapping her foot.

"You mentioned your dad. Is your mom still living?"

"Yes, but they are divorced. My dad gambles and drinks too much. When my mom confronted him on it, he divorced her and married another woman. I was six years old when my mom and I went to live with her parents, but they were desperately poor. My grandmother was sick, and they spent what little money they had taking her to the shaman. I was thirteen when my grandmother died. My grandfather had to sell his small house to pay off his debts, and went to live with one of his other children."

Inne placed six round pieces of banana leaf on the table, and scooped out servings of rice, fish, half a boiled egg, hot sauce, and a few vegetables on each banana leaf. She folded the banana leaves, stapled the edges shut, and arranged the six bundles on the table for Eka to take to her roommates. After pouring Eka a glass of water, she sat down beside her. "Go on."

"In my village, rice is dried, bagged, and stored at a warehouse. There was an unused room at the warehouse so my mom convinced the manager to let us live in it. Oh, the rats in that room!

"My mom and I had nothing to eat, so she started stealing. At first she stole mangoes or papayas to give to me. Then she started stealing clothes people hung out to dry. My mom would take these clothes to the neighboring village and sell them to a man who sold used clothes. One day a policeman brought a shirt my mom had stolen to the warehouse where we lived. He arrested my mom, and took her to the jail at the police station. They don't serve food at this jail so I had to beg food from my relatives so that my mom wouldn't starve.

"I was still attending school but I couldn't concentrate. All the kids at school mocked and laughed at me. They said our family was cursed by God. They called my mother a thief, and predicted I would turn out just like her. They ridiculed my school uniform because it was dirty and torn. They held their noses when they passed me because I hadn't taken a bath. The teachers did nothing to help me. I hated my life, my mom, my dad, the kids at school, and the teachers. Then the police released my mom."

"They just released her?"

Eka frowned like she was hiding a dark secret she didn't want to admit even to herself. Finally she said, "They just released her."

Inne got up and refilled Eka's glass of water. As Eka stared into the glass, Inne stood behind her and gently massaged her shoulders. "I had no idea you had been through such a difficult childhood. What happened next?"

"In my village, there was an older man whose wife had died. He wanted a new wife to take care of his children. My mom didn't love him but she married him anyway, even though he was fifteen years older than her. After a few months, my step-dad started yelling at me and beating me because he claimed I was eating too much food. The truth was he gave all the food to his own kids, and very little to me. He never bought me a new school uniform. I had to wear old uniforms from his kids. They were torn and stained, and didn't fit. I begged my mom to let me go live with my aunt. This aunt didn't really want me, but she felt sorry for me so she agreed to take me in. I was fourteen years old at the time.

"My aunt and uncle don't own any land. They are rice farmers, and hire themselves out to plant and harvest rice. Sometimes the rice harvest was too little so we had to travel to other areas to get work. We lived in tiny tents near the fields we harvested. It was hot and exhausting work. Usually there wasn't clean water nearby, and the food was scarce. I had to drop out of school during those times. In fact, I was twenty years old when I finished high school.

"Both my aunt and uncle were very poor and got angry easily. I always felt on edge, trying to keep from making them upset. When they were mad they called me a 'dog' or a 'monkey.' Or, if they were really angry, they called me 'Satan.' I vowed that when I grew up, I would never be poor."

"So, where do you consider home?"

"I don't have a home," Eka said bitterly, swallowing hard. "I would never live with my mom and step-dad. I haven't lived with my dad since I was six years old. I should be grateful he is paying for my college. My aunt lets me stay with her during school breaks, but I never feel welcome there. I don't belong anywhere."

Eka paused, looked at the floor, then back at Inne. Her eyes filled with tears. "So college is my only hope for a better life."

"If I've learned one thing in life," Eka continued, regaining her composure, "it's that you can't trust anyone. People use you, and then they let you down. You must trust in yourself.

"If I'm going to be happy, I have to get a good job. And in order to get a good job, I have to finish college. But right now, I'm failing my accounting course, and I may have to drop out of college. I don't know what to do." She started crying again.

Inne could feel Eka's hopelessness. *I had no idea Eka came from such a difficult background. No wonder she always seems so stressed!*

Inne sat down, placed her hand on top of Eka's, and patted it gently. "I'd like to tell you a story about the prophet Isa."

Eka nodded okay.

After telling how Isa calmed the storm, Inne added, "Isa can calm your storms too."

Eka looked puzzled. "What do you mean?"

"I'm in the midst of a storm too. I can't get pregnant, and my husband is thinking of taking a second wife. Somehow I'm comforted knowing Isa cares and can calm my storm. One more thing: I read that Isa was very poor. In fact, He didn't even own a bed,[83] so I'm sure He understands your situation."

Eka leaned her head to one side, thinking about what Inne had just said. She didn't yet believe it, but it was an interesting thought.

"Well, I must be going. My roommates are probably getting hungry. Oh, and thanks for listening."

Inne placed the six bundles of food in a plastic bag and handed them to Eka. "I've been reading some stories about the prophets which have really helped me. I think they could help you too. Next time you come back, I'd like to share another story with you."

"Sure. It can't hurt." Eka turned to go.

---

[83] Luke 9:58

* * *

Eka returned the next day to pick up that day's food. This time Inne had the food already prepared. The bundles were already stapled and placed in a plastic bag.

"I promised to tell you another story. Are you interested?"

"Sure!"

"Okay, please sit down." Inne pointed to the couch.

"As you know, God sent the prophets to teach us how to live. This first story is about the prophet Adam. In a moment, we are going to read this story twice and retell it, but first, let's each share something we are thankful for, and then we'll share something we are currently struggling with."

When they concluded their discussion, Inne asked, "Eka, what do you think of this story about Adam?"

"It's wonderful. I didn't know all those things."

"Who else needs to hear this story?"

"My roommates and I hang out together a lot. I think they would like this story."

"Why don't you share it with them?"

"I think I will." Eka stood and picked up the bag with her food. "See you tomorrow!"

Discuss and apply

1. How did you obey what you concluded God wanted you to do from the previous chapter?

2. Describe Eka's "storms." Do you know anyone with similar problems? What can you do to minister to them?

3. How did Inne show care and compassion for Eka?

4. Who is Eka's oikos?

5. Did you notice Inne's skill at asking questions? Asking questions is the best way to discover someone's felt needs. For others to be vulnerable with us, we must often be vulnerable with them first. In what ways was Inne vulnerable with Eka?

6. Form groups of two for a role play, with one person a non-believer experiencing a "storm" and the other a follower of Jesus who asks questions until he discovers the first person's "storm." Have the non-believer share their "storm." Then have the follower of Jesus tell the story of Jesus calming the wind and the waves, and pray for the non-believer. At the conclusion of your prayer don't forget to invite the first person to discuss chronological Bible stories with you. Switch roles and repeat the role play.

7. Share what you believe God wants you to do in the next 24–48 hours from what you learned in this chapter.

8. Close in prayer with your team for those with whom you are each going to share this Jesus story.

15

Encountering Radical Muslims

Abdullah (radical Muslim) accepts prayer for his demonized son

Nasrudin finished his last bite of fried rice and carefully crossed his fork and spoon upside down on his plate. He leaned across the table, kissed Amina on the cheek, and thanked her for breakfast.

Every night, much to his wife's displeasure, Nasrudin brought his motorcycle into the front room so no one would steal it during the night. Now he carefully backed it through the front door, onto the porch, and into the yard. Then he returned into the house to fetch bottles of honey.

Nasrudin had built a carrying case to hold twelve bottles on each side of the back tire of his motorcycle. He raised the lid, and systematically placed the bottles into the slots in the carrying case.

Once a year, Nasrudin and his co-workers would go into the forests in the mountains behind their village to gather honey. It was dangerous work, climbing trees and avoiding angry bees. He would never become rich as a honey salesman, but so far he had been able to provide for his family.

Kick-starting his motorcycle, Nasrudin prayed, "Lord, please give me today my daily bread. I ask You to direct me to people who will buy my honey. Give me eyes to see situations where You want me to minister. Watch over and protect my family while I'm away. Amen."

And with that he sped off to a new neighborhood to begin going door to door.[84]

* * *

Abdullah and his friends sat cross-legged on the floor in a circle. Smoke from their cigarettes hung heavy in the room. The windows and doors were all closed so no one could hear what they were discussing.

Abdullah was part of a secret group. They were disgusted by what was happening in their country, Indonesia. It was following in the way of the west: moral decay, materialism, immorality, drunkenness, and gambling. They were convinced only Sharia law would save their country.

Tall and overweight, Abdullah was an imposing figure. He had acne scars on his face and thick bushy eyebrows. His parents had given him the name Budiman when he was born, meaning "good character," but when he joined this group he took the name Abdullah because it means "servant of God." Abdullah wanted to live up to his name, so he sought meticulously to follow the example of the Prophet. He disliked violence, but had come to believe that violence was sometimes necessary to overthrow governments and establish Sharia law.

To Abdullah and his friends, the time for action had come. They had no choice. Abdullah and his friend Saleh had secretly travelled to Afghanistan to receive training in bomb making. Now, they were teaching their friends how to make bombs, and planning their first attack.

Suddenly Abdullah's phone rang. His son's name appeared in the caller ID. "What do you want?" Abdullah barked, angry at being interrupted during this important meeting.

"Hello, Mr. Abdullah? This is Mr. Lukman, Ali's teacher. I'm sorry to inform you that Ali has had another attack. I need you to come to school to pick him up."

---

[84] Selling door-to-door creates many opportunities to find persons of peace (POP). It is one form of *access business* (Appendix A).

Abdullah was embarrassed that he had snapped at Mr. Lukman. "I'll be there as soon as I can," he replied politely.

Abdullah turned to his friends, "I'm sorry but this training will have to be continued another day. My son has had another attack, and I have to pick him up from school." The men nodded they understood and excused themselves.

Abdullah got on his motorcycle and drove to school. *Why is God testing me? What more can I do to please Him?*

When Abdullah arrived, Ali was waiting in the teacher's room. He stared at the floor, shame written across his face.

Ali did not dare look at his father as he followed him to the motorcycle. They rode home in silence; then Abdullah demanded, "What happened?"

Still avoiding his father's eyes, Ali muttered, "It was just like all the other times. I was talking to my friends. Then suddenly the room started spinning. I fell to the floor, and my arms and legs started shaking uncontrollably. My head began shaking too, banging against the floor. Several friends grabbed me, and someone called for our teacher. He held my head until I stopped shaking, then called you."

"Go rest until I figure out what to do," Abdullah commanded. Dutifully, Ali shuffled to his room.

These attacks had started about six months earlier. At first they were short and rare, but recently they had become more frequent and severe. Abdullah had taken Ali to several shamans. They would write verses from the Qur'an on a piece of thick paper and then wash the ink into a glass of water. They would whisper and blow over the water and then tell Ali to drink. Each shaman promised Ali would be cured, but each "cure" was only temporary.

At first Abdullah went to cheaper shamans, but when Ali continued to have attacks Abdullah felt compelled to go to more expensive ones. The more powerful the shaman the more money they demanded. Abdullah resented paying them money when his son didn't get better. *What am I going to do?*

Suddenly he heard a voice calling from the yard, "Assalam wa'alikum." He opened the front door and stepped onto the porch.

* * *

Nasrudin was startled by Abdullah's long beard, turban, and long white robe. His beard and clothing made him look more Arab than Indonesian. Some people who dressed like this had committed acts of violence.

Nasrudin stammered his normal sales pitch, "I ... I ... I'm selling 100 percent pure honey. I gathered it myself, and I didn't add any water to it. If you have allergies local honey will help."

Abdullah turned red. "Get out of here! I'm having a horrible day. My son is being attacked by demons, and I don't know what to do!" Abdullah flung his arms in the air and turned to go inside.

"I can help."

Oh my gosh! Why did I say that? What a fool? Why didn't I keep my mouth shut?

Abdullah turned slowly and stared scornfully at Nasrudin, rage evident on his face. They stood facing each other for an awkward moment. Then Abdullah asked doubtfully, "Do you really think you can help?"

Nasrudin took a deep breath. The sun suddenly felt very warm against his back, and a trickle of sweat ran down his face. "Yes, I do," he said, surprised at his own boldness.

Abdullah began to soften. He was desperate; nothing he had tried had helped his son. "Okay. Come in."

Abdullah invited Nasrudin to sit in the front room. "How does this work?"

"First of all, I'm not a shaman. I'm a person just like you, but I believe God is all powerful, and Isa Al Masih has authority to drive out all kinds of evil spirits."

"What does this cost?"

"Nothing. I would never think of taking payment for prayer."

Abdullah raised his eyebrows in surprise. "Okay. My son just had an attack this morning. Go pray for him," he commanded, pointing to the bedroom.

"I can't. I only pray with my partner."

"Well, when can you get your partner and come back?" he asked impatiently.

"It's not that easy. You must promise to stop going to shamans. I don't want you to be confused about who heals your son."

Abdullah's rage returned instantly. "How dare you tell me not to go to other shamans? I'll do what I want when I want for my son. How do I know you can do anything to help him?"

"Those are my conditions." Nasrudin refused to budge.

"Very well. You may leave now." Then, as an afterthought, he said, "Give me your phone number."

Nasrudin scribbled down his number and handed it to Abdullah. As he walked to his motorcycle, Nasrudin could feel his hands shaking and his knees trembling.

* * *

About two weeks later, Nasrudin was on his motorcycle driving to another neighborhood to try to make a sale when he heard his cell phone ring. He had a reputation for honesty, so customers regularly called him when they ran out of honey. Nasrudin looked at the phone, but there was no name.

"Assalam wa'alikum."

"Wa alikum salam. This is Abdullah. My son has had another attack. I took him to the most powerful shaman around. It cost me a fortune, and it didn't do any good. I'm ready to accept your conditions. I won't take my son to another shaman. Just please come pray for my son."

"Okay. I will come by tonight after *magrib*."

Nasrudin immediately called his wife. "Amina, phone our teammates and ask them to come to our house. We need to have an emergency meeting in one hour."

* * *

Amina had not told the others what this meeting was about. She only told them it was important and urgent.

When they arrived Nasrudin wasted no time in telling his teammates about his conversation with Abdullah. A palpable heaviness fell on the group. They all understood the potential risks of sharing with a radical Muslim like Abdullah.

"The risks are just too great."

"But Yusuf, this man might be like the Apostle Paul."

"We need to pray!" Amina said.

They poured out their hearts with fresh intensity, pleading with God for the salvation of the Sayang people. They cried out for wisdom, and pledged themselves to do whatever God might ask.

An hour passed and they kept praying. After another hour, they grew silent.

"Amen," Faisal said. "What do you hear the Holy Spirit saying?"

"I think we should pray for Abdullah's son," Nasrudin said.

One by one, they all agreed.

"I believe this is an opportunity we must take," Yusuf declared. "We are called to be Isa's witnesses, and to trust God regardless of what happens."

"Okay then. Who will go with me?" Nasrudin asked.

"I think I should go," Faisal said. "But I would ask everyone to be in prayer while Nasrudin and I are praying for Ali."

They all agreed.

Discuss and apply

1. How did you obey what you concluded God wanted you to do from the previous chapter?

2. How would you respond if you encountered a radical Muslim?

3. Remember that many radicals are looking for truth, and are simply misguided. What approaches can you use to discover if a radical Muslim is open?

4. We have learned six ways to seek out POPs. Practice two of these with a partner:
   - making shema statements,
   - sharing your personal salvation story,
   - asking others if they know anyone who has had a dream from God,
   - offering prayer for healing, demonization, and "storms of life" (with a Bible story showing Jesus' power),
   - using verses in the Qur'an as a bridge to the Bible, and
   - sharing a *Creation to Christ* gospel presentation.

5. Do you agree with refusing to pray for a demonized person if he is still visiting shamans? How would you explain your reasons? When might you pray if he was still visiting shamans?

6. Share what you believe God wants you to do in the next 24–48 hours from what you learned in this chapter.

7. Pray with your team, and daily on your own, for God to bring radical Muslims to Himself, to recognize their lack of assurance of forgiveness for their sins, and to seek God's mercy in Jesus.

16

Delivering a Demonized Boy

God uses Nasrudin to deliver Abdullah's son and disciple Abdullah

After magrib, Nasrudin and Faisal mounted their motorcycles and drove the few miles to Abdullah's house. Excitement and dread filled their hearts as they pulled into his front yard. Abdullah heard them arrive and came out to meet them.

Nasrudin and Faisal took off their helmets and placed them on their motorcycles. "Assalam wa'alikum," they called toward the house.

"Wa alikum salam."

Abdullah ushered them into the house and pointed them towards a bedroom. Nasrudin and Faisal pushed aside the curtain and entered the room. Abdullah followed.

Ali lay on his back on a low, handmade wooden bed, his T-shirt drenched with perspiration from his thrashing. One arm covered his closed eyes, and his breathing was shallow and rapid. His mother, Titin, sat on the edge of the bed holding Ali's other hand.

Another man stood at the foot of the bed. He was dressed just like Abdullah: a turban, a long beard, and a long white robe. He squinted and frowned as Nasrudin and Faisal entered.

"This is my friend, Saleh."

Saleh nodded but said nothing.

Nasrudin turned to Abdullah. "We are not shamans. We are ordinary people who believe in the extraordinary power of Isa Al Masih as explained in the Qur'an and the Injil."

At the word "Injil," Saleh's face contorted, "I knew it," he exploded. "These men are Christians! What are you doing, Abdullah? Are you crazy?"

"Shut up. Ali is my son, not yours!"

Abdullah turned to Nasrudin. "Continue."

"When Isa walked the earth, He healed many who were afflicted by evil spirits. This example comes from Luke 4:31–37 in the Injil:

> One day Isa was teaching in the synagogue, and everyone was amazed by His teaching. In the synagogue that day was a demon-possessed man who cried out in a loud voice, "I know who You are. You are the Holy One sent from God." Isa rebuked him saying "Be quiet and come out of him." The demon threw the man to the ground and left without harming the man. Those in the synagogue were amazed and said, "With authority and power Isa commands the demons, and they obey Him."

Nasrudin looked to see if anyone had questions or comments. Saleh glared at Nasrudin but no one spoke.

In a calm but firm voice, Nasrudin declared, "Bismillahi arrahmani arrahim. I praise and exalt You, O Lord, most merciful and benevolent. You alone are God, and there is no other. You sent Isa Al Masih to earth. He lived a sinless life and always submitted to Your will. You willed that He shed His blood on a wooden cross to cleanse man of their sins. On this cross, Isa defeated the power of the evil one."

At the mention of the "cross," Ali immediately started thrashing his arms and legs. His whole body convulsed. He uttered loud groans and animal noises. Saliva spilled from his mouth, and his eyes rolled back into his head.

"In the name and power of Isa Al Masih, I command any and every evil spirit residing in Ali to be still."

Suddenly Ali became perfectly still, like he was in a deep sleep.

"On the cross, Isa defeated the power of the evil one. Through His resurrection and ascension he publicly disarmed Satan and all demons and *jinn*.[85] He sits at the right hand of God Almighty, where He has absolute authority over all powers and principalities. I am a child of God, seated with Al Masih in the heavenly realm. As His child, Isa has given me authority to exercise His power on earth. In the name and authority of Isa Al Masih, I command every evil spirit residing in Ali to flee."

Ali resumed wailing and flailing his arms and legs.

Nasrudin continued praying, "Isa Al Masih has all authority in heaven and on earth. All evil spirits are subject to His authority. These spirits may not linger or resist. They must obey. I command every demon to flee in the name of Isa."

Ali's body convulsed a couple of times then fell still.

Nasrudin stood. He and Faisal sang a worship song in the Sayang language, praising God for His love, goodness, and power.

Ali shrieked in an unnatural voice, "Stop singing. Stop singing that awful song!"

Nasrudin again knelt beside Ali and prayed, "All lingering spirits, you may not hide, you may not delay. I command you, by the authority, power and blood of Isa, to leave."

Again Ali's body convulsed a couple of times and then he was calm. Nasrudin and Faisal sang the same song again. This time Ali remained still.

Nasrudin gently took Ali's hand. Ali opened his eyes, and smiled weakly.

"Are there any more spirits inside you?"

"I don't think so."

Nasrudin turned to Abdullah. "The boy is weak. He should eat something."

---

[85] Identified in the Qur'an as spirit beings with free will, different from humans, angels, and demons.

While Titin went to the kitchen, Abdullah, Faisal, Nasrudin, and Saleh went into the front room. When the others sat down, Saleh stomped out the front door.

"I can't thank you enough for what you've done for my son. I've never seen power like that."

"You're welcome."

"Can I pay you something?"

"No. The Injil says, 'Freely you have received, freely give.'"

After feeding Ali, Titin brought a tray with three cups of hot tea into the front room. She placed one in front of each man. Abdullah pulled out a pack of cigarettes and offered some to Nasrudin and Faisal, but they declined. Abdullah took one and lit it. He inhaled deeply and exhaled slowly. He took the lid off a can of snacks on the low table in front of them, and motioned for each person to help themselves to tea and snacks.

"I need to warn you about something," Nasrudin said. "The Injil is very clear that if a spirit is cast out of a person, it will roam about trying to find a place to dwell. If it can't find a place, the spirit will return to the place from which it was cast out. If the spirit finds the place empty, it will invite seven other spirits more evil than itself to come and dwell in that place. The person's new condition will then be worse than his previous one.[86] This is what will happen to Ali unless he 'fills' his place."

"What do you mean?"

"Ali is like a house which is empty. He needs his mind and heart filled with truth so that there is no room for spirits to return and occupy his house."

"Well, how do I do that?"

"There is only one way. He needs to learn who Isa is and Isa's power to protect him. Before I prayed, I told you a story about Isa. I

---

[86] Luke 11:24–26

know many more stories about Isa and the prophets. May I come back tomorrow[87] and discuss one with you?" [88]

"Yes, I would like that."

The three of them talked a bit longer, then Faisal and Nasrudin excused themselves.

* * *

Nasrudin returned the next day and shared the story of creation and Adam and Eve's fall into sin with Abdullah, Titin, and Ali.

When they concluded their discussion, Nasrudin said, "Abdullah, it is best if I don't keep coming back here. My presence would raise too many suspicions."

Abdullah understood immediately. "You're right. What do you suggest?"

"We need to find different places and different times to meet." After they agreed on when and where to meet next, Nasrudin left.

This began a pattern of meeting once or twice a week. Each time Abdullah would explain how his meeting with his family had gone and how they had applied the story. Often Abdullah brought questions from his family that he had been unable to answer. Nasrudin always pointed Abdullah back to the text to find the answers. Nasrudin would then facilitate their next discussion and prepare Abdullah to lead his family in it.

In their discussions, they became increasingly open with one another about their struggles and challenges, and the two men came to trust each other deeply.

---

[87] The church planter should arrange to meet with the family again as soon as possible. Often after just two days the crisis has passed, the family has returned to their daily routines, and the opportunity for follow up is gone.

[88] One essential CPM principle is "begin with the end in mind." An oikos that experiences deliverance (or healing) may be ready to follow Jesus immediately, in which case we present a *Creation to Christ* invitation as described in Appendix C. If they are not ready to follow Jesus, they may still want to learn about Him after witnessing His power, in which case we start with the ninth prophet story. However in this story Nasrudin perceives that Abdullah has deep misconceptions about Jesus and God's plan of salvation. To fully equip Abdullah to follow Jesus, lead his oikos, and endure persecution, Nasrudin starts him with the first prophet story.

Discuss and apply

1. How did you obey what you concluded God wanted you to do from the previous chapter?

2. Why is it best to have a believing friend along for casting out demons? Why is it important to have others praying when driving out demons?

3. Do you agree with the approach Nasrudin used to pray for Ali? What would you have done differently?

4. What warning did Nasrudin give to Abdullah if Ali didn't "fill" his house?

5. What did Nasrudin say was the best way to prevent Ali from ending up in a worse state?

6. Role play sharing the story of the demon-possessed man and praying for the afflicted person.

7. When someone has been delivered, why is it vitally important to follow up with them within two days?

8. Share what you believe God wants you to do in the next 24–48 hours from what you learned in this chapter.

9. Pray with your team for God to lead His people in delivering those who are demonized, and to lead those delivered in deciding to follow Christ.

17

Proclaiming Power for Forgiveness and Change

Abdullah tells Umar (alcoholic) about forgiveness, and hope for change

As a honey salesman, Nasrudin traveled around the surrounding area a great deal, so he knew many different places he and Abdullah could meet. One day they met in a grass hut on the edge of a rice field outside of town. Since it wasn't rice season, the area was deserted.

Nasrudin extended his hand to Abdullah.

"Assalam wa'alikum."

"Wa alikum salam."

As they sat down on the grass hut's bamboo floor, a lizard scurried away. The sky was overcast, and a gentle breeze was blowing. Nasrudin observed that although Abdullah's beard and clothing hadn't changed, his heart and face were softening. No longer did he always look angry. He often smiled, and liked to slap Nasrudin on the back.

They discussed how Abdullah and his family applied the last story.

"Are you ready for the next story?"

"I am."

"Please read John 8:2–12, then retell the story to me in your own words."

After reading the story aloud, Abdullah said, "One day as Isa was teaching, some religious leaders brought to Him a woman who had been caught in the act of adultery. They said to Him, 'The Law demands that we stone such a woman. What do You say?' Isa replied, 'Let the person with no sin cast the first stone.' One by one the religious leaders went away until Isa was left alone with the woman. He asked her, 'Did no one condemn you?' 'No,' she replied. 'Neither do I. Go and sin no more.'"

"That's good. What do you learn about Isa from this story?"

Abdullah read over the story again silently. "Isa forgave the woman, and told her to stop sinning."

"That's right. Isa forgave her sins." Nasrudin emphasized each word. "In the other story we read, Luke 5:18–26, we observed that Isa forgave the sins of a lame man. God has given Isa authority to forgive sins."

Nasrudin paused to let Abdullah absorb what he had just said, then glanced at the darkening sky as a few raindrops began to fall.

"How could you apply this story to your life?"

"Do you think Isa could really forgive me?"

"I'm absolutely sure He would."

"But you don't know what I've done."

"It doesn't matter. Isa forgives all sins."

"He could never forgive mine."

"Of course He can."

Abdullah, too, looked at the sky. "I better go. It looks like it's going to rain hard."

Nasrudin was surprised at Abdullah's sudden decision to leave, and wondered if he might be avoiding something. "Is everything okay?" he asked.

"Yeah, some other time I need to tell you about my past."

Abdullah wheeled his motorcycle around and headed toward the main road. By the time he got there the rain was coming down harder. He saw a tin shelter beside the road. He parked his motorcycle next to it, and decided to wait in the shelter until the rain passed.

While Abdullah waited, a man came walking down the road. He was staggering, and soaking wet.

"Hey," Abdullah yelled, "get out of the rain, or you'll get sick."

The man stumbled over to the tin shelter and sat down next to Abdullah. The man smelled strongly of alcohol, and his eyes were blood shot. His hair was uncombed, and his well-worn T-shirt partially obscured a tattoo.

They sat in silence until Abdullah said, "You shouldn't drink. That's a sin."

"I know, but it relaxes me."

"There are other ways to relax. It is a sin, and you should stop."

"I've tried." The man shook his head sadly. "But I can't."

"You should ask God for help."

"I've done that too, and it didn't do any good. I'm a sinner, and there is no hope for me." The man pulled his knees up to his chest, put his arms around his knees, and bowed his head.

Abdullah was disgusted with anyone who drank alcohol. In earlier days, he would have beaten up this man and felt like he was serving God. But today he felt sympathy for him. He wasn't used to speaking kindly, yet he couldn't leave this man with no hope.

"I'm Abdullah. What's your name?"

"Umar."

"Look, Umar, there is always hope with God. I just heard an interesting story. Can I tell it to you?"

"Sure. I'm not going anywhere until this rain lets up."

"This story is about a woman caught in adultery. She was probably drinking too."

Abdullah shared the story concluding, "Isa forgave her sins. I believe He will forgive you of your sins if you truly seek Him."

"That is a good story. Where did you get it?"

"That story came from the Injil, but I also know stories from the Taurat and Zabur. Would you like to hear them?"

"Okay."

"Meet me back here at the same time tomorrow."

* * *

"Hi Umar."

"Hi Abdullah."

"In the state you were in yesterday, I'm surprised you remembered our meeting, and that my clothes didn't scare you off!" Abdullah laughed and slapped Umar on the back.

By habit, Umar brought two fingers to his mouth as if to take a drag on a cigarette. "I'll admit I had second thoughts, but I kept thinking about that story you told me yesterday. It gave me hope."

"I brought a piece of paper with another story. It's about Adam and Eve, and their sin. But first, what are you thankful for, Umar?"

The two men enjoyed a dynamic discussion of the story.

When they concluded, Umar said enthusiastically, "That is a really good story, Abdullah!"

Abdullah stroked his long beard. "Umar, who else needs to hear this story?"

"I don't know what you mean?"

"Who lives in your home with you?"

"My wife, our two children, and my wife's sister."

"Tonight, I want you to gather everyone around and do with them what I just did with you."

"There's no way I could do that. No one in my family takes me seriously. They think I'm a good for nothing drunk." Umar's shoulders slumped, and he stared vacantly ahead.

Abdullah saw that Umar's alcoholism masked a shattered self-image, and felt a sudden wave of compassion for the pitiful man sitting next to him. "Do you want to change?"

"Of course!" Umar looked at Abdullah. "But everything I do ends in failure. It's all hopeless. It's better to not try than to try and fail again!"

"No person and no situation are ever hopeless with God. Isa gives the power to change, and that change starts today with a small step. I believe you can do this. You need to share this story with your family regardless of what they think. Trust me; they will like this story. Will you try?"

"Okay, I'll try. What do I have to lose?"

Discuss and apply

1. How did you obey what you concluded God wanted you to do from the previous chapter?

2. This chapter deals with two important themes: the power of forgiveness and the power to change. Why was Abdullah interested in the story about the woman caught in adultery?

3. If you were Abdullah, what would you have said to Umar so he would want to discuss Bible stories with you?

4. Why do you think the story of the woman caught in adultery gave Umar the hope that he could change?

5. Umar felt like a complete failure and was afraid to lead his family because he thought he would fail at that too. What would you say to Umar so he would at least try?

6. Share what you believe God wants you to do in the next 24–48 hours from what you learned in this chapter.

7. Pray with your team that Muslims would recognize their lack of power to change themselves, and be drawn to the power Jesus gives. Pray together for your own lives to draw on God's power to change you in areas you need to change.

18

Witnessing through Healthy Families

Nur ministers to Aysha (a hurting wife)

Nur checked her shopping list for her weekly trip to the market. She rejoiced that Faisal, Fatima, Yusuf, and Nasrudin had each had the privilege of discussing chronological stories with an oikos. She was thankful that God's Word was going out, and that the Sayang people were being transformed. Nur longed to start her own discovery group, and was faithfully praying and diligently sharing, but so far she hadn't found a person of peace.

The recent rain had left the market muddy. Fortunately someone had arranged discarded boards to form a path from stall to stall. As Nur balanced on one of the boards, she said to a bystander, "I guess God knew the farmers needed rain!" The other woman just shrugged her shoulders.

The food sellers, all wearing head coverings, were well known to Nur, so she didn't need to bargain for her groceries. She purchased the food she needed: vegetables, fish, fruit, chicken, spices, and rice, along with a broom. She also had the soles of Yusuf's shoes replaced. Loading her wares in two sturdy bags she had brought with her, Nur decided to go home the long route so she could pray for new people along the way.

She reached an intersection and set her bags down. *Why did I go the long way on a day when my bags are so heavy?*

Most homes in this neighborhood were similar—two-bedroom houses with small porches and yards ringed by half cinderblock and half metal fences painted Islamic green, although a few fences were painted bright purple or orange. The poorer homes had bamboo fences. Most doors were open, with sandals on the porches.

As she wiped the sweat from her brow, Nur heard someone crying in a nearby house. *Lord, please help me know what You want me to do in this situation.*

Nur walked up to the porch of the house. "Excuse me. I couldn't help hearing you crying. Is everything okay?"

A short, overweight woman wearing a faded T-shirt and sarong came to the door. Her long hair was rolled up into a bun and pinned. She wiped tears from her red and swollen eyes with the back of her hand, and took a deep breath. "It's my husband. He yelled at me again."

"Would you like to talk about it?" Nur asked tenderly.

The woman nodded and invited Nur to take a seat in her front room. "He went to get dressed this morning and I hadn't ironed the shirt he wanted to wear. I was planning to do it after I finished getting breakfast ready.

"He exploded and called me a 'dog,' and a 'lazy bum.' He screamed that he works hard all day long, and the least I could do is iron his shirts. He said he was sorry he married me. He yelled, 'Why can't you do anything right?' and stomped out of the house." The woman's eyes again filled with tears, remembering afresh the stinging rejection of her husband's cruel words.

"Something like this happens almost daily. If he doesn't yell at me he yells at the kids. When I try to protect them, he beats me. He says that he must teach me a lesson for interfering with his parenting.

"It doesn't help that the imam told my husband he must discipline me so that I will behave. The imam thinks women are only good for sex and cleaning the house. My brother said I should visit the shaman and send black magic against my husband. I don't know what to do." The woman cried in despair, burying her face in her hands.

Trying to compose herself, she straightened up and crossed her legs. "I just want a family like yours."

"Like mine?"

"Yes. We met at an *arisan*[89] last year. You were very kind to me, and I've been watching you and your family ever since."

"I'm sorry. You do look familiar. Tell me your name again."

"Don't worry. It was a brief meeting. My name is Aysha."

Nur extended her hand and they shook warmly.

"May I pray for you?"

"Okay."

"God whom we call Father, It is Your will for families to experience joy, peace, and intimacy, yet Aysha's family is being ripped apart by anger and cruel words. Please intervene in their situation and change both of them so that their home will be a place of love and acceptance. Deliver them from their frequent fighting. We know that nothing is impossible for You through the power of Isa Al Masih, in whose name we pray. Amen.

"Aysha, I'm so glad to meet you again."

"Me too. Would you stay for tea?"

"Certainly."

Aysha led the way past a pile of unironed clothes into the kitchen and struck a match to light the stove. "I don't want to be rich. I don't want a fancy house, nice clothes, expensive vacations, or the latest electronics. I just want a husband who will love me, and value me for who I am."

"I think most women want that."

Aysha handed Nur a cup of tea, and sat down next to her.

"I noticed your family enjoys doing things together. I've seen you all at the beach, playing in the sand and the waves. Usually men and women only talk to each other when they are dating. When they get married, they just speak about the house and the kids. All romance is gone. But you and your husband are different; you talk and laugh together. I've even seen him drive you to the market in his taxi."

---

[89] Indonesian for a monthly neighborhood meeting with a program and food.

Nur thought, *We do enjoy each other. That's true. Wow, you never know who is watching you.*

Aysha opened a can of snacks.

"I often walk by your house, and look with envy on your family. On one occasion I saw your husband bring you a cup of coffee. My own husband would never do that. Another time, I saw your husband playing a game with your kids. My husband never pays attention to our kids except to punish them. My husband and I visited you for Idul Fitri.[90] I watched as your husband actually listened to you."

Aysha blushed as she realized how long she had been talking. "Forgive me for going on and on about my problems. I'm sorry to burden you."

"Oh, don't be. My family is far from perfect. Yusuf and I argue and even get angry at each other."

"Does he ever beat you?"

"No."

"Do you and your husband talk over what made you angry and resolve the problem?"

"Yes. We are committed to resolving issues as soon as possible."

"That's what I'm saying. I want a family like that. Is that too much to hope for?"

"My family hasn't always been this way. Several years after Yusuf and I were married, all the fun evaporated from our relationship. We just functioned together. We often argued, and didn't resolve anything. Then through stories about the prophets we started learning how God wants us to live our lives. We applied the truths from these stories to make our lives and family better. We are still learning and growing, but these stories have made a big difference in our lives. In fact, Yusuf and I have begun learning how to help others through these same stories."

"Would you come and teach me?"

"Sure! I can come back tomorrow and share the first one."

---

[90] A two-day holiday following Ramadan, during which families, friends, and neighbors typically visit each other.

* * *

Several weeks later, Nur was washing the breakfast dishes when Aysha arrived. They had discussed all the prophet stories, and several Isa stories, and Aysha had shared them with her family.

"You were right! These stories really do transform a family. And guess what?"

Nur dried her hands on a dish towel. *With Aysha, it could be just about anything!* Nur stared at her own pile of ironing and recalled the time she had found Aysha crying. "I don't know. Tell me."

"My neighbor, Meri, has seen the change in my family, and asked what shaman I had visited to cast a spell on my husband. I told her I didn't go to a shaman, but am learning about God's power through prophet stories I'm studying with you. She then asked if she could join us. What do you think? Can I start bringing her to our studies together?"

"It's a beautiful thing to watch God at work. How thankful I am God brought us together. I have seen the transformation in you. I'm not surprised your neighbor noticed it too."

"Thanks," Aysha blushed.

"If Meri were to start with the stories we are discussing now about Isa, she wouldn't have the benefit of the prophet stories."

"Well that's true."

"It would be better if she started at the beginning and discussed all the stories with her family. Why don't you help her, like I'm doing with you?"

"I'm not sure I'm ready, but if you'll help me, I'll do it."

"Of course I'll help you."

"Thanks."

Nur then directed Aysha to the next Isa story, about what Isa taught. "Please read Mark 7:14–23 aloud twice, and then retell it in your own words."

After reading the story, Aysha said, "Isa taught that what we put into our mouths defiles us. For example, eating pork or drinking alcohol defiles us."

"Are you sure? Why don't you read the text again?"

After rereading the text, Aysha exclaimed, "Wow! I sure misread this the first time, didn't I! What we put into our mouths *doesn't* defile us. Rather it's what comes out of our mouths, like unkind and judgmental words, that defiles us!"

"Yes, and why is that?"

Aysha looked at the text once again. "'For from within, out of the heart of man, come evil thoughts, immorality, theft, murder, coveting, deceit, slander, and pride. These come from the heart and these defile a man.' In other words, what a person speaks reveals what's in his heart."

"Good. How can you apply this to your life?"

"I have to admit that I say many unkind things to my husband and children. This is what my mother did to me, and I'm no different. I never thought about the fact that what I say comes from my heart. I want God to change my heart so that my words will be kind and uplifting."

"I'm sure He will. I'll pray for you."

Discuss and apply

1. How did you obey what you concluded God wanted you to do from the previous chapter?

2. Are you aware that people are watching you? Is your life a good witness to the power of Jesus? If not, what needs to change?

3. What examples do you see in this chapter of a shema statement, and of offering prayer?

4. What can your family do to be a better witness for Christ?

5. What message of hope do we have for women who are mistreated?

6. Nur prayed for Aysha's need. What other needs do people have that you can pray for? Role play in pairs praying for the other person and then inviting them to discuss chronological stories with you. Switch roles and repeat.

7. Were you surprised that Nur told Aysha her neighbor Meri shouldn't join them? What reason did Nur give? Why else is it better for Aysha to teach Meri than bring Meri to Nur?

8. According to Jesus' teaching, what defiles a person and why?

9. How did Nur correct Aysha when Aysha's retelling of the story was incorrect?

10. Share what you believe God wants you to do in the next 24–48 hours from what you learned in this chapter.

11. Pray together for your lives to bring glory to God and draw others to Him.

19

Healing the Sick

Nur follows the MAWL pattern to develop Aysha as a leader

Aysha hurried over to Nur's house with the good news; Meri and her family had been very receptive to the first prophet story, and Aysha's own family had discussed and applied the next Isa story.

Aysha is a doer, Nur thought. *When God gets hold of someone's heart, there is no telling what He will do through them. She still needs guidance, but step by step she is becoming a fine leader.*

"Shall we start today's story?" Nur asked.

After reading and discussing Luke 5:18–26, Nur said, "Isn't it remarkable that Isa can heal the sick?"

"Yes! That is so amazing!"

"How can you apply this story to your own life?"

"I won't go to the shaman if I or anyone in my family gets sick. I will ask Isa to heal me directly, or by the wisdom He gives doctors."

"That's good. How can you apply this to help others?"

"I have a neighbor, Wati, who is sick, but no one likes her, including me!"

"What do you hear Isa telling you to do?"

Aysha looked down, knowing the answer but not wanting to say it. Finally she said quietly, "I think He wants me to pray for her."

Nur patted Aysha's hand. "I think He does too. When can we visit her?"

* * *

When Nur and Aysha arrived at Wati's house, her nine year old son was burning the family's trash in a corner of the yard.

"Would you take us to your mom?"

The boy led them inside the house to one of the bedrooms, then quickly scampered back outside.

Wati was lying on the bed, dressed in a T-shirt and faded sarong, with a wet washcloth on her forehead. She opened her eyes and smiled weakly at Nur and Aysha, her teeth stained by years of chewing beetlenut. Nur sat on the edge of the bed and took Wati's hand in hers. "Can you tell me how long you've been sick?"

"It's been almost a month now. I used to be active in caring for my family. Then I came down with this cough and fever. I have grown weaker and weaker until now I can barely get out of bed. My husband took me to a shaman, but it didn't help.

"Then my husband took me to a doctor, but he didn't talk to me. In fact, he barely even looked at me. And his prescription didn't help."

A tear rolled down her cheek. "There is nothing else we can do. My fate is in God's hands."

Nur patted Wati's hand reassuringly. "I'm sorry you have suffered so much. Aysha and I are followers of Isa Al Masih. Both the Qur'an and the Injil say Isa has power to heal the sick. May we pray for you in His name?"

"Yes, please do."

"Before we pray, you should know we're not doctors, and there is much we don't know about medicine. And we aren't shaman; we have no power in ourselves. We're normal people who know that God cares. Let me tell you a story about Isa's power to heal.

One day, many crowded into a house where Isa was teaching. Four men carrying a lame man on a mat tried to bring him to Isa, but the house was so full with people they couldn't get inside. So they went onto the roof and let their friend down through the roof, right in front of Isa.

When Isa saw the lame man, He felt compassion for him, so He said, "Your sins are forgiven." The religious leaders who heard this began to grumble to one another, "Who can forgive sins but God alone?" But Isa, knowing their thoughts, said, "Which is easier to say, 'Your sins are forgiven,' or 'Get up and walk?'" The religious leaders were silent. Then Isa said, "In order that you may know that I, as the Son of Man, have authority on earth to forgive sins," He looked at the lame man, "I tell you, get up, take your mat, and go home."

Immediately, the lame man was healed. He stood up, picked up his mat and went out glorifying God. The people who witnessed this miracle said, 'We have certainly seen remarkable things today.'[91]

"Wati, the Injil teaches that Isa has the power to heal. The power is not in my words but in Isa Al Masih, who has given His authority to those who follow Him."

Again, Wati smiled weakly. Nur and Aysha placed their hands on Wati's arms while Wati held her palms up for prayer.[92]

Nur prayed, "God, most merciful and gracious, we thank you that You are full of love and compassion for those who suffer. We pray today for Wati who has suffered so much. Thank You for giving Isa authority to heal every kind of illness. If this sickness is caused by an evil spirit, then by the authority and power of Isa Al Masih we command that evil spirit to flee.

"If this illness is caused by a curse, we break the curse and render it powerless by the authority and power of Isa Al Masih.

"If this illness is caused by a germ, virus, or infection, we ask You to heal Wati by Isa Al Masih's authority and power. If Your will is to heal Wati through medicine, would You make the medicine effective. Whatever the cause of this illness, we humbly ask that You would be moved with compassion and mercy as You look upon Wati's misery.

---

[91] Luke 5:17–26

[92] This is the common position of prayer for Indonesian Muslims.

"We don't ask because of any merit of ours. We ask in simple faith, believing nothing is impossible for You. Demonstrate how much You love and care for Wati by restoring her to health. In the strong name of Isa Al Masih we pray."

Aysha, Wati and Nur each touched their lips with their hands and whispered, "Amen."

Nur stood up. "We'll check on you again in a few days."

Wati smiled gratefully. "I'd like that."

Once outside Nur said to Aysha, "Be sure to wash your hands as soon as you get home. You don't want to catch Wati's illness!"

* * *

Nur and Aysha prayed and then walked to Wati's house. As they reached the gate, they were surprised to see Wati sweeping her porch. When Wati saw them she dropped her broom, let out a scream, and ran to embrace them. She clung to them for a long time with tears running down her cheeks.

"I can't believe I'm well. I had given up all hope of ever being cured. Thank you, thank you, thank you."

"It wasn't us that healed you. It was the power of Isa Al Masih."

Wati turned her eyes toward heaven, exclaiming, "*Al hamdulilah!*[93] Thank You, Isa Al Masih!" Then Wati grabbed both women by the hand and led them inside. She made tea and placed snacks in front of them. As they chatted, Wati described how the fever had gradually left her and her cough had gone away.

"Did you like the story we told you about Isa Al Masih?"

"Yes, I did. I liked it a lot."

"Aysha and I know more stories about Isa and the other prophets.

---

[93] Arabic for "Praise be to God."

Can we come back and share more with you?" [94]

"Yes, please do!"

"We'll come back tomorrow.[95] Would you gather your family together so we can share with them too?"

"My husband will be home at five. Can you come then?"

"We sure can."

* * *

"We shouldn't keep Wati waiting," Nur said. "Are you ready to meet her?"

Aysha nodded and began gathering her belongings.

"And are you ready to lead the meeting?"

"Me? I'm not ready!" protested Aysha.

"Sure you are. You led Meri and her family, didn't you?"

"Yeah."

"This is no different. Come on!"

---

[94] With an adult who has experienced a healing or deliverance in Jesus name, it is not always necessary to study all the prophet stories. Since Wati's family observed the miracle of her healing, they may be ready to follow Jesus in response to a *Creation to Christ* invitation (Appendix C). If Wati and her family follow Jesus and are baptized, Aysha will then equip Wati to facilitate all the prophet and Jesus stories with her oikos. Or, if Wati and her family aren't ready to follow Jesus, Aysha may start with the sacrifice (ninth prophet) story, then study all the Jesus stories. Nur and Aysha will choose the best place to start the storying sequence in order to bring Wati's oikos to faith and establish them firmly enough to withstand persecution.

[95] The church planter should arrange to meet again as soon as possible. Often after just two days the crisis has passed, the family has returned to their daily routines, and the opportunity for follow up is gone.

Discuss and apply

1. How did you obey what you concluded God wanted you to do from the previous chapter?

2. What did Nur say to Wati before she prayed for her? What would you say in a similar situation?

3. Read Matt. 10:7 and Luke 10:9. Are these commands Jesus expected the disciples to continue obeying and teaching others to obey?

4. Role play with a partner: Person A is sick; B tells Luke 5:18–26 and prays for A, then concludes by inviting A to discuss chronological Bible stories with B. Switch roles and repeat.

5. When someone has been healed, why is it vitally important to follow up with them within two days?

6. The goal is not just to win an individual, but to reach an oikos so they can withstand persecution together. With this in mind, discuss the pros and cons for each of the three starting points we have learned for the storying sequence (see Appendix C):
   - the first prophet story for most of those we initiate with,
   - the sacrifice (ninth prophet) story for those eager to learn about Jesus right away, and
   - a *Creation to Christ* story for those ready to follow Christ.

7. Praying with nonbelievers for their needs is one of the most effective ways to identify persons of peace. Make a list of needs people have (e.g. in their families, neighborhoods, or at work), then role play praying for one of those needs.

8. A key CPM leadership development principle is to model what you want others to do, then let them do it. (This is sometimes abbreviated MAWL, for Model, Assist, Watch and Leave.) In this chapter and the previous one, what specific skills did Nur help Aysha develop to lead her family, Meri, and Wati? What did Nur say to build Aysha's confidence?

9. Share what you believe God wants you to do in the next 24–48 hours from what you learned in this chapter.

10. Pray together for God to lead each member of your team into more effective prayer for healing.

20

Telling a "Creation to Christ" Story

Amina shares the gospel with Lily (patient) and her mother

Amina paused outside the door of the economy class hospital room. To the right children were chasing each other down the hallway, and to the left a peanut salesman was shooing a cat out an open door. A stale smell of urine mixed with sweat hung in the air. Inside, six patients were crowded into one room, with family members sleeping on straw mats on the hard floor next to the bed. Only a thin curtain separated the beds. *Lord, help me to be Your instrument of hope and healing.*

Stepping over a pile of sandals, Amina entered the room and approached the first bed. She picked up the chart and read "Dengue Fever." A woman of about 30 lay on the bed, hooked up to an IV. An older women, probably her mother, waved a bamboo fan over her daughter as sweat trickled down her face. On the floor sat a plate of half eaten rice.

Amina approached one of the patients, read her name from the chart, and smiled cheerfully. "How are we doing today, Lily?"

"A little better I think."

"I need to draw some blood so we can check your platelet count." Amina took out a needle and prepped the arm.

"With dengue fever, it is important to drink lots of water." Turning to the older woman, Amina asked, "Are you her mother? Are you making sure she is getting plenty of water?"

"Yes, Lily is my daughter. And I'm trying."

As she watched the blood fill the needle, Amina asked Lily, "Do you know anyone who has ever had a dream from God?"

"No, but I frequently have bad dreams."

Amina raised her eyebrows. "Really! I used to have bad dreams all the time too. Now before I go to sleep I pray in the name of Isa Al Masih. I ask Him to watch over and protect me through the night. Now I rarely have bad dreams, and if I do have one I simply pray again in Isa's name."

Lily and her mother looked puzzled, and Amina gathered they had never heard of Isa Al Masih.

"Let me tell you a story. God created the heavens and the earth. He made all the plants and animals too. Last of all, He formed Adam and Eve, placed them in paradise, a garden named Eden, and gave them responsibility to tend the garden. God told them they could eat from any tree in the garden except Kholdi, the tree of the knowledge of good and evil.

"One day the devil, inhabiting the body of a serpent, spoke to Eve, 'God knows that if you eat from this tree your eyes will be opened and you will be like God, knowing good and evil.' Eve gazed at the tree and saw the fruit looked delicious, so she picked a piece of fruit, ate a bite, and gave the fruit to Adam who also took a bite. Suddenly both their eyes were opened, and they realized they were naked. Because of their shame they sewed leaves together and hid themselves. Just then they heard the sound of God calling out to them, 'Where are you?'

"Adam replied, 'We realized we were naked so we hid ourselves.' Then God asked, 'Have you eaten from the tree I forbid you to eat from?'

"Realizing they couldn't hide anything from God, they confessed their sin. God punished the serpent by decreeing that it would crawl on its belly forever. He punished the woman by giving her pain in childbirth, and He punished the man by making him work hard for his food. Then God provided animal skins to cover their nakedness, and expelled Adam and Eve from the garden!

"In this story, we see the severity of sin in the presence of a holy and all-knowing God. Adam and Eve committed only one sin, yet God punished them. Think of the punishment we deserve who have committed so many sins!"

Both women shuddered at this thought.

Amina removed the needle, labeled the vial, and placed it in a tray. "Yet in this story, we also see God's incredible mercy. Adam and Eve already had clothes they had sewn together from leaves, so why did God make new clothes for them out of animal skins?"

Lily and her mother both shrugged.

Amina placed a cotton ball on the wound and applied pressure. "God's Word says, 'Without the shedding of blood, there is no forgiveness of sins.' For this reason, God in His mercy shed the blood of animals to cover Adam and Eve. You might be thinking, 'Why is blood necessary for the forgiveness of sins?' There is another verse which says, 'The life of the creature is in the blood.'

"We read in the Holy Books that every prophet offered sacrifices for this reason, 'Without the shedding of blood there is no forgiveness of sins.'

"Then Isa Al Masih was born of a virgin and never sinned. He healed the sick, cast out demons, raised the dead, and taught about the Straight Way. One day the prophet John saw Isa walk by and cried out in a loud voice, 'Behold the lamb of God who takes away the sins of the world.' Do you know what he meant?"

Again, both women shook their heads.

"Do you remember when I said all prophets offered sacrifices? That's true, except for one. Isa Al Masih *never* offered a sacrifice. Do you know why?"

"No."

"Because *He* was the sacrifice! He died on a wooden cross. Because He never sinned His blood was holy; therefore, His blood alone is capable of cleansing us from our sins. After His death, people placed His body in a tomb, but after three days He rose from the dead. He taught His followers for forty days, then God took Him to heaven.

Now, Isa forgives the sins of His followers because He shed His blood for the forgiveness of their sins.[96]

"What did you think of this story?"

"Well, it was interesting."

"I know more stories from the holy books. Would you like me to come back and tell you another story some time?"

"We have our own beliefs."

Amina placed tape on the cotton ball to hold it in place. "No problem. May I pray for Isa Al Masih to heal you before I leave?"

"That would be okay."

Placing her hand on Lily's shoulder, Amina prayed, "O God, most merciful and gracious, I ask You to heal Lily in a way that shows her how much You love her. Please heal her supernaturally, or through the wisdom You give doctors. Use the medicine she is taking to its maximum effect. In the name of Isa Al Masih. Amen."

Amina made a note on Lily's chart and went to the next bed.

---

[96] Many ministries use some variant of *Creation to Christ* (*C2C*) to discover persons of peace. Various written and video versions of *Creation to Christ* can be found with a quick internet search. Appendix C contains the outline for our adaptation of *C2C*.

Discuss and apply

1. How did you obey what you concluded God wanted you to do from the previous chapter?

2. Do you sometimes have bad dreams? Do you pray in Jesus' name before going to sleep?

3. Amina told a *Creation to Christ* story to test for spiritual interest. Practice in pairs telling this story in your own words.

4. This week follow Amina's example and ask a Muslim (or anyone) if they know anyone who has ever had a dream from God. What will you say to invite them to discuss a prophet story with you if they respond positively?

5. Although Lily wasn't interested in more gospel stories, Amina blessed her with prayer. How else can you think of to bless those who show no immediate interest in the gospel?

6. Review the Critical Elements of CPM listed in Appendix A. What examples of these principles do you observe in this chapter?

7. Share what you believe God wants you to do in the next 24–48 hours from what you learned in this chapter.

8. Pray together that God would give dreams to your people. Pray by name for those to whom you are ministering. Share with one another what you are thankful for, along with your struggles, then pray for one another.

21

Answering Muslim Objections
to the Death of Jesus[97]

Yusuf and Haji Ishmael explore the Qur'an's teaching about Jesus' death.

"Haji Ishmael, today's story is about Isa's death."

"Then it will be a very short story, because Isa didn't die. God would never allow such a great prophet to suffer such a humiliating death on a cross. God substituted the betrayer Judas for Isa at the crucifixion, and God took Isa directly to heaven."

"I expected you to say that, so I did some research and found some very interesting verses from the Qur'an. Could we take a look at them together before we begin our story from the Injil?"

Over their weeks of studying together, Yusuf and Haji Ishmael had developed a good rapport. They both found it quite comfortable now to read and discuss verses from the Qur'an and Injil.

"Haji Ishmael, please read An Nisa 155."

Haji Ishmael read the Arabic and the translation, then explained the meaning.

---

[97] This chapter condenses to a single discussion what might in real life take several conversations.

فِيمَا نَقْضِهِم مِّيثَـٰقَهُمْ وَكُفْرِهِم بِـَٔايَـٰتِ ٱللَّهِ وَقَتْلِهِمُ ٱلْأَنۢبِيَآءَ بِغَيْرِ حَقٍّ وَقَوْلِهِمْ قُلُوبُنَا غُلْفٌۢ بَلْ طَبَعَ ٱللَّهُ عَلَيْهَا بِكُفْرِهِمْ فَلَا يُؤْمِنُونَ إِلَّا قَلِيلًا ﴿١٥٥﴾

Qur'an 4:155 And [We cursed them] for their breaking of the covenant and their disbelief in the signs of Allah and their killing of the prophets without right and their saying, "Our hearts are wrapped." Rather, Allah has sealed them because of their disbelief, so they believe not, except for a few.

"God cursed them for killing the prophets."

"Who killed the prophets?"

"The Jews."

"So you are saying that, according to this verse, the Jews killed Jewish prophets."

"Yes."

"Isa was a Jewish prophet. Did the Jews kill Isa?"

"No."

"But the Jews killed other prophets."

"Yes."

"So, it is possible for prophets to be killed."

"Yes." Haji Ishmael spoke with all the authority of an Islamic scholar. He had, after all, studied at the world's most preeminent Islamic University, Al-Azhar University in Cairo, Egypt.

"Haji Ishmael, please read Maryam 33."

وَٱلسَّلَـٰمُ عَلَىَّ يَوْمَ وُلِدتُّ وَيَوْمَ أَمُوتُ وَيَوْمَ أُبْعَثُ حَيًّا ﴿٣٣﴾

Qur'an 19:33 "And peace is on me the day I was born and the day I will die and the day I am raised alive."

"This verse says three things would happen to Isa: He would be born, He would die, and He would be raised up."

"All Muslims know that Isa was born and He was raised to heaven by God. So the first and third events are past events; that is, they have already happened. Muslims also believe Isa's death is still a future event, right?"

Haji Ishmael nodded.

"But don't we usually speak in the order events occur? If Isa hasn't yet died, shouldn't the word order be different: was born (past event), was raised (past event), and will die (future event)?" [98]

Haji Ishmael looked up from the Qur'an in front of him and stared out the window, evaluating what Yusuf had just said. Finally Haji Ishmael said, "God chose this word order: was born, died, and was raised. I must study this further."

"Haji Ishmael, please read Ali Imran 55."

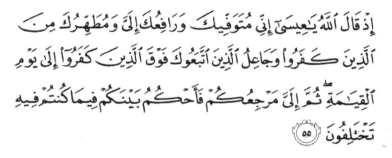

Qur'an 3:55 Thus, Allah said "O Isa, I am terminating your life, raising you to Me and ridding you of the disbelievers. I will exalt those who follow you above those who disbelieve, till the Day of Resurrection. Then to Me is the ultimate destiny of all of you, then I will judge among you regarding your disputes." [99]

"God terminated Isa's life and raised him to Himself."

"You said 'God terminated Isa's life.' Is that really what the Arabic says?"

"Yes, the Arabic is *mutawaffika*, a variant of *tawaffa*, which always means 'to die.'"

"So you are saying Isa did die?"

"Not so quickly, young man!" Haji Ishmael spoke as an Islamic

---

[98] To say Jesus was born, will die, and was raised is like saying, "I ate breakfast, I will eat lunch, and I ate dinner." This violates the common practice of speaking in the order events occur.

[99] *Qur'an: The Final Testament*, translated by Rashad Khalifa (Tucson, AZ; Universal Unity, 2001).

scholar teaching a pupil, but not harsh or demeaning. "You are forgetting about An Anisa 157. This verse proves Isa did not die."

وَقَوْلِهِمْ إِنَّا قَتَلْنَا الْمَسِيحَ عِيسَى ابْنَ مَرْيَمَ رَسُولَ اللَّهِ وَمَا قَتَلُوهُ وَمَا صَلَبُوهُ وَلَكِن شُبِّهَ لَهُمْ وَإِنَّ الَّذِينَ اخْتَلَفُوا فِيهِ لَفِي شَكٍّ مِنْهُ مَا لَهُم بِهِ مِنْ عِلْمٍ إِلَّا اتِّبَاعَ الظَّنِّ وَمَا قَتَلُوهُ يَقِينًا ﴿١٥٧﴾

Qur'an 4:157 And [for] their saying, "Indeed, we have killed the Messiah, Jesus, the son of Mary, the messenger of Allah." They did not kill him, nor did they crucify him; but [another] was made to resemble him to them. And indeed, those who differ over it are in doubt about it. They have no knowledge of it except the following of assumption. And they did not kill him, for certain.

"This says, 'They did not kill or crucify Isa. They killed a man who was made to look like Isa, probably Judas who betrayed Isa.'"

"I'm glad you brought up this verse. I've done some research about it. From history we know Muhammad (pbuh) lived 600 years after Isa. In the time of Muhammad (pbuh), some people apparently claimed the Jews killed Isa. Since 600 years had passed no one could prove the Jews were wrong. But God who knows the truth said, 'No, they did not kill him or crucify him' because God knew the *Romans* killed him. Furthermore, this verse says there was disagreement among the Jews over who died. Some said Isa, and others said another man."

Yusuf leaned back against the wall and took a deep breath. "You have studied at Al-Azhar University, so you know Islamic scholars don't agree on how to interpret this verse."

Haji Ishmael nodded.

"The interpretation that the Romans killed Isa, and not the Jews, is consistent with Qur'an 3:55, 3:181, 4:155, 5:117, and 19:33. This interpretation is also consistent with many verses from the Injil. As we have discussed before, we can trust the Injil because no one can alter the words of God. In addition, this interpretation is consistent with a vast amount of historical evidence."

Haji Ishmael opened his mouth to object but realized he had nothing to say. He was accustomed to teaching, so the experience of being taught by a simple lay person made him uncomfortable. Yet over their months of meeting together Haji Ishmael had come to respect and trust Yusuf. In addition, Haji Ishmael had an independent mind, and refused to simply accept what he had been taught without considering the evidence for himself.

"I'd like to discuss another passage, As Saffat 102–107."

فَلَمَّا بَلَغَ مَعَهُ ٱلسَّعْىَ قَالَ يَٰبُنَىَّ إِنِّىٓ أَرَىٰ فِى ٱلْمَنَامِ أَنِّىٓ أَذْبَحُكَ فَٱنظُرْ مَاذَا تَرَىٰ ۚ قَالَ يَٰٓأَبَتِ ٱفْعَلْ مَا تُؤْمَرُ ۖ سَتَجِدُنِىٓ إِن شَآءَ ٱللَّهُ مِنَ ٱلصَّٰبِرِينَ ﴿١٠٢﴾

فَلَمَّآ أَسْلَمَا وَتَلَّهُۥ لِلْجَبِينِ ﴿١٠٣﴾

وَنَٰدَيْنَٰهُ أَن يَٰٓإِبْرَٰهِيمُ ﴿١٠٤﴾

قَدْ صَدَّقْتَ ٱلرُّءْيَآ ۚ إِنَّا كَذَٰلِكَ نَجْزِى ٱلْمُحْسِنِينَ ﴿١٠٥﴾

إِنَّ هَٰذَا لَهُوَ ٱلْبَلَٰٓؤُا۟ ٱلْمُبِينُ ﴿١٠٦﴾

وَفَدَيْنَٰهُ بِذِبْحٍ عَظِيمٍ ﴿١٠٧﴾

Qur'an 37:102–107 And when he reached with him [the age of] exertion, he said, "O my son, indeed I have seen in a dream that I [must] sacrifice you, so see what you think." He said, "O my father, do as you are commanded. You will find me, if Allah wills, of the steadfast." And when they had both submitted and he put him down upon his forehead, We called to him, "O Abraham, You have fulfilled the vision." Indeed, We thus reward the doers of good. Indeed, this was the clear trial. And We ransomed him with a great sacrifice.

"Abraham was told in a dream to sacrifice his son. When he and his son submitted, God Himself ransomed Abraham's son with a great sacrifice."

"I'm sure you remember that in the sacrifice study we observed that all the prophets offered animal sacrifices because without the shedding of blood there is no forgiveness of sins. In the verse we just read, Abraham was commanded to make a blood sacrifice, in this case, his own son. However, the last verse, As Saffat 107, says God ransomed Abraham's son. In other words, God provided an animal for Abraham to sacrifice so he didn't have to kill his son. Just as God provided the sacrifice for Abraham, God has also provided the sacrifice for mankind.

"In one of our stories about Isa, we learned that the Prophet John called Isa 'The Lamb of God which takes away the sins of the world.' [100]   We also observed that all the prophets offered animal sacrifices except one: Isa. Nowhere in the Injil or the Qur'an does it say Isa offered an animal sacrifice. Why?"

Yusuf leaned forward and looked at Haji Ishmael, his eyes ablaze with intensity. "Because *Isa* was the sacrifice!

"Those who know history will see this parallel: The mountain on which Abraham was told to offer his son as a sacrifice is located in modern day Jerusalem. The mountain on which Isa offered Himself as a sacrifice is also located in modern day Jerusalem. Do you think it is a coincidence that God provided a sacrifice for Abraham and He provided a sacrifice for mankind in the same part of the world?

"All the prophets made animal sacrifices, but we commemorate only one sacrifice each year, the sacrifice of Id Al-Adha. Why, with all the sacrifices the prophets made, do we commemorate only one sacrifice? Because God wants us to see that He provided a sacrifice for all mankind, just as He provided the sacrifice for Abraham.

"Historical evidence, the Injil, the Qur'an, and the example of Abraham provide four strands of evidence which lead to one conclusion: Isa Al Masih died." [101]

Haji Ishmael had no response. It was clear that Yusuf had done his homework and presented a compelling case. What Haji Ishmael had

---

[100] John 1:29

[101] Appendix J provides a detailed explanation of how the Qur'an affirms that Jesus died on a cross.

believed and taught for years had been challenged with logic and evidence he couldn't refute.

"Let's study the story together, and then you can make up your own mind." Yusuf handed Haji Ishmael the story of Isa's death.

Discuss and apply

1. How did you obey what you concluded God wanted you to do from the previous chapter?

2. Outline the main points of what Yusuf said to Haji Ishmael to convince him Jesus really did die. What else would you add to convince a Muslim that Jesus died?

3. Read John 8:32, 16:13, and 1 Cor. 2:14. Despite our most persuasive arguments, the natural man can't understand spiritual truth without the Holy Spirit's enlightenment. Pray for those with whom you are seeking to share, asking especially that the Holy Spirit would make them understand that their good works will never fulfill the righteous standard of a holy God, and that they need a Savior.

4. Review the Critical Elements of CPM listed in Appendix A. What examples of these principles do you observe in this chapter?

5. Share what you believe God wants you to do in the next 24–48 hours from what you learned in this chapter.

6. Pray together for Muslims to accept that Jesus died for them.

22

Beginning the Harvest

Faisal Leads Ahmad in committing himself to follow Jesus

Faisal stood as Ahmad entered their regular coffee shop. His mind drifted to their first meeting, when he had shared his personal salvation story and invited Ahmad to discuss chronological stories from the Taurat and Injil with him. He remembered the first four meetings when he had facilitated stories with Ahmad and his family, and how beginning with the fifth story he had equipped Ahmad weekly to facilitate the stories with his family. Now they had discussed ten prophet stories and thirteen Isa stories.

"Assalam wa'alikum."

"Wa alikum salam."

Faisal and Ahmad shook hands and ordered their coffees. "We should get a discount for all the coffee we have ordered here." Faisal laughed as he blew on his coffee to cool it down.

They chatted a bit, then discussed how Ahmad's family had applied the previous week's discussion.

"Are you ready to discuss the next Isa story?"

"Of course."

Ahmad took the paper and read twice from John 9. "Now tell me the story in your own words," Faisal said.

Ahmad sat back in his chair and crossed his legs. "Isa's disciples saw a blind man and asked who sinned that this man was born blind. Isa said the blindness wasn't because of sin, but for God's work to be displayed. Then Isa spat on the ground and formed mud, applied it to the blind man's eyes, and told him to go and wash in a pool of water. When the blind man returned he could see! This miracle was reported to the religious leaders, who summoned the man born blind. They interrogated him to find out how he had been healed. The man carefully described what Isa had done for him, but the religious leaders doubted he had been born blind, so they called his parents.

"They asked, 'Was your son born blind?' 'Yes,' the parents replied. 'Then how does he now see?' The parents were afraid to answer that Isa healed him, so they said, 'Ask him. He is an adult.'

"The religious leaders again called the man born blind and asked him to make clear how he was healed. The man explained again how Isa healed him, and then asked, 'Do you want to become His disciple too?' The religious leaders scoffed and said they would never become Isa's disciples. Then they insulted him and drove him from their presence."

"Good job! I want you to observe the three responses to Isa.

"The religious leaders couldn't deny that a miracle had taken place, but they refused to believe in Isa.

"The parents knew a miracle had taken place. Maybe they secretly believed in Isa, but they wouldn't express their faith openly for fear of the religious leaders.

"The man who had been born blind experienced the miracle, and boldly proclaimed his faith in Isa.

"These three groups represent three possible responses to Isa: to deny Him like the religious leaders, to believe secretly but not confess Him like the parents, or to believe and confess Isa publicly like the man born blind."

Faisal paused to let Ahmad consider these responses. Cigarette smoke drifted past from a nearby table.

Then Faisal leaned forward, looking directly into Ahmad's eyes. With great intensity he asked, "Ahmad, which person do you want to be like?"

Ahmad shooed a fly from his coffee and took a slow drink, savoring the bitter sweetness before swallowing.

"When we discussed the sacrifice story, we observed that all the prophets offered blood sacrifices because there is no forgiveness of sins without the shedding of blood.

"Then we studied the life of Isa. I learned He was born of a virgin, healed the sick, raised the dead, cast out demons, and taught the way of God. John the Baptist said Isa is the Lamb of God who takes away the sins of mankind. As the Lamb, Isa shed His blood on the cross. He was buried and raised to life again after three days.

"This is very difficult for me because I don't want to bring shame on my parents and my family. Yet if all these things are true about Isa, and I believe they are, then there is only one honorable choice. I must follow the Truth. I want to be like the man born blind!" Ahmad said confidently.

Faisal grinned. "I was hoping you would say that.

"Now, I have a few questions for you:

- Do you believe Isa Al Masih is the eternal Word of God?
- Do you believe Isa is the Son of the living God, with the fullness of deity dwelling in Isa as described in the Injil?
- Do you believe Isa Al Masih lived a sinless life, that is, he never committed a single sin?
- Do you believe Isa Al Masih died on a cross, was buried, rose again on the third day, and ascended into heaven?
- Do you believe Isa Al Masih shed His blood for you on a wooden cross so you could be cleansed from your sins?
- Are you prepared to confess your sins to Isa and ask for His forgiveness?
- Are you ready to follow Isa as your Savior and obey Him as your Lord and Master?"

As Faisal asked each question, Ahmad affirmed his faith in Isa and his determination to follow Him.

"If you are ready to trust in and proclaim Isa Al Masih like the man born blind, you can pray a prayer like this:

God, most gracious and most merciful, I confess I am a sinner and I deserve punishment for my sins.

I believe all that is written in the Taurat, Zabur, and Injil.

I believe that without the shedding of blood there is no forgiveness of sins.

I believe Isa Al Masih came from heaven, lived on earth without committing a single sin, was the perfect Lamb of God, and shed His blood on a wooden cross. I believe He was buried, was resurrected to life again, and was taken to heaven.

With my mouth I confess Isa Al Masih as my Lord, and with my heart I believe God raised Him from the dead.

I ask You, O God, to forgive my sins, not because of any good deeds I have done, but solely based on the shed blood of Isa on the Cross.

O God, most kind and benevolent, forgive my sins, cleanse me from all unrighteousness, and make me Your child.

By faith, I surrender my entire being to You, Isa Al Masih, as my Savior and Lord. I want to live from now on to bring glory and honor to Your name. In Isa's name. Amen.

Ahmad said, "I am ready to give my life to Isa, but do I have to use this exact prayer?"

"Of course not. This prayer is only an example. All true prayer comes from the heart. Let's pay our bill and go to a secluded spot to pray."

After Ahmad finished praying the two men spontaneously embraced, overcome by the significance of what had just taken place.

"This is so exciting! Welcome to the family of Isa Al Masih! Not only are we close friends, now we are spiritual brothers."

"Ahmad, can you do with your family what I just did with you?"

"I can."

"I know you have also been meeting with Dr. Hasan. Can you lead him through this story, as I led you just now?"

"I'll try. Please pray for me."

Discuss and apply

1. How did you obey what you concluded God wanted you to do from the previous chapter?

2. Role play with a partner the fourteenth Jesus story (about the three responses to Jesus illustrated in this story), and invite this partner to follow Jesus like Faisal did with Ahmad. Then switch roles.

3. In your ministry what keeps people from deciding to follow Jesus? What can you say to invite them to make this decision?

4. What questions do you consider important for a new believer to understand and be prepared to answer?

5. Once someone follows Christ, what are the next things you would encourage them to do?

6. Share what you believe God wants you to do in the next 24–48 hours from what you learned in this chapter.

7. Pray together for those you know, asking God to guide each member of your team in offering to discuss chronological Bible stories with others and their oikos.

23

Gathering the Harvest

Many boldly follow Jesus Christ for a wide variety of reasons

Ahmad knocked on Dr. Hasan's door.

The previous day Ahmad had shared the story about Isa and the blind man with his own family. Together they had all asked Isa to forgive their sins and reign over their lives.

Now, Ahmad was ready to train Hasan to do the same thing.

Hasan opened the door and greeted Ahmad warmly. Hasan was still just as overweight, and perspired just as profusely, as the day they first met cleaning up the yard at the neighborhood mosque.

Hasan sat down in his usual seat, a large padded chair with big armrests. Ahmad took his usual seat, also a large, comfortable chair. Between them was a low table with elegantly carved legs. The room was furnished with expensive curtains and wall hangings. Above the door that led to the rest of the house was a plaque displaying verses from the Qur'an.

They talked about the heavy rains and the frequent power outages until Hasan's maid brought them cold soft drinks. Then Ahmad turned to the topic of the day. "We've discussed ten prophet stories and thirteen Isa stories. Today, I brought with me the next Isa story. Would you mind reading it?"

When they finished their discussion, Ahmad reviewed the responses of the religious leaders, parents, and the man born blind.

"In this story we see three responses to Isa.

"Hasan, which person do you want to be like?"

Hasan glanced at his expensive watch, then stood and walked to the front window. He looked outside at his new car, the two motorcycles parked next to it, the beautifully manicured yard, and the high fence that protected all his treasures.

Turning to face Ahmad, Hasan pointed around his house. "I grew up poor, but I was fortunate to be able to attend medical school. There I determined to become as wealthy and comfortable as I could.

"I worked hard, and have reached that goal. Now I own a car, motorcycles, cell phones, TVs, computers, the latest video games, jewelry, a big house, and the best of everything."

"When I was in medical school I thought owning many nice things and living well would make me happy. So I became very materialistic, always wanting more. But when I got those things I realized how empty my heart was. I knew there had to be something more to life.

"We discussed the prophets and Isa, and now I see my priorities were all wrong. Isa was poor, yet He was always joyful. Isa has taught us how to live full and meaningful lives.

"Before we started discussing these stories, my family never talked with one another. Each of us was either watching TV, checking Facebook, or texting a friend. We may have been in the same room, but we weren't relating to each other. We might as well have been strangers living under the same roof. Plus, my kids were being influenced by friends to do things they shouldn't be doing.

"Ahmad, discussing these stories as a family has helped us see what is truly important, and how to have meaning and purpose in life. Now we talk to one another on a deeper level. The teachings of Isa have changed my life and the lives of my wife and kids. I want to be like the man born blind!"

"That's wonderful, Hasan! Can you share with your family as I have just shared with you?"

* * *

"Assalam wa'alikum," Yusuf said as he entered Haji Ishmael's yard.

"Wa alikum salam."

Haji Ishmael soon appeared and invited Yusuf in.

They took their usual seats, with Haji Ishmael beneath the large picture of pilgrims crowded around the Kaaba.

"Are you ready to discuss the next Isa story?"

When they concluded their discussion, Yusuf said, "In this story we see three responses to Isa: the religious leaders, the parents, and the man born blind. Haji Ishmael, who do you want to be like?"

Haji Ishmael was an intelligent man, and a critical thinker. He was not willing to accept what others had taught him. He wanted to study for himself and make up his own mind.

"When you first came to my house and offered to share stories from the Taurat, Zabur, and Injil I told you they had been corrupted. But you showed me from the Qur'an that I was mistaken. God protects His Word from change.

"From the Qur'an, I already knew Isa was different from every other prophet. He was born of a virgin, did more miracles than any other prophet, and is called 'distinguished in this life and the next,' but I learned more about Him from the Injil.

"After that you told me Isa died on a cross. I said you were wrong, but you showed me from the Qur'an that Isa did die.

"We pray seventeen times a day, 'God, show us the Straight Way.' [102] You showed me from the Qur'an and the Injil that God has already raised Isa up to heaven. Isa knows the way to heaven, so Isa is the answer to our prayers.

"We are so afraid of death because we have no assurance that God will accept our good deeds. Now I know my most righteous deeds are like filthy rags in light of God's infinite holiness.[103] I realize God accepts me as his child when I am cleansed by Isa's blood, and Isa will take me to heaven when I die.

---

[102] Qur'an 1:6

[103] Isa. 64:6

"I have always had an emptiness in my heart, even though I have fasted and prayed all my life. I have obeyed every command I have ever known. I have taught the Qur'an and helped others in every way I could. I have longed to know that God accepts me, loves me, and cares for me.

"Yet this desire in my heart to know my Creator was never satisfied. I knew there must be something more. Now I know I need Isa in my heart.

"I want to be like the man born blind," Haji Ishmael concluded.

"Great!" Yusuf said. "I'll pray for you as you share with Sharif."

* * *

Sharif arrived at Haji Ishmael's home for their weekly meeting.

"Assalam wa'alikum."

"Wa alikum salam."

Haji Ishmael invited Sharif into his home. "Do you remember the first time you came to talk to me?"

"I'll never forget. I was so desperate. I am a headmaster, and I have dedicated my life to changing my world by changing my students. I thought, 'students are the future, if I can influence them, they will improve their world.' But no matter how hard I tried, no one seemed to change. Even religious people, including those who had gone on the Hajj pilgrimage, were all hypocrites."

Sharif suddenly felt embarrassed. "Except you, Haji Ishmael."

Haji Ishmael smiled. "Do you remember what I told you?"

"I'll never forget. You said change comes from the inside."

"Good. What do you remember from the stories about Isa?"

"He is called the Light of the world, the Good Shepherd, the Bread of Life, the Teacher, and the Savior of the world. He came to give people hope and peace, and to relieve their burdens." [104]

"Excellent insights! Are you ready for the next Isa story?"

As they concluded their discussion, Haji Ishmael spoke with his scholarly voice. "In this story we see three responses to Isa: the

---

[104] Jesus stories 8 and 9, listed in Appendix C.

religious leaders, the parents, and the man born blind. Sharif, which one do you want to be like?"

"When you told me that change comes from the heart, I knew that was true because I had tried my best to change on my own. Now we are letting God change our hearts. My family and I read these stories and apply them to our lives. Little by little we are changing with His help.

"I want to give my life to Isa," Sharif said, "and I want Him to come and change me and my family from the inside out. I want Him to rule over every thought, emotion, decision, and action. I want to be like the man born blind."

* * *

Aysha beamed as she stepped through the doorway. Nur thought back to the first time they met. *She was crying because her husband had just insulted her. Then we began discussing chronological stories in the Taurat and Injil, and Aysha shared these with her husband.*

"Are you ready to discuss the next Isa story?"

After their discussion, Nur said, "We see three responses to Isa in this story: we can be like the religious leaders and refuse to believe in Him, we can be like the parents and secretly believe but tell no one, or we can be like the man born blind and tell others.

"Aysha, who do you want to be?"

"I never wanted to be rich, to have nice clothes, or to own a big house. I only wanted a husband who loved me and my kids. I only wanted a home filled with joy, peace, and laughter.

"Before I met you I thought those things were only in movies. I thought they didn't exist in real life. But then we began to learn about the prophets and about Isa, and to apply the truth we were learning. Slowly, almost imperceptibly, joy and peace crept into our home.

"We're not perfect by any means, but I have seen the transforming power of God's Word. How could I deny Isa after He has done so much for my family and me?

"Nur, I want to be like the man born blind!" Aysha said.

* * *

"Hi Wati. I just met with my spiritual mentor, Nur. You're going to really like this next story about Isa!"

Wati eyed Aysha expectantly. "I've liked every other story, I'm sure I'll like this one too!"

When they finished Aysha said, "This story shows three ways we can respond to Isa: like the religious leaders, the parents, or the man born blind.

"Wati, who do you want to be like?"

"With each Isa story, I have felt more and more drawn to Isa. He is strong yet tender, brave yet compassionate, wise yet humble. He is both highly exalted and approachable. His teaching cuts to my heart but is never cruel or crushing. He rebuked the hypocrites, and forgave the penitent. He came to complete a task, yet people were His priority.

"I was on my deathbed when you and Nur came to pray for me. No doctor or shaman could heal me. I had completely given up hope, but then I experienced Isa's power.

"He restored me to health, and I have experienced His power in other ways as well. I know He has power over death, disease, evil spirits, and nature. I believe Isa is the Son of the living God. He is my Lord and Savior.

"I want to be like the man born blind."

"I am so pleased! Will you share this story with your family as I have shared it with you?" Aysha asked.

"I definitely will!" Wati said.

Discuss and apply

1. How did you obey what you concluded God wanted you to do from the previous chapter?

2. In this chapter, five people place their faith in Jesus. Discuss the different motivations of Hasan (the doctor), Haji Ishmael (the imam), Sharif (the headmaster), Aysha (who wanted a happy family), and Wati (who was bedridden).

3. Share your own initial motivations for following Jesus.

4. In these examples, each person is challenged to follow Jesus. What is the danger when people learn about Jesus but don't commit their lives to Him? In your ministry, do you hesitate to invite people to surrender their lives to Jesus? What in this chapter encourages you to be more direct?

5. Describe what Jesus has done for you. How does this make you want to love and obey Him even more?

6. Share what you believe God wants you to do in the next 24–48 hours from what you learned in this chapter.

7. Pray together for God to give each member of your team boldness in inviting others to follow Jesus.

24

Resolving Fear, Shame, and Guilt

Inne and Eka discover the gospel meets all of their deepest needs

"Today we will discuss the next Isa story, and I have a gift for you." As they sat at the kitchen table, Fatima handed a package to Inne.

Inne slowly unwrapped and stared at a beautiful picture of a massive waterfall pouring into a pool below, sending spray in all directions. Waves rippled toward the banks of the pool. Rugged mountains jutted up in the background, and lightning streaked across the dark, ominous sky.

Inne was puzzled. "What does this picture mean?"

"Do you remember when you shared with me that you can't get pregnant and you are afraid your husband might take a second wife?"

Inne nodded.

"I shared with you that Isa calmed a storm which was threatening to swamp the boat He and His disciples were in. I explained that Isa can calm the storms of your life, and free you from fear."

"I understand that, and Isa has calmed many storms in my life. But what does that story have to do with this picture?"

"Look closely behind that waterfall. Do you see the baby bird in the nest? It doesn't matter that there is a storm raging all around. That baby bird is at perfect peace. It reminds me that, because Isa is here, we too can have peace and freedom from fear even in the midst of our storms. Sometimes Isa calms our storms; at other times He gives us the strength to endure them."

Inne took a close look at the picture. Sure enough there was a tiny bird at perfect peace surrounded by a violent storm. "Thank you. I will hang this picture next to my bed so I will see it the first thing when I wake up."

"Shall we start the story?"

When they concluded, Fatima said, "We see from this story three responses to Isa.

"Inne, do you want to be like the religious leaders, the parents, or the man born blind?"

"I still haven't been able to get pregnant, but my husband isn't talking about taking another wife right now. Of course, who knows the future?

"Isa has helped me so much. I never would have believed I could have such peace and freedom from fear in the midst of this storm. Besides, He died for me, and then He rose again. With power over storms and power over death, I know I can trust Him with whatever happens.

"Fatima, I want to be like the man born blind," Inne said.

* * *

Eka knocked on Inne's door to pick up the food she and her roommates had ordered.

In their first meeting Eka had revealed she was from a broken home, and grew up desperately poor. She had believed her only way out of poverty was to rely on herself, and get a college education. At that time she was failing a class, and was afraid she might have to drop out of school because she didn't have money to pay her professor for tutoring.

Inne had shared how Isa had freed her from fear, and calmed the storm she was in because she couldn't get pregnant.

Inne had also come up with an idea that had helped both her and Eka. As a caterer, Inne prepared meals which she delivered each day. So Inne had offered to pay Eka a commission for each new customer Eka brought her.

During the time she and Eka had been studying stories in the Taurat and Injil, Inne's business had tripled. As a result Inne had extra money, and Eka had enough money for her tutoring. *God is providing for both of us, but does Eka realize this?*

"Are you ready to discuss the next Isa story?"

When they concluded their study, Inne said, "As you can see from this story, Isa performed a great miracle. The religious leaders, the parents, and the man born blind each responded differently to this miracle. Eka, who do you want to be like?"

"My parents, my extended family, my teachers, and my community have all let me down.

"I came here to go to college, determined to trust no one. I believed I had to rely on myself. I knew if I depended on others they would eventually let me down.

"These stories have shown me there is One whom I can trust. He keeps His Word, and He is always faithful. We have read that Isa is a friend of sinners, and He intercedes for us to God. Also God's Word says that Isa can make us clean before God, and that He shares His honor with us.

"I don't know how all this works, but I feel you are an answer to my prayers. God used you to meet a very real need I had. He taught me I don't have to rely on myself. I can rely on Him. "

Eka paused and took a deep breath, "But I can't become Isa's follower," she uttered dejectedly.

Inne sat back in her chair stunned. "What do you mean you can't become His follower?"

"You don't know what happened to me. I am defiled and covered with shame. I am unworthy to be His follower."

Inne shifted her position on the chair. "Let me tell you a story about God's love and grace. All glory and honor come from God. In the beginning, He created a magnificent and beautiful garden to reflect His glory and honor. This garden, which He named Eden, was perfect in every way, with no disease or death. In creating Adam and Eve, God crowned them with glory and honor, and gave them responsibility to cultivate this garden. Adam and Eve even enjoyed sweet fellowship and communication with God. He was their Father, and they were His children. They were naked but not ashamed because sin had not yet entered their world.

"Satan entered the body of a serpent and deceived Eve into eating fruit from Kholdi, the tree of the knowledge of good and evil, from which God had forbidden them to eat. She gave some of the fruit to Adam, who also ate. Immediately their eyes were opened, and they realized they were naked. They sewed fig leaves together to cover their private parts.

"Just then, God called out to them, but Adam and Eve hid themselves because of fear and shame before a holy God. In punishment, God drove them out of the garden; in mercy, He clothed them with animal skins."

"Let's think for a moment about what happened." Inne glanced at Eka to see if she was following the conversation.

"Because of one sin, Adam and Eve were defiled and alienated from God. They were chased out of the garden. The honor and privilege of walking with God and speaking with Him face to face was gone forever. What could be more shameful?

"All people throughout history have been defiled because of their sin. Then God sent Isa Al Masih who was born of a virgin. He healed the sick, cast out demons, raised the dead, and taught the Straight Way of God. He lived His entire life without committing even one sin, which brought great honor and glory to God. Yet Isa's enemies arrested Him, stripped Him naked, beat Him mercilessly, and then killed Him by nailing Him to a cross. What could be more humiliating and shameful than to be ridiculed by your enemies, rejected by your friends, and then die naked on a cross?"

Eka shuddered at the thought, and nodded in agreement.

"You may be thinking, 'Isa was a mighty prophet of God. Why did God allow Him to die in such a humiliating and shameful way?' If that were the end of the story, we would call it an awful tragedy, but the story doesn't end there. Isa's body was taken down from the cross and laid in a tomb. Three days later, He rose again to life. The shame of Isa' death was covered by the glory of His resurrection!"

Eka looked puzzled. "What does this have to do with me?"

"How does one get rid of defilement?" Inne asked.

"I don't know."

"Do you clean a dirty plate with a clean or dirty towel?"

"A clean one, of course." Eka chuckled at the thought of trying to clean a dirty plate with a dirty towel.

"That is exactly what Isa did. Sin causes defilement, and since all people are sinful, all people are defiled. Isa is the undefiled One who took our defilement upon Himself to cleanse us and make us worthy before God. Do you understand?"

"No, not really."

"Isa never committed a sin, so He is the undefiled One. Like a clean towel takes on the filth of the plate, Isa took our defilement when He died on the cross. When He rose from the grave, He left the defilement in the tomb. God willed it this way. Because Isa was completely loyal and obedient even unto death, God has crowned Him with glory and honor. The Injil says 'Isa endured the cross, despised the shame, and is now seated at the right hand of the throne of God.' [105] At the cross Isa embraced our shame; in the resurrection, He broke its power. God's glory was magnified, and His honor was vindicated!"

"Despite all our best efforts and all our rituals, we cannot drive defilement from ourselves any more than darkness can make itself light. Only light can drive out darkness. That is why Isa is called 'the light of the world.'

"Remember when I said Adam and Eve were expelled from God's family?"

Eka nodded.

"What happens when a child does something shameful and is alienated from his parents? It often takes a mediator to reconcile the child to the parents. In the same way, Isa is the mediator who reconciles us to God.[106]

---

[105] Heb. 12:2, also John 1:4,14, Rom. 10:11, Heb. 2:7, 4:16, 7:26–27, 9:13–14, 13:13

[106] 1 Tim. 2:3–6

"Isa is also the perfect sacrifice. Remember we learned that all the prophets offered sacrifices except for one: Isa never offered a sacrifice because He became the sacrifice! God does not require good works, He requires the shedding of blood for the forgiveness of sins. Why blood? Because the life of every creature is in its blood. Only Isa never sinned, so only Isa's pure and holy blood could cleanse man from his sins.

"Not only did Isa cleanse us from defilement, when He rose from the dead He also defeated the greatest enemy, death. Isa overcame sin, shame, and death.

"God is saying, 'I want to make you clean forever. I want to heal our relationship. I want to share with you My honor.' Isa makes all this possible by offering to take our sin and shame upon Himself. He paid the penalty for our sin by His death. Then He rose, defeating death and shame to live forever with the highest honor and glory. When we repent, confess our sins to God, ask His forgiveness, and determine to follow Isa, several wonderful miracles happen. God cleanses us and makes us His children. He frees us from our shame and guilt. And He shares His limitless honor with us, along with His approval and acceptance."

Eka's face beamed. "I've always felt unclean and defiled. I never felt worthy of God's love and help. How could I reject such a wonderful gift? Inne, I want to be like the man born blind."

Discuss and apply

1. How did you obey what you concluded God wanted you to do from the previous chapter?

2. In this chapter, two more people place their faith in Jesus. Discuss the motivations of Inne (the caterer) and Eka (the college student).

3. What are the dominant concerns of those you are seeking to reach: guilt, fear, or shame/defilement? How will these people best understand the effect of Adam and Eve's sin?

4. What do the people you are seeking to reach fear most? How does the gospel address that?

5. Isa's death on a cross was very shameful (Heb 12:2). Why was this shame necessary? How did Jesus death honor God? How did God honor Jesus?

6. Why are human efforts to remove defilement ineffective? How does Jesus cleanse us from our defilement?

7. What did Jesus do to bring us back into God's family?

8. What does Jesus' death accomplish for you?

9. Share what you believe God wants you to do in the next 24–48 hours from what you learned in this chapter.

10. Pray once more for God to give each member of your team boldness in inviting others to follow Jesus.

25

Bringing Forgiveness to the Unforgivable

Abdullah and Umar learn no sin is too great for God to forgive

Finding places to meet hadn't been easy. Dressed like a hard-core radical, Abdullah was not the kind of person with whom one wanted to be seen. As a traveling honey salesman, Nasrudin knew many secluded places, so they had varied the times, days, and places where they met.

Arriving at the appointed place at the agreed upon time, Abdullah and Nasrudin greeted each other warmly. "Are you ready to discuss the next Isa story?"

After discussing the story, Nasrudin said, "This story teaches three ways to respond to Isa: deny Him like the religious leaders, believe in Him but fear to confess Him to others like the parents, or believe in Isa and confess Him like the man born blind.

"Abdullah, which person do you want to be like?"

"Do you remember the day you and Faisal came to my house and cast the demon out of my son, Ali?"

"How could I forget?" Nasrudin laughed. "I was terrified of you, yet I knew God wanted me to come to your house."

"I probably wouldn't have been open to Isa in any other way, but I saw His power with my own eyes. I had to know who Isa is."

Suddenly Abdullah shifted nervously in his seat and began bouncing his knee. He scratched the back of his neck, and looked blankly off into the distance. His expression intensified, and his eyes narrowed.

"Do you remember the day we sat in the grass hut, and you told me Isa forgave all my sins?"

"I remember it well. I also remember you said there was something in your past you needed to tell me."

"My parents wanted me to grow up to be a good Muslim, so they sent me to a Muslim boarding school. There I studied more diligently than all my classmates. When my teachers saw my devotion to God, they started giving me special instruction. I was taught it is the duty of every Muslim to fight for God to establish Sharia law. If an unbeliever wouldn't submit to God's will, we were obliged to kill him.

"When I finished high school I was sent to Afghanistan for further training. My friend, Saleh, went too. There we studied verses about jihad in the Qur'an. Our teachers taught us Muhammad (pbuh) was a great military leader. When he conquered a people, he gave them three choices: convert to Islam, pay a special protection tax, or be killed. I wanted to follow the example of the Prophet, and became convinced violent jihad was the only way to establish Sharia. I learned how to make bombs, too.

"I returned to Indonesia and trained with jihadist groups. We were armed with guns and machetes, and went to the Maluku islands to kill Christians there. We would approach a village in the middle of the night, charge into the village, and go house to house killing people.

"One time, Saleh found the baby of a Christian, but he couldn't bring himself to kill it. So I took the baby and put it in a bag and began beating it against the wall. The baby screamed and blood began to run out of the bag, but I kept hitting it against the wall. When the crying stopped I threw the bag onto a rubbish heap.

"We also raped girls, cut babies from pregnant women, crucified children, forced circumcision on both sexes, played soccer with severed heads, and took women captive and forced them to marry Muslim men.[107]

---

[107] Details based on events reported in interviews conducted by the author.

"In one village, all the Christians fled to a church building. We surrounded it and threw in Molotov cocktails. The building caught fire and burned to the ground, killing 170 Christians.

"We even kidnapped Christian children and sent them off to Islamic boarding schools to train them as jihadists like ourselves.[108]

"The day you came to my house, Saleh and I were teaching others how to make a bomb." Abdullah bowed his head, his face covered with deep remorse, guilt and shame. Quietly he said, "Isa could never forgive me for all I have done."

Nasrudin glanced up at the overcast sky as the light rain became a downpour. Nasrudin shivered in the brisk breeze. He felt nauseated by all the atrocities Abdullah had committed in the name of Islam. He had read about these brutal murders, and now he was sitting with a murderer who was asking for forgiveness. *A person like this deserves the worst form of torture, not mercy.* Waves of anger, shock, revulsion, disdain, and horror cascaded over Nasrudin as his mind raced with competing thoughts. *What do I say? Do I run? Do I call the police?*

Then he thought of his own life. *I haven't killed anyone, but I am still a sinner in need of forgiveness. I too have dishonored God by breaking his law.[109] Isa forgave me, didn't He? God's love and forgiveness know no bounds. No sin is too great to be forgiven. Isa died for everyone's sins. Even Paul participated in putting believers to death.*

As if on cue, the rain stopped and a ray of light pierced through the dark clouds.

"Isa forgave the woman caught in adultery, and Isa forgave those who crucified Him, so I'm sure Isa forgives even you. Would you like to pray right now and ask God to forgive and cleanse you forever?"

"Yes, I would."

---

108 This reflects actual events which took place in 1999–2000. en.wikipedia.org/wiki/Laskar_Jihad and ea.org.au/ea-family/religious-liberty/maluku--eastern-indonesia--anarchy--jihad---cleansing-

109 Rom 3:23

* * *

Abdullah waited for Umar to arrive.

They were an unlikely pair. One a former radical Muslim who disdained all things irreligious, the other a former alcoholic who despised all things religious; one the epitome of legalism, the other the embodiment of debauchery. Yet they were drawn together by their thirst for forgiveness, and then bonded together in their quest for new life.

Starting as polar opposites, they were each attracted to the person of Al Masih, hearing the words of Isa as being spoken directly to them: "Neither do I condemn you; go and sin no more." [110]

Together they basked in freedom from shame and guilt like men just released from prison, passionately seeking Isa and experiencing His transforming power to change them from the inside out.

After discussing the next Isa story, Abdullah said, "As you can see in this story, there are three responses to Isa, that of the religious leaders, the parents, or the man born blind.

"Umar, which person do you want to be like?"

"I was stone drunk the day you found me on that road. I didn't always drink, but then I went from one failure to another. I got drunk to forget my problems, but each time I awoke my problems were still with me. I used to rationalize 'Everyone has weaknesses. My weakness is alcohol; those who judge me, their weakness is being judgmental.'"

"I wanted to change but I was powerless to give up alcohol. I felt deep shame every time I took money and used it to drink, but I couldn't stop. I never did anything right. The fear of failure and being rejected always haunted me.

"Others ridiculed me. I was a big shame to my parents and friends. Worst of all, I let my wife and kids down. I felt like a worthless stray dog.

"What gave me hope was the story Isa told about the son who squandered his inheritance on wild parties until all his money was

---

[110] John 8:11

spent. Then he had nothing to eat except what was given to pigs. As Muslims, we can't eat pork, so to eat the food pigs eat is the lowest humiliation imaginable. Nevertheless, the son gathered his courage, returned home, and asked his father for a job. He said to him, 'I am no longer worthy to be your son, treat me as one of your hired servants.'"

"But what did this father do? He saw his son coming from a long distance and ran to meet him. He embraced his son, and prepared a feast for him.[111] The father covered his shame and restored his honor.

"If God is like that, and forgives us when we repent and turn to Him, if He gives us power to break bad habits and be transformed, if He heals families that seem beyond hope, if He removes our shame and gives us honor, and if He gives us purpose and direction in life, then I want to follow Isa.

"I want to be like the man born blind."

---

[111] Jesus story 8, listed in Appendix C.

Discuss and apply

1. How did you obey what you concluded God wanted you to do from the previous chapter?

2. Discuss the different motivations of Abdullah and Umar in placing their faith in Jesus.

3. Read 1 John 1:9. Abdullah confessed his sins to God and experienced His forgiveness. Take time now to confess your own sins to God, and receive His forgiveness.

4. How does knowing God has forgiven you increase your love for Him, and your desire to obey Him?

5. Read Matt. 18:21–35. According to this parable, God forgives our sins and expects us to forgive others. Whom have you not forgiven? Take time now and forgive that person.

6. Umar had a pattern of failure and believed he couldn't change. As a result he was filled with shame, and struggled with a low self-esteem. How did the gospel message help Umar?

7. What else would you say to a person like Umar?

8. Share what you believe God wants you to do in the next 24–48 hours from what you learned in this chapter.

9. Pray together for God to convict people of their sin so they will seek His forgiveness. Pray for opportunities for each of you to minister to people with low self-esteem, and to those already conscious that their sins have separated them from God.

26

Celebrating Baptism Together[112]

Ahmad and his family get baptized

Faisal met Ahmad at their usual coffee shop. "You shared about Isa and the blind man with your family last night. How did it go?"

"It went great. I did exactly what you taught me to do. When I asked them which person they wanted to be like—the religious leaders who knew a miracle had taken place but who were unwilling to confess Isa, the parents who knew a miracle had taken place and probably believed in Isa but were afraid to confess Isa, or the blind man who boldly confessed Isa—they all said 'the blind man who was no longer blind.'"

"And what did you do next?"

"We each prayed a prayer asking Isa to forgive our sins, and committing ourselves to obey Him as our King."

"I'm so proud of you. You led your family well." The two men smiled as they shook hands, Faisal choking back tears.

After regaining his composure, Faisal said, "Well, shall we get started? Isa taught, 'If you love Me, you will obey My commands.'"

---

112 In Muslim cultures baptism is often perceived as rejection of family and community, and those baptized may be killed or kicked out of their family. It is often advisable to delay baptism to win an oikos. However if, after some patient waiting, an oikos still refuses to believe, new believers should obey the command to be baptized despite the risk. Many in this situation report that baptism strengthens their faith.

One of His commands is to be baptized. We have two lessons[113] to prepare you and your family.[114] In this first lesson you will learn how to tell your own personal salvation story and we will study verses to prepare you for suffering." [115]

Faisal and Ahmad worked through the lesson. "Now I want you to teach this to your family, and do just what we have done."

* * *

In their second meeting, Faisal said, "Our next lesson explains the meaning of baptism. Let's study these verses."

When they concluded their discussion, Ahmad asked, "Every Friday we go to the mosque. After we are baptized, can we still go to the mosque?"

"Wow, Ahmad, that's a great question. The more important question is, 'Does *God* want you to continue going?' Let's take this next week to look through the Taurat and Injil for everything we can find regarding this question, then talk further next week.

Now, before I baptize you, I have asked my friends Nasrudin and Amina to interview you to make sure you understand the meaning of baptism[116] and what you are getting into. This is our standard practice for those who choose to follow Isa."

Before parting, Faisal and Ahmad scheduled a time for Ahmad and his family to meet with Nasrudin and Amina. They also discussed where and when to hold the baptism.

---

[113] Appendix D lists the related scriptures.

[114] Sometimes the group will separate into mens and womens groups for the baptism and Spiritual Foundations studies. These smaller groups allow more focused attention on the Spiritual Foundations and practicing the personal salvation story.

[115] The content of personal salvation stories is discussed in Chapter 2.

[116] In some Muslim contexts, a third-party interview may be counterproductive because of fears new believers may carry regarding persecution. However in our context, to protect against syncretism, a third party listens to the personal salvation story (requesting clarification as needed), invites the other person to explain their understanding of baptism, and asks the seven questions which will be used at the baptism.

* * *

The big day had arrived! Faisal and Fatima picked up Ahmad and his family in a borrowed car and drove to the beach, making sure not to park under a coconut tree. The sun was just coming up over the horizon, and a light breeze blew off the ocean. The place was secluded except for a few fishermen in the distance cleaning their nets after fishing all night. Yusuf and Nur were already there, along with Nasrudin and Amina.

The group stood in a circle near the water's edge. Excitement filled the air as Faisal opened to Matthew 28:18–20 and read:

> And Isa came and said to them, "All authority in heaven and on earth has been given to me. Go therefore and make disciples of all nations, baptizing them in the name of the Father and of the Son and of the Holy Spirit, teaching them to observe all that I have commanded you. And behold, I am with you always, to the end of the age."

"Baptism is one of the commands Isa gave His followers. Ahmad and his family have come to obey that command today. Ahmad, what did you discover when we studied together about baptism?"

"First, baptism is a public statement that I have made Isa my Savior and Lord. I show my love for Him by obeying His command to be baptized.

"Second, baptism is an outward symbol of the inner change in my life. When I placed my faith in Isa I became a new creation and a change occurred in my heart. Being immersed under the water symbolizes that I have been washed and changed on the inside. Baptism 'into God's name' also reminds me that the shame of my sin has been removed and I have received the honor of being adopted into God's family.

"Third, just as in the days of Abraham, where circumcision joined a person into the family of faith, so now baptism into the name of the Father, Son and Holy Spirit joins me to every other person who has obeyed God in this way. Together we become members of one worldwide family in Al Masih.

"Finally, baptism doesn't save us; faith does. Baptism is not a work to 'earn' salvation. It is a command to obey."

"Great!" Faisal said. "Now I want you to each share your personal salvation story, starting with Ahmad."

When each of them had finished, Faisal asked Ahmad and his family:

- Do you believe the Taurat, Zabur, and Injil are inspired by God and free from error?
- Do you believe Isa Al Masih is the eternal Word of God who became a human being?
- Do you believe Isa is the Messiah, and the Son of the living God as described in the Injil?
- Do you believe Isa Al Masih shed His blood on a cross to cleanse you of each of your sins, cover all your shame, and share His honor with you?
- Do you believe God raised Isa from the dead and took Him to heaven, and when you die Isa will take you to heaven?
- Have you confessed your sins and asked God to forgive you? Have you embraced Isa as the King who has rescued you from sin and shame? Will you be loyal to Him forever, even to death?
- Have you confessed and renounced all involvement with the occult, ancestor worship, and idolatry?"

They responded to each question with an exuberant "Yes!"

Then Faisal prayed, "Bismillahi arrahmani arrahim, O God most merciful and most gracious, our Father in heaven. We praise and exalt You for the way You have worked in Ahmad and his family's life.

"Thank You for calling them to be Your children, and for giving them the courage to obey You in baptism. Strengthen them so they will be faithful to You when persecution comes.

"May You always be glorified in their lives. In the name of Isa Al Masih, our divine master and king. Amen."

It was high tide, and the waves were small. A seagull landed and pecked at something on the beach. Faisal, Yusuf, Ahmad, and

Ahmad's family waded into the sea. The water was cold, and took their breath away.

Faisal stood in front of Ahmad. Yusuf stood behind Ahmad to steady him because he couldn't swim. Faisal placed his hand on Ahmad's head. "I baptize you into the name and honor of the Father, and the Son, and the Holy Spirit." Ahmad lowered himself under the water. Then he jumped up with a huge grin and gave Faisal a giant bear hug!

Ahmad then stood in front of Hajar, with his hand on her head, and declared, "I baptize you into the name and honor of the Father, and the Son, and the Holy Spirit." Hajar lowered herself under the water, with Faisal and Yusuf each holding an elbow to steady her. Ahmad then proceeded to baptize the rest of his household.

When they exited the water, the men moved to one clump of trees to change into dry clothes while the women went to another. Gathering again, Fatima, Nur and Amina spread out food on a woven grass mat. All eyes turned to Faisal to bless the food.

"Hey, am I the only one around here who can pray?" Faisal joked. "Let's ask Ahmad to pray!"

Discuss and apply

1. How did you obey what you concluded God wanted you to do from the previous chapter?

2. What is the meaning of baptism?

3. Why is it important for a new believer to be baptized?

4. Why do some delay baptism? What can you say to encourage them to get baptized?

5. How do you answer Ahmad's question about attending the mosque on Fridays? What passages in Scripture guide your decision?[117]

6. Was it right for Ahmad to baptize his family, or should Faisal have baptized all of them? What benefit is there in Ahmad baptizing his family?

7. Baptism ceremonies should be adapted to the local culture and circumstances as much as possible. What else could be done to make baptism more culturally appropriate in your context?

8. Review the Critical Elements of CPM listed in Appendix A. How do you see these principles demonstrated in this chapter?

9. Share what you believe God wants you to do in the next 24–48 hours from what you learned in this chapter.

10. Pray together for those who have believed in Jesus but are afraid to get baptized, asking God to give them courage. Also ask God to protect from the attacks of the evil one those who have already been baptized.

---

[117] Consider: Exod. 20:3, 2 Kings 5:1–19, Dan. 3:1–30, 6:1–27, Ps. 34:13, Matt. 5:14–16, 10:32–33, Luke 6:31, John 12:42–43, 15:20, Acts 9:20–25, Rom. 10:9–10, 1 Cor. 1:22–23, 9:20–21, 2 Cor. 6:14, Eph. 6:19–20, 2 Tim. 3:12, Heb. 12:1, and 1 John 2:22.

27

Laying a Foundation
for Spiritual Development

Faisal and Ahmad study how to grow spiritually

Faisal sat with Ahmad in the coffee shop again, sipping his usual coffee. *I can hardly believe Ahmad and his family were baptized just a week ago!*

"How are you doing, my friend?"

Ahmad forced a smile. "Fine."

Faisal set down his coffee and leaned forward. "How are you really doing, I mean, since your baptism?"

A shadow crossed Ahmad's face. For a moment he was silent. "We have now met twenty-six times, counting the prophet stories, the Isa stories, and the baptism lessons. My family and I were all really happy and everything was going well." Ahmad paused and motioned downward with his hands, "And then last week everything fell apart."

Faisal leaned forward. "I know the feeling. Tell me about what happened."

"Hajar and I hadn't argued for months, but the day after our baptism we got into a huge argument over something very petty. Then my kids got sick and started fighting with each other. But the worst part is these fears that keep plaguing me. I am most worried about my family being attacked. I am also having intense struggles with lust, jealousy, and envy.

"And I am filled with doubts about all we have discussed. I have this gnawing feeling that it is all a lie, and I have made a huge mistake. I feel so confused and depressed I want to give it all up. I didn't want to meet you today."

Faisal nodded. "I actually expected this, and you may recall we studied verses to prepare you for suffering in our first baptism lesson. We have an enemy, Satan, who attacks us ruthlessly when we decide to be baptized. I experienced the same thing when I was baptized. Prior to placing our faith in Isa we were part of Satan's kingdom, the kingdom of darkness. If he can't keep us out of God's kingdom, he does all he can to rob us of the blessings of God's kingdom. He plagues us with troubling thoughts like lust or doubting our salvation. He arouses negative feelings like despair or anxiety. He attacks our families, seeking to divide husbands and wives, and parents and children. He knows where we are vulnerable, and exploits that weakness. It's not fun to go through this, but it is actually quite common for new followers of Isa."

"So I'm not losing my mind?"

"Not even close! Losing your good looks maybe, but definitely not your mind!" Faisal teased.

Ahmad smiled with obvious relief.

"Our first response to such attacks must be prayer, informed by God's word. Let's pray together, Ahmad, and then we'll start the first of five lessons called Spiritual Foundations to help you learn how to grow spiritually and defend yourself and your family against such attacks." [118]

After prayer Faisal continued, "You are already quite familiar with the discovery approach we have used to study the Taurat and Injil with others. In this lesson we will review how and why we use this same approach to feed ourselves in our daily time with God.[119] We will also discuss how to pray, and you will practice telling your personal salvation story again."

---

[118] Appendix D lists the related scriptures.

[119] Group cultures often prefer to have their daily devotions with others.

After a brief discussion, Faisal asked, "Would you summarize what we just learned about how and why we use the same discovery method for personal study of the Taurat and Injil?"

"I read the story or passage aloud twice, then retell it in my own words. Next I ask three application questions, 'What do we learn from this passage?,' 'How do I apply it to my own life?' or 'How do I obey it?,' then 'How do I apply it to help others?'

"I do this to learn the story accurately enough to meditate on it and retell it with confidence, and to obey all Isa commanded."

"Great! Now we will use this method to discover that our salvation is guarded by God Himself, and that suffering is a normal part of life, even an honor, for everyone who follows Isa."

After this discussion and a break, Faisal continued, "In the final part of our lesson today we will study what is often called 'the Lord's Prayer,' and discover how Isa taught his disciples to pray." [120]

After they had read and retold the passages, Faisal asked, "What do we learn here?"

"We start by praising and honoring God as our Father and asking for His Kingdom to come into our lives and into the lives of people we know. In other words, we pray specifically for ourselves and others to do God's will. Then we remind Him of our immediate needs, and confess our sins one by one, asking for His forgiveness as we have forgiven others. Then we ask for protection from the enemy. And finally we praise and honor God again for who He is."

"Excellent! Do you have any questions?"

"No."

"Great. Then let's pray this way. You start."

Before they parted, Faisal also had Ahmad practice his personal salvation story again.

---

[120] Matt. 6:9–11, Luke 11:2–4

* * *

At their second lesson, Faisal said, "In this study we'll learn about the Great Commandments, the Great Commission, and what to do if we sin. We will also practice your personal salvation story again."

After they worked their way through the lesson, Faisal said, "Now let's put this into practice. I want you to make a list of fifteen people you know. They can be family members, friends, or acquaintances. Then I want you to rank them in order of who you think would be most open to discussing chronological Bible stories with you."

When Ahmad finished, Faisal said, "So, you think your uncle would be the most open?"

"Probably."

"What could you say so your uncle would want to hear you tell your story of how you came to follow Isa?"

"I'm not sure."

"Try something like this: 'Uncle, you have known me all my life. Something happened recently that has changed me. May I share it with you?'"

"That will feel very awkward, but I'll try."

"Let's practice now. Pretend I am your uncle. When you finish telling me your story, ask if you can share with me a story about the prophets.

"Practicing now will help you when you go to talk with your uncle. Then if he isn't interested in studying the prophet stories with you, approach the second person on your list. You'll find it gets easier each time you talk to another person. Talk to at least one new person each day until you find someone who wants to discuss the prophet stories with you.

"Also teach this lesson to your family, and have them do exactly what we have just done."

* * *

When they met for the third Spiritual Foundations study, Faisal was pleased with how Ahmad was applying what they had been studying and teaching it to his family.

"Today's lesson will help you understand the power available to you for living the victorious life of faith in Isa Al Masih."

After their study, Faisal asked, "Tell me in your own words what you've just learned about how to be filled by the Holy Spirit?"

"Isa said, 'I came that they may have life, and have it abundantly.' How do I live this full and rewarding life? Through the power of the Holy Spirit who indwells every true believer in Isa.

"The Holy Spirit comes and lives inside me from the moment I ask Isa to forgive my sins, cover my shame, and be my Savior and Lord. Being filled with the Spirit comes through being aware that the Spirit is present in me, and yielding to His guidance. He teaches me what to do, and gives me the power to do it. He fills my heart with joy and peace, and reminds me of God's great love for me.

"The Holy Spirit is like a wind that is always blowing. If the captain of a sailboat wants his boat to be driven by the wind, he must raise his sails. The wind then fills the sails, and the boat is carried along. In the same way, the Holy Spirit is always ready to guide us, and to empower us to obey His will."

"Excellent! Do you remember the steps for being filled by the Holy Spirit?"

"I think so. First we surrender ourselves to Isa so He reigns over our thoughts, attitudes, and actions. Then we confess all known sin. Next we ask in faith to be filled by the Holy Spirit, believing in His promise."

"Great! What did we learn about what happens when we sin?"

"When we sin or ignore God's command we quench the Holy Spirit. It's like when our leg falls asleep from sitting on it. As soon as we straighten our leg the blood begins to circulate again, and the feeling returns to our leg. In the same way, when we confess and repent of our sins, and take time to talk with God and hear from

Him, the Holy Spirit flows through us again to produce the fruit of the Spirit in and through us."

After their study, Faisal led Ahmad again in practicing his personal salvation story. Then they reviewed Ahmad's experience in sharing with his uncle, and discussed when Ahmad would share his personal salvation story with the next person on his list.

* * *

Faisal opened their next study by saying, "In our last lesson, we discussed how to be filled by the Holy Spirit. The point of being filled is to be guided and empowered by the Spirit, so we need to also learn to discern His voice as He whispers to us. Let's study these verses together and note principles of discerning His voice."

When they concluded Faisal asked, "What have we learned from this study about listening to Isa, our Savior and King?"

"We need to worship God, confess our sins, quiet our hearts before Him, meditate on His Word, submit to Him, resist the devil, believe God will speak, and obey all He tells us to do."

"Not only are you a good teacher, you are also a good student!" exclaimed Faisal. "What caution did this lesson give?"

"The devil also whispers to us, so we must test everything we 'hear' according to God's Word with others who are also seeking and being loyal to God."

* * *

At the end of their final Spiritual Foundations study, Faisal asked Ahmad to summarize the main points of living as a child of God.

"We observed that I am now a member of God's Kingdom, with a high and noble calling to live as God's child. The Injil says I am a new creation, and the Holy Spirit is dwelling in me; therefore I can no longer live like I used to live. Isa taught that if we love Him, we will obey Him.

"I am an ambassador for Al Masih, and represent Him at all times. There are no days off from being a friend of God, and there are no vacations from my privilege of being a servant of the King. I must surrender every part of my being to His Lordship, and always strive to live like I belong to a royal family: I am a child of the King of kings and Lord of lords, so I must act like one!

"This will transform my relationships (how I treat my family, neighbors, and co-workers), my attitudes (such as patience, humility, and thankfulness), my performance at work (like my work ethic and personal integrity), and my spending. I will be more truthful and kind toward my family, neighbors, and co-workers. I will be more humble, grateful, and patient. I will be honest and diligent instead of cutting corners or cheating. And I won't waste my money, but give more, and spend more wisely."

"What a high calling it is to be an ambassador for Al Masih! With that privilege also comes great responsibility. These Spiritual Foundations lessons have taught you how to grow spiritually for the rest of your life."

Discuss and apply

1. How did you obey what you concluded God wanted you to do from the previous chapter?

2. When you were baptized, did you experience any spiritual warfare? Describe it. What helped you get through that time? What would you say to a new believer to encourage him or her in the midst of spiritual warfare?

3. Explain the discovery method taught in this chapter for personal study of the Scripture, and why it is so important.

4. Pray now following the pattern of the Lord's Prayer as taught in this chapter.

5. Persecution is a normal part of following Jesus. What would you say to encourage a new believer encountering persecution?

6. State the Great Commandment[121] in your own words. Share how you can love God and others practically this week.

7. Say the Great Commission[122] in your own words.

8. Update your list of fifteen family members, friends, and acquaintances who don't know Jesus, then rank these individuals in order of who you think would be most interested in discussing Bible stories with you. Practice again what you can say to invite these individuals to meet with you.

9. One way to find persons of peace is by sharing your personal salvation story. Practice presenting your personal salvation story to each other in three minutes or less.

10. What does it mean to be filled by the Holy Spirit? What steps did Ahmad give? What principles and cautions did Faisal and Ahmad discuss regarding listening to the Holy Spirit?

11. Share how God wants you, because you are His child, to live differently this week?

12. Share what you believe God wants you to do in the next 24–48 hours from what you learned in this chapter.

13. Meditate on these verses, listen to the Holy Spirit, and then share what you heard: 1 John 3:1–3, 3:16–18, 4:4, 4:11, 4:19–20.

---

[121] Matt. 22:36–39

[122] Matt. 28:18–20

28

Incorporating Healthy DNA
into House Churches

Faisal's team learns how healthy churches should function

Faisal tightened the laces on his jogging shoes. So many things were happening in their little movement. He needed time to think about where they had come from and where they were headed. Maybe an early morning jog would help. Faisal headed down his street, and turned at the mosque. The road rose gradually. There were few people and vehicles, and the view was inspiring. On one side of the road, he could see terraced rice fields. On the other, cows and goats grazed.

The original group had gotten off to a slow start. They had tried every way they knew to find a person of peace—incorporating shema statements in their conversation, sharing a personal salvation story, asking others if they know anyone who has had a dream from God, praying for needs, saying a prayer of blessing, discussing references to Isa in the Qur'an, and recounting a "Creation to Al Masih" story. They had faithfully shared with others, but at first no one was interested in discussing the prophet stories with them. Then spiritual attacks had nearly wrecked their group. After Faisal had rallied them in prayer, God had answered in dramatic ways.

Everyone on the team had started one or more discovery groups to discuss chronological stories in the Taurat and Injil. Recently, Ahmad and his household had been baptized. What a joy and privilege it was to be used by God to lead people to Al Masih and see the beginnings of multiplying house churches.

The team had learned there are two key but difficult transitions for the house church planter: first to gather the oikos together to begin discussing the prophet stories, and second to stop attending the group after appointing and equipping a leader from within the oikos.

It helped that they had established a clear goal of planting healthy, independent, multiplying house fellowships led by oikos leaders, and a deep commitment to seeing those house churches reproduce to four generations and beyond.

Their experience had confirmed that they needed to continue relying on the Word of God and the Spirit of God. Their study had also taught them that followers of Isa are blessed to be a blessing; consequently they were actively seeking ways to bless others.

Their meetings were encouraging. They prayed, supported each other, and held one another accountable. They laughed and enjoyed one another, and were a team in the fullest sense of the word.

Up the road Faisal could see several women carrying baskets of vegetables on their heads, walking toward the market.

Now that Ahmad and his family had been baptized and become a house church, it was time to discuss with his team the essential ingredients of a healthy church, so the right DNA would be present in these groups from the outset.

Faisal suddenly saw that he had run farther than he had planned. *What an adventure this has been!* he thought as he headed home.

* * *

Faisal, Fatima, Yusuf, Nur, Nasrudin, and Amina gathered for their weekly meeting. There was excitement in the air; God was on the move. They were experiencing a sense of awe, perhaps like what the early disciples felt.

Following their usual pattern, they shared what they were thankful for, and what they were struggling with. Each one also shared what was going on in the groups they were facilitating, and they prayed for each other and their respective groups.

Faisal then directed them to the day's topic, *Essential Church Ingredients*.[123] "Once a household is baptized it becomes a house church.[124] This study will help us discover from the Injil what must be present for this church to become healthy. It is also important to note that house churches can become stronger when several oikos join together."

Afterward Faisal said, "This discussion has been very fruitful. Let's summarize these verses."

Together the group listed these essential ingredients of healthy churches:

1. worship,
2. prayer,
3. discussion of the Word,
4. fellowship (applying the "one-another" commands),
5. the Lord's Supper,
6. giving,
7. baptism,
8. evangelism leading to new churches,
9. godly leadership, and
10. regular meetings.

Faisal asked Nasrudin to pray, then Fatima brought out tea.

---

[123] Lesson 1 under *Healthy Church Studies* in Appendix F.

[124] Dedicated church buildings were uncommon in the first 300 years after Jesus commissioned the disciples. Instead of reinforcing the synagogue model of dedicated buildings and professional leaders, Jesus labeled His new movement with the Greek *ekklesia*. According to Vine's Expository Dictionary of New Testament Words, the Greeks used *ekklesia* to refer to "a body of citizens 'gathered' to discuss the affairs of State," commonly at the city gates (with no building at all!).

Discuss and apply

1. How did you obey what you concluded God wanted you to do from the previous chapter?

2. What methods for finding persons of peace are mentioned in this chapter? Are there new ways you could try to find a POP?

3. What did this group learn about prayer and spiritual warfare?

4. What two difficult transitions did Faisal mention? What has your experience been with these two transitions? How have you overcome obstacles to these transitions?

5. What role does accountability play in Faisal's team?

6. Was the goal of Faisal's team to win individuals or groups? How did this affect their strategy?

7. Review the essential ingredients of a healthy church listed at the end of this chapter. If you are already mentoring house churches, which of these ingredients are absent or weak?

8. Churches become stronger when several oikos combine. If you are mentoring single oikos house churches, discuss how you might combine these to form stronger churches.

9. Share what you believe God wants you to do in the next 24–48 hours from what you learned in this chapter.

10. Pray together for your discovery groups to persevere to become healthy, independent, multiplying house churches.

29

Developing a Simple Pattern
for House Churches

Ahmad's family transitions from a discovery group to a house church

When they met again in their usual coffee shop, Faisal began, "Ahmad, now that you and your family are baptized believers, you are actually a house church. Today we will start studying Acts to observe what the early disciples did, and how we can imitate them."

"I have no idea what you just said." Ahmad replied, half-joking and half-serious.

"This should make sense as we study further. As a church you'll continue to meet weekly, and we will build on the pattern we used in our Discovery Groups.[125]

"Do you recall the first question we asked in every study?"

"Sure. What are you thankful for?"

"Right. Worship is the first part of our house church gatherings, and giving thanks is a key part of worship. We should worship God in all that we do, but our gatherings start with a focus on worship that can take a variety of forms: thanking God, praising Him for His attributes (like wisdom and justice), singing[126], praying verses from Zabur, and giving.

---

125 Appendix H provides a simple pattern of worship for a church.

126 Where our churches don't sing because the houses are too close to neighbors, they still worship using the other methods described here.

"Let's spend a few minutes worshiping from Zabur. We'll read a few verses, and pray them back to God."

Faisal handed Zabur 29 to Ahmad. "Read verses 1 and 2."

Ascribe to the LORD, O heavenly beings,
  ascribe to the LORD glory and strength.
Ascribe to the LORD the glory due his name;
  worship the LORD in the splendor of holiness.

"Now I'll model praying this back to God.

"O Lord, You are strong and glorious. We serve you as Lord. We worship You in holiness. Amen.

"The next part is sharing," Faisal continued. "Do you recall the second question we asked in our studies?"

"Yes. What are your struggles?"

"Exactly. In our sharing time, we share our struggles and burdens but also how God is changing and helping us. We also share about our attempts to find POPs, and about the groups we are mentoring.

"Our sharing leads naturally to prayer, the third part of our house church. In prayer we bring our burdens and concerns to God, and thank Him for how He is helping us. We also ask God to give us opportunities to share with those who don't yet know Him. Through our sharing and prayer we are expressing care for one another.

"The fourth part of our house church gathering is studying God's Word with the same discovery approach we used with the prophet and Isa stories. When we ask the question, 'How did you apply the last story?' we are holding people accountable to obey God's Word. And when we ask 'How can we apply the story to help others?' we are casting vision and calling everyone to consider how they will obey God's Word. Finally we ask the Holy Spirit to help us obey what we have read."

"Each time we meet in our house church we follow this pattern: worship, sharing, prayer, and God's Word. So the pattern we followed in the Discovery Group is expanded in our house church."

Discuss and apply

1. How did you obey what you concluded God wanted you to do from the previous chapter?

2. What are some ways Faisal suggested they could worship?

3. Take a moment and worship using Ps. 66:1–5.

4. It is helpful to vary the questions to keep the sharing time lively. Take a look at Appendix H. Which of these questions haven't you used before? What other questions could you use?

5. The leader should involve others in praying aloud for needs. What would you say to people who are hesitant to pray in front of others?

6. What elements of this pattern are common to groups you have been part of in the past? What is new? How do the additional elements encourage obedience and multiplication?

7. Discuss Acts 2:38–42 together, following the pattern of studying God's Word outlined in Appendix H.

8. Share what you believe God wants you to do in the next 24–48 hours from what you learned in this chapter.

9. Pray together that your growing house churches will practice lively worship, heartfelt prayer, application-oriented discussion of the Word, genuine love, and bold evangelism.

30

Discovering Freedom in Jesus Christ

Inne and Fatima help Eka discover her identity and authority in Jesus

When Eka arrived, Inne and Fatima were sitting in the living room, a modest room with a polished concrete floor, a few old chairs, a TV, and a faded picture on the wall. Eka seemed surprised at Fatima's presence.

"This is Fatima," Inne said. "She's my spiritual mentor."

Eka and Fatima exchanged smiles, and shook hands.

Usually Eka came to Inne's directly after class to help with food preparation, and then delivered the food after their discussion.

"Where's the food?"

"I wanted extra time to talk with you today, so I got up early, prepared the food, and delivered it myself. Come, sit down.

"Eka, you have obeyed Isa Al Masih by being baptized. As you know, we are involved in a fierce spiritual battle. Today in our study of *Steps to Freedom in Al Masih*[127] you'll learn more about your identity and authority as a child of God in Al Masih, and how to be victorious over attacks from the evil one.

"Fatima has trained me in how to use this material. She is joining us today to pray over us as we study. Let's begin."

---

[127] Because of the intimate nature of ministering to personal brokenness, an oikos may split into separate mens and womens groups for the Freedom and Healing studies (detailed in Appendix E). The full oikos resumes meeting together for the Acts Studies and beyond (Appendices E and F).

After their study, [128] Inne asked, "What did you learn today?"

"I learned that I am no longer in a place of shame before God. Because of Isa, God has covered my shame and shared with me his honor. I am a new creation in Al Masih, the Holy Spirit lives in me, I am seated with Al Masih in the heavenly places, my salvation is guaranteed by God's power, I have been blessed with every spiritual blessing, and in Al Masih I have authority over evil spirits."

"No wonder you are such a good college student. You catch on very quickly." Eka blushed at Inne's compliment.

"Knowing who you are in Al Masih is important for walking in victory and exercising authority over evil spirits. There are at least seven ways, or doors, through which Satan gains access to deceive, influence, and control us.

"The first door is involvement with unclean spirits. We come into contact with these spirits by possessing amulets, visiting shaman, making offerings, and attending ceremonies to protect ourselves from spirits or seek their blessings. Let's pray and ask God to reveal any such involvements you may have had. Then you'll write them down."

Eka was surprised at how quickly her page filled up.[129]

"Let's see your list."

- When I was a baby my parents bought an amulet with a verse from the Qur'an, and tied it around my neck to protect me from evil spirits.
- My parents whispered verses from the Qur'an in my ear when I was young.
- There was a cultural ceremony for my first haircut.
- I suffered female circumcision.
- Every year my grandfather gathered us to wash the keris.[130]
- Growing up, my parents took me to shamans when I was sick.

---

[128] Matt. 10:1, 16:19, 28:18; Rom. 8:16–17; 2 Cor. 5:17; Eph. 1:3–8,13–14, 20–22, 2:4–6,10; Col. 2:9–10,15; Heb. 2:14, Jas. 4:7–8, 1 Pet. 2:9, 1 John 3:8, 4:4, 5:18

[129] Evil spirits can gain access to afflict individuals through animistic practices such as those in this list.

[130] A special type of sword believed to possess power to protect the family.

- Every morning my mom made an offering to the spirits around our house.
- My aunt and uncle sacrificed a chicken before planting or harvesting rice.
- I went to the shaman to ask for help for an upcoming test."

"These are good examples of involvement with spirits. Satan will use any one of these to get his foot in the door in order to control your life. As a child of God, you are a child of light. Light can have nothing to do with darkness. To be free from any influence of Satan, you need to confess and renounce one by one all of your past involvement with spirits, and ask God's forgiveness."

Eka nodded.

"Pray something like this, 'I confess that I was taken to a shaman when I was eight. By the authority and power of Isa, and by virtue of my position in Him in the heavenly realm, I command any evil spirit attached to me through this visit to the shaman to flee right now in the name of Isa.'

"Are you ready to pray?"

One by one, Eka confessed her involvement with spirits, asked for forgiveness, and commanded the spirits to flee in the name of Isa Al Masih.

"Eka, Do you own any amulets?"

"Yes, my mom gave me an amulet when I went to college. She promised it would protect me and bring me luck."

"If you want to be free from any influence from the evil one, you must sever all ties with powers not from God. We need to burn that amulet. Would you bring it the next time you come?"

"Sure."

"Great. I think we've covered enough material for today. There are still six more ways Satan enters our lives to influence, deceive, and control us. We'll continue next time." [131]

The three women hugged each other, and Eka went home.

---

[131] All seven steps are found in Appendix E.

Discuss and apply

1. How did you obey what you concluded God wanted you to do from the previous chapter?

2. Why is it important to minister in pairs when involved in spiritual warfare?

3. Why is it important to know your position in Christ when it comes to spiritual warfare?

4. Summarize in your own words what the chapter said about your identity in Christ.

5. The first step in the material entitled *Steps to Freedom in Christ*[132] is forsaking involvement with spirits. What practices or ceremonies have you participated in? Make a list, then confess them one by one, adapting the sample prayer given.

6. Do you possess any amulets? Ask your spiritual mentor to discard or burn them with you.

7. Share what you believe God wants you to do in the next 24–48 hours from what you learned in this chapter.

8. Take a few minutes together to thank God for who you are in Christ. Pray together for those you know who need to be set free from the chains of the evil one.

---

[132] Appendix E.

31

Moving Toward Emotional Health[133]

Inne and Fatima assist Eka in inviting Jesus to heal her deepest wounds

Inne, Fatima, and Eka sat down again in the living room. "We have completed the material in *Steps to Freedom in Al Masih*," Inne said. "Today[134] I want to cover *Toward Emotional Health*." [135] She excused herself and returned with a box of tissue, which she placed in front of Eka. "You might need this," she said casually.

Eka eyed the tissue apprehensively, yet knew she could trust her friends. *Inne is like the mother I never had; she always wants the best for me. Besides, Fatima is here too. I can trust these two women.*

"Many times, people are wounded in their childhood by things others say and do. This often brings deep shame and hurt. These things leave lasting scars on our hearts, and often influence how we relate to others. These deep wounds express themselves *mentally* through disturbing thoughts and difficulty in concentrating, *emotion-*

---

[133] Emotional Health is not a critical element of CPM; however, discipleship is. In our context, so many have been abused or experienced trauma as children that we find we need to address emotional healing as part of our discipleship.

[134] We usually plan several extra hours in one block to study this material and, because of the personal nature of the sharing, separate into mens and womens groups.

[135] This approach (Appendix E) tests all impressions and images against Scripture, and does not explore repressed memories or suggest trauma or abuse. In severe cases (like sexual abuse), an individual may have suppressed memories. In such cases it is best to involve a trained professional as revisiting the event may expose serious psychological issues.

ally through depression, moodiness, or hypersensitivity to comments, or *physically* through headaches, ulcers, or loss of appetite.

"When someone didn't receive love from their parents, often they will seek love in inappropriate or even destructive ways. When someone experienced a lack, they will often overcompensate to make up for that lack. For example, if someone didn't receive much attention when they were young, they may try to be the center of attention when they become an adult. Healing will require you to face the hurt, feel the pain, and release the wounding to God. Hence the box of tissue."

Inne reached over and tenderly stroked Eka's arm. Eka felt nauseated, with a knot growing in her stomach. *Is this the time to tell Inne my most closely guarded secret?*

Inne handed Eka a piece of paper. "On the top left write 'sorrows,' and on the top right put 'thankfulness.' Then think about your past, and write down everything you can think of under each heading."

When Eka finished, she handed her paper to Inne.

Sorrows
- Abandoned and rejected by dad
- Shamed by mom
- Ridiculed by friends at school
- Unprotected by school teachers
- ???

Thankful
- Opportunity to go to college
- Met Inne

"These are deep wounds. They must cause you great pain."

Eka nodded. She could feel anxiety building up inside.

"We will follow four steps in *Toward Emotional Health*."

"The first step is to *Recall*. Here you remember all the details or facts about the event as well as your feelings, such as what you felt then, and feel now toward those who hurt you, the ones who didn't help you, the situation, yourself, and God.

"The second step is to *Repent*. Repentance means confessing your sins and asking God to change you. People may have hurt you deeply, and you may have responded in unhealthy ways. For your own healing you must take responsibility for your wrong thoughts, attitudes, and actions. Part of repentance is forgiving the people who wounded you. This may seem impossible and unfair now, so we will discuss this later. Under certain conditions you must also apologize to those you have hurt.

"The third step is to *Renew* your mind by renouncing lies you have believed about yourself, the situation, and God, especially lies about His goodness. You must replace these lies with truth from God's Word.

"The fourth step is to *Receive* God's touch, and to thank and worship Him."

Eka nodded that she understood and was ready to start. One by one, they discussed the deep emotional pain Eka felt from each of the items she had listed as Sorrows.

Coming to the final entry on the left, Inne probed further. "What do the three question marks mean?"

Eka took a deep breath and let it out slowly. She glanced over at Fatima, who was smiling warmly at her. Eka knew she was praying for her. "Do you remember when I told you the police just released my mom when she was in prison for stealing?"

"Yes."

"Well there is more to the story. One day when I brought food to my mom, the policeman who arrested her told me there was a way to make all of her charges go away. I said, 'Can you help me?' Remember, I was a naïve fourteen-year old. The policeman led me to the back of the police station and into a small room. There was a desk on one side and a mattress on the other. He closed the door and locked it. 'Take off your clothes and lay there' he said, pointing to the mattress. He raped me. Then he said, 'Get dressed. If you say anything about this to anyone, I know where you live. I will come and kill your mom in front of your eyes.'

"I was devastated. I felt violated and dirty. I thought 'How could anyone love me?' When I came here to college, I wanted nothing to do with guys. I hated men, yet I craved their attention. I met a guy and he seemed to like me. He pressured me to sleep with him, so I did. For a short while I felt close to him, but soon I hated him and myself. Not long afterwards he dumped me.

"From then on I felt lucky if a guy would give me attention. Word got out I was 'easy.' Soon lots of guys were paying attention to me, but as soon as they got me into bed they left me and pretended they didn't even know me.

"I've never told anyone what that policeman did to me."

Eka leaned forward in her chair, grasped her stomach as if in pain, and started to weep uncontrollably. Shame, anger, and regret crashed upon her like a tsunami. Then she fell to the floor, curled up in a fetal position, and wept and groaned in deep agony. Inne slipped out of her chair and pulled Eka close to her. Eka buried her face in Inne's chest. Inne just held her tightly and whispered, "It's okay. It's okay. Cry all you want."

Inne stroked Eka's hair like a mom strokes the hair of a young child who has just fallen down. Eventually Eka stopped crying. The burden of concealing this secret had finally been lifted. For a moment Eka felt relieved. But then the realization of her sinful responses to what she had suffered gripped her with a new and heavier burden. Raw emotions of self-loathing and condemnation overwhelmed her. Feelings of uncleanness and unworthiness she had long suppressed brought forth despair, helplessness, and hopelessness. With horror she thought, *Will Inne reject me now that she knows my secret? Will I lose the one true friend I have?*

Inne looked reassuringly into Eka's tear-stained eyes, melting Eka's fears.

"Do you want to stop for today, or do you want to go on?"

"Can I go to the bathroom first?"

Inne pointed toward the bathroom. "Well, of course."

Eka emerged ready to proceed. "I've been carrying that burden far too long. I want to be free. I want to be clean."

"As I said before, we use a four step process of healing. The first step is *Recall*, which you have just done in remembering this place of excruciating pain and wounding, along with your feelings about what happened. What else did you feel?"

"I felt used up and discarded like an old rag. Because I felt unworthy of love and respect, I let guys sleep with me."

"The second step is *Repent*. What that policeman did to you, and the ways men have used you since then, are absolutely wrong. They are evil and inexcusable, but you must choose to forgive."

Instantly Eka's mind was bombarded with thoughts. Her whole being revolted at the thought of forgiving that policeman. She blurted out, "Forgive! After all he did to me? Never! I hope he burns in hell!"

Eka crossed her arms insolently and stared straight ahead. A minute passed. Then two. The clicking of an oscillating fan filled the silence.

In a quiet yet firm voice, Inne spoke again. "Do you want to be free?" She reached over with her finger and tucked Eka's hair behind her ear. Impulsively, Eka slapped her hand away in anger, then crossed her arms again.

More minutes passed with only the fan making a noise. Eka stared ahead defiantly. She swallowed hard, but said nothing.

Fatima prayed.

With her arms still crossed, Eka turned slowly toward Inne. "I don't feel like forgiving."

"Of course you don't. You'll never feel like forgiving. Forgiveness is a choice."

"I can't do it."

"Is your way working?"

"What do you mean?" Eka snapped.

"Can you free yourself from your anger and bitterness?"

"No."

"No one is pushing you. You can stay angry and bitter. Maybe, today is not the day you want to deal with this wounding. Perhaps, you don't really want to be free."

Eka exploded. "Of course I want to be free, but he doesn't deserve forgiveness!"

"Right! He doesn't deserve forgiveness, and neither do you!"

"What do you mean?"

"You don't deserve forgiveness for your sins, yet God mercifully forgives you. You forgive others because God forgave you.

"You don't forgive someone for their sake. You forgive them for yours. That policeman hurt you many years ago, and he is still hurting you through your anger and bitterness. Forgiving him doesn't release him from punishment, it turns him over to God, who will judge him with perfect justice. You may not see His judgment, but you can be sure God will punish him in His way and in His timing. That policeman won't escape God's judgment."

Eka bit her lip, wanting God to punish the policeman now.

"Forgiveness is accepting onto yourself the results of someone else's sin. You choose to forgive him in order to be free from your anger, bitterness, and hate. Look at what the anger is doing to you. Your mind races with uncontrollable thoughts, while your anger and bitterness churn within. You lash out at your friends and drive them away. Is this how you want to live? There is a better way."

Tears welled up in Inne's eyes. She wanted this dear one whom she loved so much to be free of the pain, but she understood the struggle within to forgive this monstrous evil.

Everything in Eka screamed, *This isn't fair!* Every fiber of her being cried out for revenge, but she could see Inne was right. *This policeman is still hurting me. Six years have passed, yet not a day goes by that I don't think about that horrible event. I am filled with anger and hatred. I feel unlovable and unworthy. Half the time I don't even like myself. I can't relate to guys in a healthy manner, and I drive my friends away with outbursts of anger. I really do want to be free. But this is so hard!*

By a sheer act of will, Eka declared, "I am ready to forgive."

"I don't want to rush you. Before you forgive you must feel the full weight of the hurt. You must also realize you are suffering due to someone else's sin. In this way, you are like Isa. He never sinned, so He was innocent. Yet He died on the cross for man's sins. In doing so, He took upon Himself the sins of others. The sins of the policeman have already been laid upon you. You must accept that you can't change the past. What you can change is the future. When you forgive this policeman you release him to God's judgment and choose to not seek revenge upon him personally, although the government may still prosecute him. Are you sure you are ready?"

"He's hurt me too long. I want to be free. I'm ready to forgive."

"Okay. Prayer is talking to God from the heart. Use your own words. Even when you don't make sense, your loving heavenly Father understands."

"Oh God, what that policeman did to me was horribly wrong and indefensible. He is not worthy of forgiveness. For that matter I'm not worthy of forgiveness, but Isa Al Masih forgave me. Now I see forgiveness is the only way I can be free. I choose to forgive the policeman. I release him to You, believing You will punish him with perfect justice. In Isa's name. Amen."

Inne continued leading Eka through the steps to emotional healing. "Forgiving others is part of repentance. Another part is taking responsibility for your own wrong thoughts, attitudes, and actions in response to what happened to you."

"I understand. I've carried bitterness, anger, and hatred toward that policeman. He stole from me what he had no right to, my virginity. I've had evil thoughts of torturing him until he begged for mercy, then watching him die a slow, painful death.

"I allow guys to disrespect me when I let them sleep with me.

"I'm quick to get angry at my friends now, and say all kinds of cruel and ugly things to them. But I know it's not my friends I'm really angry with. My anger at the policeman spills out on those around me."

"It is understandable that you have those thoughts, feelings, and actions," Inne replied compassionately. "Are you ready to confess them, and ask God for forgiveness and His help to change?"

Eka nodded yes and prayed, "Gracious heavenly Father. I confess that I am trapped in anger, bitterness, and hatred. I confess that I say all kinds of cruel things to my friends. I confess that I explode over the slightest thing. Would You forgive me? Would you help me to change? Amen."

"1 John 1:9 says, 'If we confess our sins, He is faithful and just to forgive us our sins and to cleanse us from all unrighteousness.' Based on this verse, you can be certain that God not only forgives you from your own sin, but He also cleanses you from the defilement of what others have done to you!"

Eka burst out crying again, but not from pain. These were tears of joy in the freedom of forgiveness and of relief that such a crushing burden had been lifted from her shoulders. They were tears of gratitude at the love of Isa flowing into her and cleansing all the filth away. They were tears of triumph and victory. They were tears of celebration and hope.

Again, Inne slipped her arm around Eka's shoulders. Now all three women were crying, and wiping tears from each other's eyes.

"The final part of repentance is asking forgiveness from those you have wronged unless they can still hurt you emotionally or physically. Are you willing to apologize to those you have wronged?"

"Yes. I can do that."

"Maybe, we should take a break before we continue."

"I'd like that."

Eka stood and walked to the front porch. She moved her head from side to side to stretch out her neck, and rolled her arms and shoulders. A little bird flew down from a nearby tree and landed in the yard. It picked up a small piece of trash and flew away. *That bird just took away the trash. That is like what God just did. He carried away the trash from my life!* Eka smiled, and a new hopefulness welled up inside. *My life can be different. I have finally found the right path.*

Eka went back inside and sat down next to Inne. "The third step in *Toward Emotional Health* is to *Renew* our mind. In this step we both renounce the lies of the evil one, especially lies against God's goodness, and replace those lies with truth from the Scriptures. Can you think of some lies you have believed?"

"That I was to blame. That I am unworthy of love. That I can never be happy. And that God abandoned me."

"Now replace those lies with the truth; in other words, reclaim the ground which formerly had been given over to the evil one."

"I did nothing wrong when the policeman raped me. I was just a young girl trying to help her mother. I've always felt that I was somehow to blame, but now I know that isn't true.

"God has made me new. Nothing is beyond His forgiveness. No one is so dirty that God cannot clean them and make them whiter than snow.[136] What Christ did covers not only my own sins but also the sins of others against me! Because I am valuable in God's eyes, I have worth no matter what happened to me. I *can* have a meaningful relationship with a guy which isn't based on sex."

"I hope you hear what you are saying. Those truths are so powerful!"

"Now it's time to look at the thankfulness side of your paper. Maybe you want to add a few more things to your list."

"I do. I'm thankful the policeman didn't kill me. I'm thankful I met you, Inne. I'm thankful God loves me unconditionally, and that I am valuable and worthy in His eyes. I'm thankful He heals all my pain, and gives me hope for a better life."

"That's beautiful. Now that your eyes have been opened, you'll want to continue adding to your "thankfulness" list as you see more ways God has helped you. I don't have enough paper in this house to write down all of God's goodness to you!"

Eka, Inne and Fatima looked at each other and laughed. The laughter felt good, really good.

"The fourth step in *Toward Emotional Health* is to *Receive* God's touch, then respond to Him in thankfulness and worship. This looks different for each person because each person's pain is different. God knows just how to speak to us because He knows us so well. Talk to Him, then listen to what He says."

"I don't know what to say. I'm just a brand new believer!" Eka protested.

"God is like the perfect parent, so just speak from your heart. Tell Him what you have learned about yourself and your situation. Tell Him what lies you accepted, then restate the truths you now believe.

---

136 Isaiah 1:18

Express your sadness at all the years you spent in anger and bitterness, and how grateful you are to finally be free. Review how He sees you as His beautiful daughter, and express your gratitude that He is your heavenly Father. Tell Him other things you are thankful for. When you are ready, start talking to Him."

"O God, this is Eka. I really don't know what to say, but I'll try. I am so thankful ..."

As Eka finished praying, Inne said, "Keep your eyes closed Eka, and focus on listening to God. Your heavenly Father is deeply pleased by the honesty with which you poured out your heart to Him. He delights for His children come to Him in this way. Now let's simply be quiet in His presence. God often responds by giving us a verse or an image. Let me pray again.

"In Isa's powerful name I bind Satan in any way he would try to plant a false vision or impression in Eka's mind. I cover Eka with the blood of Isa Al Masih as a protection against all interference from the evil one. Amen.

"Now, I'm going to play a worship song. Just listen to the words and dwell in God's presence."

As the song finished, Eka said, "This verse just came into my mind 'You have taken account of my wanderings; Put my tears in Your bottle.'" [137]

"That is so like God. He is near to us, so near He collects every tear and saves them in a bottle. Have you ever thought about that? When you wept, you were not alone. God was right there with you."

Eka felt very peaceful, sitting in the chair with her eyes closed, breathing calmly. "When we took a break, I went outside and saw a bird come down in your yard and carry away a piece of trash. I felt like that is what God has done for me, He has carried away my trash. I can still see the bird in my mind, but as it flies higher and higher it is getting smaller and smaller. I feel like God is saying to me the initial healing has begun but complete healing will take time, and the pain won't disappear overnight."

---

[137] Ps. 56:8

"That's very insightful. The healing has begun. The deeper the wound, the longer it may take to be completely healed. Sometimes God heals instantly, but at other times He gives us the initial breakthrough and then heals us completely as we apply truth to our situation. It is important for you to continue talking with wise and mature people who can help you unlearn destructive patterns and learn constructive ways to handle negative emotions.

"It's also important to remember forgiving is not forgetting. You will remember for the rest of your life what that policeman did to you. But over time the emotional intensity will decrease. For a while you may still feel great emotion when you think of that event. But as you walk out truth and victory you will be able to think of that event without feeling the same intense emotions. Is there anything else God is speaking to you?"

"I see Isa on the cross. He is bleeding from His head and His back. He is struggling to breath and suffering horribly. I see angels all around ready to rescue Him, awaiting His command, but He says nothing. He continues to endure His affliction.

"Now I see Him cry out, 'It is finished,' and His head falls forward lifelessly. Now I understand Isa's death on the cross in a way I never have before. He willingly suffered and died even though He was innocent. He understands what it means to be rejected, humiliated, and left alone. He empathizes with me because He went through suffering far worse.

"Now, I see Isa after His resurrection. He is standing over me, clothed in a dazzling white robe. I have fallen to my knees with my face to the ground, and I'm trembling all over. He takes my hand and lifts me to my feet. His hand gently lifts my chin so I am looking into His radiant eyes.

"I hear His words, 'You did not choose Me, but I chose you and appointed you that you should bear fruit, and that your fruit should remain. Whatever you ask of the Father in My name He will give you.[138] You did not choose this pain. I allowed it because I knew you

---

[138] John 15:16

would be shaped by it. Suffering is a gift, although many don't recognize it as such. It is one path to knowing me better.[139] I knew this suffering wouldn't be wasted on you. As you receive my comfort in this pain I will make you a more tender, compassionate, and understanding person.[140] I have chosen you, and appointed you to be My hands and feet. The world is filled with people who have suffered indescribable agonies. It needs people like you, who have experienced my grace amidst such pain, to be agents of healing. Rise up, dear one. There is much work to be done.'

"Now Isa is pulling me to Himself. His strong arms are holding me close. I have never felt so safe, or so loved. Now the image is fading. I want to hold on, but it is leaving."

Eka opened her eyes, her face full of joy and contentment.

"What do you understand about that image?"

Eka blinked as if awakening from a deep sleep. "Isa understands my pain because He Himself suffered terribly. He also said suffering is a gift when someone submits to God and allows Him to use the pain to mold them into a caring and kind person. He chose me because He knew I would be transformed by the suffering, and not defeated by it. Isa told me He wants to use me in the lives of others."

"I believe He does, too."

"One final thing; the evil one may pelt you with thoughts that you were just kidding yourself and you will never be free. If that happens, recognize those thoughts as coming from the pit of hell, renew your mind with the truths you know, and cultivate thankfulness for God's goodness."

---

[139] Phil. 3:10
[140] 2 Cor. 1:4

Discuss and apply

1. How did you obey what you concluded God wanted you to do from the previous chapter?

2. *Recall* involves remembering trauma details and naming feelings. If you have experienced trauma, discuss how you felt then and how you feel now. Be honest with God; He already knows everything.

3. *Repent* means confessing our sins and asking God to change us. We often act in sinful ways, in our thoughts, attitudes and actions, especially when others sin against us. How do you see this in Eka's life, and in your own?

4. Forgiving the people who wound us is one of the most difficult parts of repentance. What reasons are given in this chapter for forgiving others? How do you answer the statement, "He doesn't deserve to be forgiven?" Does your forgiveness release the person from the laws of the government, or from God's justice? Is there any way to be free from deep emotional hurt without forgiveness?

5. Repentance also means taking responsibility for our actions. Inne said Eka should apologize to those she has wronged. Discuss when it is appropriate to apologize directly to a person and when this is unwise.

6. *Renew* means renouncing lies and replacing them with truth. What lies had Eka believed and with what truth did she replace those lies? In what ways have you doubted God's goodness? How has this chapter helped you?

7. *Receive* is the step of accepting God's touch and then worshiping Him. What did you learn about how God sees you? What can you be thankful for?

8. What else did you learn from this chapter about the process of *Toward Emotional Health*? Do you have wounds from your past that need healing? Ask your spiritual mentor to help you. See Appendix E for guidance.

9. Share what you believe God wants you to do in the next 24–48 hours from what you learned in this chapter.

10. Ask God to heal those you know have had trauma, heartbreak, a difficult childhood, fractured relationships or emotional pain.

32

Paying the Price

Abdullah is confronted by his radical friends

Abdullah, the former radical Muslim now the radical follower of Al Masih, looked around at the boys in his front room. *Who would have thought nine months ago I would now be teaching students to read and understand Arabic? What a perfect opportunity to teach what the Qur'an says about Isa. God certainly knew what He was doing when He helped me learn Arabic. God has also redeemed my skill at working with my hands. Whereas before I built bombs, now I repair motorcycles. Between teaching Arabic and repairing motorcycles, I can support my family. God is indeed good.*

There was one person in the Injil Abdullah especially liked. The Apostle Paul had also been a radical until he met Isa on the road to Damascus. Paul went from being a violent persecutor to a vigorous propagator of the faith. Abdullah liked to think of himself as a junior Apostle Paul.

All of a sudden Saleh and five other men, all part of the same radical group Abdullah had been in, barged into his house. The boys all looked at Abdullah, their eyes wide with fear. Abdullah dismissed them. "Our lesson is over for today."

Instantly the boys packed their books and bolted for the door.

Abdullah wasn't surprised to see Saleh. Saleh had been suspicious of him ever since Faisal and Nasrudin had cast the demon from his son. Abdullah called for Titin to make coffee for their visitors.

Saleh interrupted. "We don't need coffee. What we have come to talk about is serious, and it can't wait."

"Okay. Go ahead."

"We have heard you were baptized. Is this true?"

"Yes," Abdullah replied clearly and calmly.

"What? You have become a Christian? You are an apostate!" Saleh roared in anger.

"No, I'm not a Christian as you understand it. I don't drink alcohol, eat pork, gamble, sleep around, or worship statues. I am not a colonialist or a crusader, and I don't support exploitation of Muslims by the West. I never wear my shoes or uncover my head when I am worshiping, and my wife dresses modestly. I still pray and fast, and give my alms to the poor. I am a Muslim follower of Isa Al Masih."

For a moment, Saleh didn't know how to respond. Then he shook his head in disgust and shouted, "You're wrong. Either you are a Muslim or you aren't. There is no such thing as a 'Muslim follower of Isa.'"

Abdullah picked up the Qur'an he had been using to teach his students just a few minutes earlier. "Yes there is, and I can prove it." He opened the Qur'an and read,

$$\text{۞ فَلَمَّآ أَحَسَّ عِيسَىٰ مِنْهُمُ ٱلْكُفْرَ قَالَ مَنْ أَنصَارِىٓ إِلَى ٱللَّهِ}$$
$$\text{قَالَ ٱلْحَوَارِيُّونَ نَحْنُ أَنصَارُ ٱللَّهِ ءَامَنَّا بِٱللَّهِ وَٱشْهَدْ بِأَنَّا}$$
$$\text{مُسْلِمُونَ ۝}$$
$$\text{رَبَّنَآ ءَامَنَّا بِمَآ أَنزَلْتَ وَٱتَّبَعْنَا ٱلرَّسُولَ فَٱكْتُبْنَا مَعَ}$$
$$\text{ٱلشَّٰهِدِينَ ۝}$$

Qur'an 3:52–53 But when Jesus felt [persistence in] disbelief from them, he said, "Who are my supporters for [the cause of] Allah?" The disciples said, "We are supporters for Allah. We have believed in Allah and testify that we are Muslims [submitting to Him]. Our Lord, we have believed in what You revealed and have followed the messenger Jesus, so register us among the witnesses [to truth]."

"As you can plainly see from this verse, the followers of Isa are called Muslims. Now, listen to this verse:

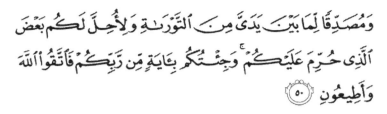

Qur'an 3:50 And [I have come] confirming what was before me of the Torah and to make lawful for you some of what was forbidden to you. And I have come to you with a sign from your Lord, so fear Allah and obey me.

"This verse says, 'Obey Isa.' What did Isa command? He commanded baptism as a sign of genuine repentance. I repented and became a follower of Isa. In getting baptized, I was following the Qur'an in obeying Isa."

Saleh turned red. He pointed an angry finger at Abdullah and screamed, "You are a blasphemer. Don't you know Christians worship three gods: God the Father, Mary, and Isa?"

Abdullah burst out laughing. "Where did you get that ridiculous notion?"

"It's true. That's what Christians believe!" As Saleh's fury grew, Abdullah's confidence increased, making Saleh even angrier.

"You haven't studied what Christians believe. You only know what our Muslim teachers told us. No Christian believes that the Trinity is God the Father, Mary, and Isa. Get your facts straight if you are going to criticize something. Otherwise, you look like a fool! I have read both the Taurat and the Injil, and both teach God is one." [141]

"I don't know about that, but I do know this: God does not have a son." [142]

Abdullah chuckled. "Everyone knows God is spirit: He could never have a biological son. The Qur'an calls Isa Kalimatullah, the

---

[141] Deut. 6:4, Mark 12:29

[142] Qur'an 72:3, 112:3

Word of God.[143] The Injil also says Isa is the Word of God.[144] God is eternal and His Word is eternal. God's Word cannot be separated from Himself. As I just said, Isa is that Word according to both the Qur'an and the Injil. Isa is called the Son of God not because He is a biological son, but because the eternal Word dwelt in the person of Isa Al Masih."

Saleh looked incredulous. "Isa was just a man, but Christians made him a god!"

"You're wrong again," Abdullah replied calmly. "Isa was not just a man. The Injil says 'in Him the fullness of deity dwells in bodily form'." [145]

"That is nonsense," Saleh scoffed. "How can that be?"

"I have no idea. But not understanding something doesn't make it untrue. Take gravity, for example. I don't understand how it works but I know gravity is true. Why do you think the older I get, the harder it is for me to get out of this chair?" Abdullah tried to lighten the atmosphere with a joke, but Saleh and his friends were in no laughing mood.

"You are wrong on something else. Isa didn't die," Saleh stated confidently. "God would never allow a prophet to be killed!"

Abdullah pointed to the Qur'an in front of him. "Have you never read this? Ten times it says, 'and they killed the prophets.' [146] Who were these prophets? Clearly Isa was one of them."

"Consider Ali Imran 54–55."

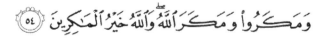

---

[143] Qur'an 3:45; 4:171, 19:34

[144] John 1:1–4, 14

[145] Col. 2:9

[146] Appendix J.

إِذْ قَالَ ٱللَّهُ يَـٰعِيسَىٰٓ إِنِّى مُتَوَفِّيكَ وَرَافِعُكَ إِلَىَّ وَمُطَهِّرُكَ مِنَ ٱلَّذِينَ كَفَرُواْ وَجَاعِلُ ٱلَّذِينَ ٱتَّبَعُوكَ فَوْقَ ٱلَّذِينَ كَفَرُوٓاْ إِلَىٰ يَوْمِ ٱلْقِيَـٰمَةِ ثُمَّ إِلَىَّ مَرْجِعُكُمْ فَأَحْكُمُ بَيْنَكُمْ فِيمَا كُنتُمْ فِيهِ تَخْتَلِفُونَ ۝

Qur'an 3:54–55 They plotted and schemed, but so did GOD, and GOD is the best schemer. Thus, GOD said, "O Jesus, I am terminating your life, raising you to Me, and ridding you of the disbelievers. I will exalt those who follow you above those who disbelieve, till the Day of Resurrection. Then to Me is the ultimate destiny of all of you, then I will judge among you regarding your disputes." [147]

"The 'disbelievers' here are the unbelieving Jews who wanted to kill Isa. This says Allah had the best plan, to 'mutawaffika' (kill) Isa, *then* raise Him up to God and exalt those who follow Him above those who disbelieve. Our Indonesian translation softens the wording, but mutawaffika in the Arabic means 'kill,' or 'cause to die.'

"The Jews planned to kill Isa and leave Him dead, but Allah's 'best plan' was for the Romans to kill Isa and then for God to raise him up and make those who follow Isa superior to those who disbelieve. This is perfectly consistent with the Injil, which says Isa died on a cross."

Abdullah sat back in his chair and let Saleh ponder his words. The late afternoon sun radiated heat into the already hot room. "Think back to what we learned at the Muslim boarding school. God has given us signs to guide us. If we neglect these signs we will be 'companions of the fire' in hell.[148] Ali Imran says Isa is a sign from God. Seventeen times a day we pray, 'show us the Straight Way.' [149] The Injil says Isa is the way. In other words, Isa is a sign from God and Isa is the Straight Way. He is the answer to our prayers!"

---

[147] *Qur'an: The Final Testament* translated by Rashad Khalifa (Tucson, AZ; Universal Unity; 3rd edition, January 2001).

[148] Qur'an 7:36, 40 Yusuf Ali translation.

[149] Qur'an 1:6

Saleh was stumped. Abdullah had countered all his accusations. Anger boiled within him until he exploded, "The Christians have bewitched you. No one in their right mind would believe this!"

Abdullah responded passionately, "Do I sound like a crazy man? Look at me. We have known each other since Muslim boarding school. We did everything together. We trained in Afghanistan together. We fought in Maluku together. We have the same goal, to honor God and bring forth His Kingdom, but we were going about it the wrong way!

"You want to establish an Islamic government. What is that? It is where God rules. I want God to rule on this earth just as much as you do. We both want everyone to submit to Him. But violence and killing people isn't God's way. Have you forgotten the ninety-nine beautiful names of God? God is loving, merciful, compassionate, kind, gracious, forgiving, forbearing, and bountiful.

"God's way is the way of love, not the way of violence. Violence only begets violence. It never ends. Love is different. Love changes people from the inside. Love conquers hate. Can't you see this, Saleh? Isa never killed anyone, never led an army, never held political office, never owned a home. He was a spiritual teacher who taught the way of God, the way of love. Please read the Injil with me and you will see for yourself," Abdullah pleaded earnestly.

The veins of Saleh's neck bulged. "You have insulted Islam! You are a traitor and an infidel. You must die!"

As if on command, the five men with Saleh stood up and began dragging Abdullah toward the front door. Titin, who had been listening behind the curtain, rushed into the front room. "Please stop! STOP!"

She grabbed Saleh and tried to pull his arm off her husband. "Abdullah has changed. For once in his life he is happy. Do you want him to be miserable like you? He is so loving now because he has experienced God's forgiveness and mercy. Please stop!"

Saleh pushed Titin to the ground as they dragged Abdullah into the yard. As the men hit and kicked Abdullah repeatedly, they yelled,

"Allahu akbar![150] Allahu akbar!" Soon a crowd gathered, horrified but unwilling to stop the six men.

Abdullah lay face down in the dirt as the blows rained down on him. Blood flowed from his arms, back, and legs. Saleh took his foot and rolled Abdullah on his back. Blood was pouring from his nose, mouth, and ears.

Saleh raised his foot and slammed it as hard as he could into Abdullah's side, breaking several ribs and puncturing his lungs. Abdullah gasped for air, but each breath sent a stabbing pain through his lungs and body. He could feel his life ebbing away.

A heavy rock landed on Abdullah's leg, shattering his knee.

Saleh grabbed a piece of wood and stood over Abdullah. Their eyes locked, and time stood still—Saleh's eyes blazing with anger and hate; Abdullah's overflowing with love and compassion. Then Saleh raised the piece of wood over his head. Abdullah thought, *Your name means devout; you think you are serving God but it is not based on knowledge.* Abdullah coughed and blood spurted from his mouth. He cried out as loudly as he could, "Father, forgive Saleh. He doesn't know what he is doing."

The wood crashed down on Abdullah's temple, ending his life.[151]

Titin shrieked and rushed to Abdullah's lifeless body. She pulled his bloodied head onto her lap and sobbed as she rocked back and forth. Through her tears she cried out, "Abdullah is in a better place, God. But what is going to happen to me?"

Titin cradled Abdullah's body as his killers congratulated themselves on their brave deed. "Let's go destroy some of the cafes in our city," one urged. "They should know better than to sell alcohol. Are you coming?" he asked Saleh.

"NO!" Saleh turned and ran down the street into the nearby woods, where he fell to his knees crying, "What have I done? What have I done? How could he forgive me after what I did to him? Is Abdullah right, that the way of God is the way of love?"

---

[150] Arabic for "Allah is great."

[151] In December 2012, an Indonesian church planter was beaten to death because of his efforts to reach Muslims.

* * *

The moment Abdullah's spirit left his body, he was surrounded by a warm radiant light. He was greeted by his Savior and Friend, Isa Al Masih, accompanied by a vast multitude.

"Where are You taking me?" asked Abdullah.

"To heaven, where I have prepared a place for you.[152] Well done, good and faithful servant." [153]

"And who are these others?

"My faithful witnesses who have preceded you," [154] said Isa.

---

[152] John 14:1–6
[153] Matt. 25:21
[154] Heb. 12:1

Discuss and apply

1. How did you obey what you concluded God wanted you to do from the previous chapter?

2. After reading this chapter, how do you feel about the persecution you might face?

3. Saleh made several accusations against Abdullah. How did Abdullah respond to each of these:
   - getting baptized,
   - being a Christian,
   - Jesus didn't die on the cross,
   - the Trinity, and
   - Jesus as the Son of God.

4. Do you agree with Abdullah that the way of God is the way of love? What proof would you offer?

5. How do you think Abdullah was able to forgive Saleh? How might forgiveness be a key to unlock the hardness of heart in some Muslims?

6. Share what you believe God wants you to do in the next 24–48 hours from what you learned in this chapter.

7. Pray together that God would prepare believers to suffer, and that He would strengthen those you know who are already experiencing persecution.

33

Suffering Persecution

Nasrudin is arrested and stands trial[155]

Nasrudin placed the last bottle of honey in the pouch on the side of the motorcycle, and closed and latched the top. Just then two policemen walked into his yard.

"Would you care to buy some honey?"

"Are you Nasrudin?"

"Yes."

"You're under arrest for proselytizing."

Nasrudin had known this day was coming. Even before Abdullah had been killed, he knew he was being watched.

The policemen handcuffed Nasrudin and led him to their police car. At the police station, they took him to an interrogation room. Nothing hung on the walls except pictures of the president and vice president of Indonesia. In the center of the room was a plain table with a chair on either side.

Nasrudin sat in one chair and a policeman sat in the other. The second policeman stood behind his colleague and glared at Nasrudin.

"This is where we find out what really happened!" The seated policeman put his hands on the table and suddenly shoved it into Nasrudin, knocking him over backwards. Nasrudin's head hit the tile floor and he was knocked unconscious momentarily.

---

[155] This follows closely an actual trial which occurred in Indonesia.

The policeman stood and walked around to where Nasrudin lay on the floor, unable to move because of his handcuffs. He gave two powerful kicks to Nasrudin's side, then grabbed his handcuffs and hauled him back onto the chair.

He pulled out his gun and held it by the barrel. He placed the handle of the gun next to Nasrudin's temple and then pulled his arm back to strike Nasrudin. Nasrudin closed his eyes and awaited the impact, but after a few seconds the policeman put the gun back in its holster.

Then he returned to his seat and said, "Now you know what we can do if you don't tell us the truth. So, tell me what you did."

"I don't know why I'm here." Nasrudin was beaten several more times. Each time he gave the same answer. Finally the policemen took him to a cell, unlocked the handcuffs, pushed him inside, and slid the heavy door shut.

Nasrudin's head was throbbing. His arms, legs, and sides ached from repeated beatings. The two-bunk cell was crowded with six prisoners, including himself. In the corner was a squat toilet that looked like it hadn't been cleaned in years. In this hot weather, the stench from the toilet and the other prisoners was unbearable.

The biggest man in the cell walked up to Nasrudin, said, "Welcome," then hit Nasrudin hard in the stomach.

Nasrudin fell down, gasping for air. "Why did you do that?"

"My name's the 'Boss.' I want you to know who is in charge here." Nasrudin later learned this man was in prison for murder, while the others were there for theft and drug use.

The beds didn't have mattresses, and were claimed by the strongest prisoners. Everyone else slept on the floor.

After Nasrudin woke from a fitful night of sleep, Amina arrived with food which she slipped between the bars. As soon as she was gone, the Boss grabbed it from Nasrudin's hands. "Nice of your wife to bring me food!"

So Nasrudin ate the grimy prison food.

Several days passed. Each morning Amina would bring food, then as soon as she left the Boss would take it. The prison food Nasrudin ate wasn't prepared properly, and he became sick with vomiting and uncontrollable dysentery. One day he was so weak he couldn't pull himself to the toilet, and soiled himself.

Amina saw that Nasrudin was getting frail and pleaded with the police to call a doctor for him, but they were unsympathetic. "No doctor would go in there. Those are violent criminals."

As Nasrudin grew weaker, Amina grew more desperate. Finally she brought antibiotics to the police station and demanded, "Let me into Nasrudin's cell to administer these antibiotics."

An officer let Amina into the cell. After receiving the IV, Nasrudin's diarrhea and vomiting stopped, and he began regaining his strength.

One day Amina was granted permission to visit Nasrudin alone in the interrogation room.

"How are you doing?"

"My body is still really weak, but my spirit is very strong. We can't do anything in those cells. At first I was bored, but then I started using the time to pray and worship. I have been able to meditate on the Scriptures I've memorized.

"Hebrews 10:32–35 has become very precious to me. Please remind our friends of this:

> But recall the former days when, after you were enlightened, you endured a hard struggle with sufferings, sometimes being publicly exposed to reproach and affliction, and sometimes being partners with those so treated. For you had compassion on those in prison, and you joyfully accepted the plundering of your property, since you knew that you yourselves had a better possession and an abiding one. Therefore do not throw away your confidence, which has a great reward.

"God has brought me to the place where I can honestly rejoice at being considered worthy to suffer disgrace for Isa's name.[156] I had always hoped I could rejoice if I suffered for Him, and I honestly can.

---

[156] Acts 5:49

God has been so real in this place. I know our friends are praying for me, please tell them His grace really is sufficient." [157]

"We are praying for you constantly, and doing all we can to get you out of here. We have hired a defense attorney for you."

"Please pray for my witness here. I have never met men who are so hopeless and helpless. I'm beginning to think God sent me here to share with them.

"And one more thing, ask our friends not to visit me, and not to attend my trial. There is no reason for them to be linked to me."

* * *

News of the trial dominated the local newspaper for weeks, so when the day came the visitor's gallery was packed as Nasrudin was led into the courtroom, hands and legs shackled. Several reporters sat in one corner.

The three judges each wore a black robe with a white tie, a legacy of the Dutch colonial period. After opening statements from the prosecutor and the defense attorney, the head judge directed the prosecutor to call the first witness.

The woman was in her mid-forties. She testified that when she was sick Nasrudin prayed for her in the name of Isa.

The second witness was in his mid-thirties. He appeared very poor, and was clearly nervous at being the center of attention. He testified that Nasrudin had paid the school fees for his son when they fell on hard times, and that Nasrudin had explained that when he helped others he was doing it unto Isa.[158]

The third witness was an old woman who needed help walking. She told the court Nasrudin had lifted a heavy object for her and explained that Isa came as a servant so he tried to follow His example.

The fourth witness testified that Nasrudin had warned his son not to use drugs and alcohol, to avoid premarital sex, telling his son if he was weak Isa would help him.

Lastly Saleh was called to the stand.

---

[157] 2 Cor. 12:9
[158] Matt. 25:32–46

According to Saleh's testimony, Nasrudin was really a shaman who had directed an evil spirit to attack Abdullah's son, then came to Abdullah's house and pretended he could cast out demons. Since Nasrudin sent the demon in the first place it was easy for him to cast it out. Nasrudin had also cast a spell on Abdullah, and tricked him into reading the Taurat and Injil. Abdullah was powerless against this spell, and even agreed to be baptized.

When Saleh mentioned baptism, the crowd became restless. Suddenly the back doors of the courthouse burst open, and several men carried in a coffin. The crowd chanted, "DEATH TO NASRUDIN! DEATH TO NASRUDIN!"

The judges looked nervously at the crowd, and motioned the policemen to the front of the courtroom. The officers faced the crowd, patting their rifles. The crowd continued to shout while the judges waited for order to be re-established. After about 30 minutes, the crowd quieted down.

The defense attorney then called Nasrudin to the stand. Nasrudin prayed silently, *Lord, you promised to give us wisdom when we are called before kings and rulers.* [159] *I really need that wisdom now.*

"Is it true you prayed for this woman in the name of Isa?"

"Yes, I did. Is it a crime in this country to pray for people? Doesn't our constitution guarantee freedom of religion? I can't pray like a Hindu or Buddhist prays. I can only pray in the way I know how, in the name of Isa."

"Did you offer to help someone financially if they followed Isa?"

"No. I never put conditions on helping people. Isa taught that God sends rain on the just and the unjust.[160] I try to obey His commands and do good to everyone. I believe we are blessed to bless others."

"Do you want to say anything further in your defense?"

"Yes. I am here today because I believe what the Qur'an says about Isa. He was born of a virgin, healed the sick, raised the dead, was

---

[159] Matt. 10:18–20

[160] Matt. 5:45

taken into heaven and will return as the final judge. I believe all these things are true.

"The Qur'an says we are supposed to obey Isa. I don't do this perfectly, but I try.

"If it is a crime to do good to people in Isa's name, and if it is a crime to believe what the Qur'an says about Isa, then I am ready to be punished. Prove to me from the Qur'an where I'm wrong!"

The crowd again raised the coffin and shouted for Nasrudin's death. Eventually the crowd quieted down, and Nasrudin returned to his seat.

In his closing argument, the prosecutor pointed at Nasrudin. "This man is evil and dangerous. He preys on those who are weak. He is so clever he takes advantage of people, and they don't even know it. He is deceptive and manipulative. He offends Muslims everywhere, and insults Islam. He disturbs the peace, and violates the customs of our people."

The crowd burst into applause.

The defense attorney rose. "This man loves his family and helps those in need. He obeys the laws of our government. Nasrudin is a reliable member of his community, and an honest businessman. The prosecutor has presented no evidence that my client has been deceptive, coercive, or violated our culture. Men like this should be looked to as an example, not sent to jail."

The trial concluded and Nasrudin was led back to his cell.

Two months later the verdict was rendered: guilty of all charges. Nasrudin was sentenced to five years, and sent to a prison five hundred miles from his family and friends.

* * *

Several months after Abdullah's death, Titin's family forced her to marry a sick, elderly Muslim widower who needed someone to care for him.

Discuss and apply

1. How did you obey what you concluded God wanted you to do from the previous chapter?

2. How does the persecution in this chapter and the previous one help you count the cost of following Jesus? What gives you strength and courage to face persecution?

3. What did Nasrudin do when he was bored in prison?

4. Are you diligent in memorizing God's promises in Scripture?

5. If you were in prison, what scriptural promises would you claim?

6. What else could Nasrudin have said to defend himself?

7. Why do you think God didn't free Nasrudin?

8. Share what you believe God wants you to do in the next 24–48 hours from what you learned in this chapter.

9. Pray together that God would prepare believers to suffer. Pray also for those you know who are experiencing persecution.

34

Persevering Stubbornly

Faisal's team grapples with the brutality of persecution

Faisal and his team had gone from euphoria over several baptisms to despair after the outbreak of persecution. They decided not meet for a few weeks after the trial.

When they gathered again, Faisal observed that they were under a cloud of uncertainty and heaviness. He knew they needed to talk.

After opening in prayer, Faisal asked, "How is everyone feeling about Abdullah's death and Nasrudin's imprisonment?"

Looking around the room, Faisal saw fear, confusion, and shock on their faces.

"I can't sleep at night," Fatima said, "I'm afraid the police will come and arrest me."

"I feel guilty for not helping Nasrudin," Yusuf said. "I wanted to help, but I didn't know what I could do."

"I never expected persecution to be ... to be ... so painful," Faisal admitted. "I had this idyllic view that persecution is glorious and heroic, but it isn't like that. It is painful and degrading, and for Nasrudin it isn't going to end for five long years. He is all by himself in that prison, and we can only visit him once in a while. Everyone knows why he is there. Who knows what the other prisoners are doing to him. He may not make it out alive."

"I'm disappointed in our government for being intimidated by a handful of radicals," Yusuf added.

"I feel so bad for Abdullah's wife, Titin," Nur said. "She was forced to marry a man she didn't love. She cares for him day and night because of his sickness, and his children order her around like a maid. She never gets time for herself, but I've heard she is remaining strong in her faith."

Fatima looked at Amina. "My heart goes out to you. You are doing the job of two parents and trying to keep Nasrudin's business going. You must be so lonely, and your kids need their dad."

As the sharing continued, the group expressed their grief, fear, regret, and anxiety. The trauma had affected each of them differently, and they needed each other more than ever.

Faisal waited until everyone had finished sharing. "The best thing we can do for Titin, Amina and Nasrudin is pray."

After they prayed, Faisal said, "Listen to these words from Paul in Acts 20:22–24:

> And now, behold, I am going to Jerusalem, constrained by the Spirit, not knowing what will happen to me there, except that the Holy Spirit testifies to me in every city that imprisonment and afflictions await me. But I do not account my life of any value nor as precious to myself, if only I may finish my course and the ministry that I received from the Lord Isa, to testify to the gospel of the grace of God.

"Paul had a choice to make," Faisal continued. "He knew that bonds and afflictions awaited him in every city. We too have a choice to make. Are we going to disband and end this ministry, or are we going to go forward despite the knowledge that more persecution is likely?"

At first no one spoke, each counting in their minds the cost of continuing.

Then Nur said, "I don't think we can stop. The people I mentor won't stand for it. They know what has happened, but their lives have been so transformed they insist on continuing our discussions."

Yusuf's clouded expression gave way to resolve. "I keep thinking of all that Abdullah and Nasrudin suffered. As terrible as their suffering is, it is nothing compared to the suffering in hell. That will be worse than any suffering on earth, and it will never end."

"I know suffering is sometimes the only way to advance God's kingdom," Fatima said. "I don't understand it, but I know His ways are higher than our ways.[161] I intend to keep following the King and trusting Him regardless of what happens to me. If the value of something can be measured by the degree to which people are willing to suffer to obtain it, then when others see us suffering for Al Masih, they will know He is of supreme worth to us."

"When we suffer persecution," Nur reminded the group, "we are merely following in the steps of our Savior, all the apostles, and countless other saints through the ages. We discussed the dangers before Nasrudin and Faisal prayed for Abdullah's demon-possessed son, and we knew persecution and suffering were a real possibility. One of the critical elements of CPMs is recognizing suffering as normal for the follower of Al Masih. Our experience only proves God's Word is true."

"Would Abdullah want us to stop? I don't think so," Amina said with conviction. "He found what he was looking for! Every time I talk to Nasrudin, he is concerned first of all for me and the kids, and he is more concerned for the ministry than for himself. He always urges me to be faithful to what God has called us to do. He gave me Romans 8:18:

> For I consider that the sufferings of this present time are not worth comparing with the glory that is to be revealed to us.

"Amina has given us a good word. Consider what Paul wrote:

> For to me to live is Christ, and to die is gain. ... For it has been granted to you that for the sake of Christ you should not only believe in Him but also suffer for His sake, ... I have fought the good fight, I have finished the race, I have kept the faith.[162]

---

161 Isa. 55:8–9

162 Phil. 1:21,29, 2 Tim. 4:7

Paul was faithful to the end. We each face the same question, 'Will we be faithful to the ministry which *we* have received from Isa Al Masih?'"

As Faisal glanced around the room, each person nodded.

"I know we just prayed," he continued, "but let's get on our knees and pray again, rededicating ourselves to this calling."

"Father, I'm so afraid," Faisal's voice quivered. "I don't want to go to jail, or be beaten to death. But more than anything I want to be found faithful. Please help me to remain strong."

"When I think of all Isa suffered for me, I feel ashamed of my fears of suffering." Fatima wept.

"O Isa, you are so worthy of all glory and majesty," Yusuf prayed. "You are worthy of any sacrifice."

"I know my sufferings will never be in vain," Faisal prayed. "You are too wise to make a mistake, and too good to afflict needlessly. You have a purpose in everything You allow." [163]

"You have so radically changed my life," Nur prayed. "You have given me joy, peace, and abundance. How could I not love and serve You?"

"I want to be faithful to Abdullah's memory," Amina prayed, "and to the cause for which my beloved Nasrudin is suffering. Give me strength, O Lord. I can't do it on my own."

Faisal closed their prayer time. "Nasrudin is no longer working, so Amina's income is greatly reduced. Though small in number, we must serve as Isa's body in caring for Nasrudin's family.

"Amina has agreed to contact Nasrudin's regular customers and find out who is willing to come and pick up their honey. We will make a schedule to deliver the rest. Amina and Nasrudin have two children. I propose Fatima and I pay the school fees for one child and Yusuf and Nur pay for the other. What do you think?"

Everyone nodded their agreement.

"These children also need a male influence. Yusuf, what if you and I include Amina's children in activities we do with our kids?"

---

[163] Lam. 3:33, Rom. 8:28

"I was already thinking the same thing. We must demonstrate practically what Isa taught, that 'All men will know you are My disciples if you love for one another.'"

"Thank you all for your love and support." Amina said. "I don't know what we would do without you."

Discuss and apply

1. How did you obey what you concluded God wanted you to do from the previous chapter?

2. How would you feel if someone you discipled was imprisoned or killed for following Christ?

3. What would you say to Amina to comfort and strengthen her?

4. Any experience that produces fear is traumatic, but often we don't talk about it. Such traumatic feelings may become buried, but they don't go away. It is vitally important to talk about your feelings with others as Faisal's team did in this chapter. Have you been traumatized? Whom can you talk to about it?

5. Vision casting is a big part of leadership. What did Faisal do to help his team focus on the task God had called them to, rather than on themselves?

6. What would you say to encourage a new believer facing persecution? What verses would you use?

7. Knowing persecution often comes when others are being saved, are you prepared to pursue this kind of ministry? If yes, stop now and pray together, expressing to God your willingness to suffer or see others suffer for the advance of His Kingdom.

8. Share what you believe God wants you to do in the next 24–48 hours from what you learned in this chapter.

9. Pray together that God would grant new believers courage to face persecution, and strengthen those already suffering persecution.

35

Transforming Families, Communities, and Cultures[164]

The team explores how to respond
when culture and biblical values collide

When they gathered the following week, Faisal said, "We need to discuss the process by which our house fellowships become healthy, independent, and reproducing."

They all agreed.

Faisal continued, "Some of our groups have been through the Baptism and Spiritual Foundations studies, received baptism, and completed the material in *Steps to Freedom in Al Masih* and *Toward Emotional Health.* Now they are in the Acts studies. What is the goal of these Acts studies?"

Nur answered, "To observe what the early believers did in the first century, and to seek the Holy Spirit's guidance in how to imitate them now, in the twenty-first century."

"Excellent," Faisal replied. "What are some points we hope they will glean?"

"Reliance on the Holy Spirit," Amina said, "leading to boldness in sharing their faith, strength in persecution, and diligence in prayer."

---

164 The progression of studies listed in this chapter is outlined graphically in Appendix B, and detailed in other appendices.

Yusuf thought for a moment. "We also want their worship to be vibrant, and their application of Scripture to be genuine, leading to sacrificial giving and joyful celebration of the Lord's Supper."

"Most of our original groups have started at least one discovery group," Faisal observed. "I'd like to challenge each of our groups to believe God for bigger things. Let's adopt 1–2–1, that is, one house fellowship starts two house fellowships in one year."

The others nodded and Fatima added, "I think 1–2–1 should be our minimum. Some of our groups could start three or four groups in one year."

"Yes!" Faisal said. "Isa said to count the cost of following Him,[165] so let's consider the commitment we are making. Achieving our vision will be costly in time *and* energy. For 1–2–1 to succeed we must each *participate* in one group *and* facilitate another! If we neglect the group where we are a member, we may lack spiritual nourishment, support and prayer. But if we neglect to facilitate another group, no multiplication takes place."

"I agree," Nasrudin said. "This is a big commitment. To achieve our vision our members may need to stop other good activities."

Faisal kept the conversation moving. "After the Acts studies we have the End Times studies. These have two purposes. First, it is important for new believers to understand God's unstoppable plan to accomplish His unchanging purpose. In the beginning God created the heavens and the earth, and in the end Isa will return to judge all mankind. All the stories in between are little stories that fit into God's one big story. Who can tell me how this helps strengthen new believers?"

"When we see the big picture we understand that God has a plan, and that He has been working throughout history and into the present to fulfill that plan," Nasrudin said.

"Great!" Faisal said. "Second, we want new believers to understand we live in the end times, and embrace their responsibility to

---

[165] Luke 14:25-33

spread the gospel until Isa returns. After our End Times studies we have a series of Healthy Church studies.

"Then we move into discipleship studies, starting with a series on Character. These focus on issues like anger and humility, and each story suggests how to glorify God through healthy living in areas like health, nutrition, sanitation, budgeting, etc.[166] Next, we have studies on Healthy Families and Freedom from Fear."

"We should always remember," Fatima said, "when others see God changing our lives in practical ways, they want to know why. Our transformation opens doors to invite others to discuss stories about the prophets and Isa with us."

"Right!" Faisal said. "And in everything our groups study, we want them to look for ways to bless their community. We have been blessed to be a blessing. Our calling is to cooperate with God's Spirit to bring His kingdom to earth."

After the group reflected on this, Fatima suggested, "I think we should call our ministry a Church-Planting Kingdom Movement."

"Why is that?" Faisal asked.

"Our goal is not only to save souls and plant house churches," Fatima explained. "We also want to transform individuals, families, and communities in a comprehensive and holistic way. In this way, we are establishing God's kingdom right where we live."

"That's right!" Faisal said. "And how might God use us to transform our Sayang culture?"

"Aysha and her husband need transformation. They always have money problems. In fact, most people have trouble managing their money. I know Yusuf and I do. What advice can you give us?"

"Often the problem isn't lack of money, but lack of discipline in using money. When people gamble, smoke, or drink, they are wasting money and showing unwise stewardship."

"Another problem is people feel they need the newest electronic gadgets," Fatima added. "They buy the newest TV, gaming device, cell phone, and computer. There isn't anything wrong with buying

---

[166] Appendix I contains a complete list of these suggestions.

new things if you sense God's leading and have the money to buy them, but we need to obey Romans 13:8, which says 'Owe no one anything, except to love each other.' Unfortunately many people buy electronics and furniture on credit, and end up paying twice the original price because of interest. They would be much wiser to save for the purchase and pay with cash. Saving is an excellent discipline to teach our children, but parents have to set the example."

"Sometimes, seeing their friends and neighbors with nice things, people become jealous and want them too," Nur said. "They don't consider that different people may have different financial means."

"People often talk about increasing their income," Amina said, "but they could also decrease their expenditures. For example, children spend a lot of money on snacks at school. They could save money by bringing a snack from home. And instead of buying all their vegetables at the market, they could raise tomatoes, chilis, cucumbers, and other vegetables in pots at home."

Nur continued, "The specific issue Aysha and her husband are facing is paying for their son's circumcision. Her husband wants to throw a big reception, and invite all their friends and neighbors. He told Aysha that Sayang people like elaborate ceremonies. 'It is who we are!' Thankfully they decided not to circumcise their daughter after I explained that Isa's followers don't circumcise females. What advice should I give them?"

Yusuf thought back to his own circumcision ceremony, and remembered that his parents had incurred a large debt. "Aysha's husband is right. Having expensive ceremonies is part of our culture. But that doesn't mean we have to continue the tradition. Everything we do must be evaluated according to Scripture. The main point is not what the community expects but what the individual family can afford. They should not go into debt to have an elaborate ceremony."

"That is exactly what Aysha's husband wants to do," Nur said. "He wants to borrow money, and hopes someday he will be able to pay it back, but he has no plan for how he will do that."

"I have seen so many relationships permanently strained because someone owes money to someone else," Faisal said. "If they have to borrow money then they can't afford the ceremony. I know this seems hard, but being in debt causes lots of problems. Aysha's situation brings up an important point for us to consider. How do we respond when our culture collides with biblical values?" [167]

"It's easy to say we have to follow God's Word," Yusuf said, "but sometimes it's hard to do."

"Yes, sometimes it's hard to obey," Fatima added, "but we're always glad after we do, because God's plan for us is always best!"

"In the Great Commission, Isa commanded us to teach all nations to 'obey all He commanded,'" Amina said. "This may mean going against culture, but we don't have to do this in our own strength. The Holy Spirit dwells in us, and gives us supernatural power to obey."

"We are all in a process of growth," Nur added. "We need to create an atmosphere of grace, where people know they are loved and accepted, even as we urge them to live according to kingdom values. Isa told the woman caught in adultery, 'I don't condemn you. Go and sin no more.' In saying this, Isa was calling her to a higher standard."

Everyone nodded in agreement.

"We also transform culture when we redeem the arts for God's glory," Fatima continued. "We Sayang love our music, dance, dress, and, of course, our food! Our life-cycle ceremonies are also important to us, like when a mother is seven months pregnant, when she gives birth, at a son's circumcision, and in marriage."

"That's right!" Yusuf exclaimed. "These ceremonies are part of who we are, so we can celebrate our distinctive Sayang culture while adapting it to God's Word. God delights in variety. This is why He created so many rich and diverse cultures. We don't stop being Sayang when we choose to follow Isa. I'm proud to be Sayang *and* a follower of Isa!"

---

[167] As this book was being written, one key indigenous leader of our movement was divorced by his wife. He remarried quickly against the strong advice of his spiritual mentor. Another example of culture colliding with biblical values is cultures where fathers are trained never to apologize to their wife or children.

"Me too!" Faisal picked up his guitar. "Let's sing a Sayang worship song." He strummed a melody while Yusuf drummed the edge of the table. Soon everyone joined in the song.

As Faisal put away his guitar, Yusuf spoke up. "In many ways, Islam crushes cultures by teaching that everything Arab is superior, and scorning our cultural ways. But a follower of Isa appreciates his own local culture without accepting everything in that culture."

Fatima added, "I think it's up to us to create new Sayang songs and dances, and to adapt our life-cycle ceremonies."

Yusuf continued, "We have our Sayang culture, but we also live in a modern culture. Who among us doesn't have a Facebook page, or enjoy modern conveniences like a cell phone and a computer?

"But we also need to be aware of the dangers of modern culture. Pornography is readily available on the Internet. Some people take sexy pictures of themselves and send them to others. Others become 'friends' on Facebook with a former girlfriend or boyfriend and end up having an affair. Many parents don't know what their kids are doing because they don't understand modern technology."

Nur added, "As followers of Isa, we need to lead the way in addressing these problems in our communities. For example, we could both serve our community and expand our search for POPs by conducting a seminar on the dangers of computers and cell phones."

Everyone agreed, and Yusuf offered to talk to the neighborhood leader about using the community center to offer this seminar.

After closing in prayer, the group enjoyed a snack together and then returned to their homes.

Discuss and apply

1. How did you obey what you concluded God wanted you to do from the previous chapter?

2. Chapter 28 ends with a list of essential ingredients of a healthy church. If you are mentoring house churches, evaluate them according to that list. Which are present in good measure, and what is lacking?

3. Faisal suggested their house churches adopt 1–2–1. Explain this goal in your own words. How can the groups you mentor fulfill this goal?

4. Discuss why everyone should aim to participate in one group while seeking always to initiate new groups?

5. Do those to whom you minister have trouble managing money? What advice do you have for them?

6. How can people avoid going into debt?

7. Can you give other examples of cultural practices which collide with biblical values? How do you help those you lead to follow what the Bible teaches?

8. This chapter discusses local ethnic culture (e.g. life-cycle ceremonies), Islamic culture (e.g. everything Arab is superior), and global modern culture (e.g. Facebook). Give examples of each in your own ministry context.

9. How can you help transform families, communities, and culture in your context?

10. Share what you believe God wants you to do in the next 24–48 hours from what you learned in this chapter.

11. Pray together for new believers to be transformed from the inside out. Pray especially that they would have courage to embrace biblical values, even when those are different than their cultural values.

36

Training Oikos Leaders

*Local leaders learn about vision casting, pastoral care,
and multiplication*

Faisal glanced at his notes. The host was welcoming everyone to the retreat, explaining the schedule, and mentioning where the bathrooms were located. This was the first-ever gathering of local leaders from their little church-planting movement.

I teach every day. So why am I so nervous about talking now? It's the investment this group has made! Some traveled all night by bus to be here. One rode a motorcycle for twelve hours. Others made and sold snacks to save up money for transportation. Many in this room have suffered for their faith, though none have been killed.

Of course if they had been killed, they wouldn't be here, Faisal laughed to himself. *Nevertheless, many have experienced extreme social ostracism. I hope everyone feels their sacrifice was worthwhile.*

It had been nine months since Abdullah had been killed and Nasrudin had been imprisoned. Faisal had expected the movement to slow down significantly, but the opposite had happened. The ministry had exploded. *Maybe it's because we have experienced the worst—death, beatings, and imprisonment—and it hasn't broken us. In fact, the suffering seems to have purified and strengthened us.*

"Faisal, I'll turn it over to you." The host gestured for Faisal to come forward.

Faisal rose, cleared his throat, and walked to the front.

"Assalam wa'alikum."

"Wa alikum salam," the crowd answered in unison.

"Some people say a church-planting movement is a leadership development movement. I think they are right. Leaders are the key to seeing churches birthed and new leaders raised up. This movement will rise or fall depending on the quality and effectiveness of its leaders. That is why you are here; you are the future.

"During our three days together, we will enjoy worship, prayer, fellowship, and fun. Yes, I said fun! We are going to play some lively games. But most of your time will be spent in small groups where you will interact with people around a given topic.

"Since this is a leaders' retreat and we are actively developing new leaders, I'm going to invite Haji Ishmael to come and introduce our first topic."

"Assalam wa'alikum wa rahmatullahi wa barakatuh." [168]

"Wa alikum salam rahmatullahi wa barakatuh." [169]

"The most important aspect of a spiritual leader is his character. Character is who you are when no one is looking. Get into small groups, discuss these verses,[170] and make a list of what's important about a leader's character."

Haji Ishmael's age and status as an imam had added great credibility to this young group. He had also modeled a willingness to learn, and a commitment to studying and applying God's Word.

Some groups formed circles in the meeting room. Others went into the courtyard. Haji Ishmael walked around to monitor the groups, which were busy reading the verses, discussing them, and making notes. After an hour and a half, Haji Ishmael motioned for a guitarist to begin singing as a signal to call the small groups back together in the meeting room.

---

[168] Arabic for "Peace be unto you, with the mercy of Allah and His blessings" (a more formal greeting).

[169] Arabic for "And peace be unto you, with the mercy of Allah and His blessings" (a more formal greeting).

[170] Gal. 6:1, 1 Tim. 3:1–13, 4:12, 2 Tim. 2:24–25, Titus 1:6–9, 1 Pet. 5:1–4

"I'd like someone from each group to write on the whiteboard what their group discovered about character and leadership." One by one people came to the front, wrote down and explained their answers, and then sat down.

Haji Ishmael read the list. "A leader ...

- studies God's Word for himself and applies it,
- is patient, humble, and has a servant's heart,
- is faithful, reliable, and trustworthy,
- always speaks the truth,
- invites the Holy Spirit to produce fruit in their life,
- is loving,
- puts others first, and
- is willing to sacrifice."

"Good work. Let's take a break, then Dr. Hasan will facilitate."

Someone brought out glasses of water while others put out plates of snacks.

* * *

"A key aspect of leadership is vision casting," Dr. Hasan said. "A leader knows where he or she is going, and rallies people to that vision. Now do two things in your groups: Write out a succinct, measurable vision statement answering these two questions: 'What are you asking God to do among your people?,' and 'What does God want to do beyond what you are asking?' Then discuss how to promote this vision."

The groups soon discovered how difficult it can be to develop a succinct and measurable vision statement.

A guitarist began singing to signal the group to gather again. As before, someone from each group wrote their vision statement and goals on the whiteboard, and then explained them.

Dr. Hasan then read their ideas for promoting their visions:

- Everyone memorize it.
- State the vision before every meeting.
- Review frequently how their activities support the vision.
- Anchor the vision in Scripture.
- Assure people that when a vision is from God, He empowers us to fulfill it.

"Excellent! Now return to your groups and discuss this question, 'How will having a clear vision unify your group?'"

When the groups had returned and listed their ideas on the whiteboard, Dr. Hasan read:

- We need each other because our vision is too big to achieve alone.
- If a soccer team's vision is winning a game, all the team members must work together to accomplish that goal.
- Praying about the vision unifies our hearts.
- Small problems between people disappear when we focus on a common vision. When we don't have a clear vision, we tend to focus on what others do that irritates us. Pursuing a shared vision takes our eyes off ourselves and focuses us on God and what He desires to do in and through us.
- We cooperate together to fulfill the vision. For example, I might ask one of my teammates to go with me to meet someone.
- We celebrate successes and failures together.
- We encourage one another when we're discouraged.
- We all sacrifice to fulfill the vision. Common sacrifice unites people.

"You guys are brilliant! Now two more ideas to keep us on track.

"First, count what counts. In other words, we keep statistics on what's important. So we track the number of discovery groups, baptisms, and house churches.

"Second, diagramming. When you meet as a team, draw a diagram of who is mentoring whom. This helps everyone understand their responsibilities, and enables you to track your progress.

"Finally, remember this work can be difficult, dangerous, and discouraging. While some of our groups have multiplied to the eighth generation, others started strong but then stopped. Worldwide, up to two-thirds of the discovery groups that get started don't finish studying all the stories. Groups dissolve for a variety of reasons, but even when they fall apart the members often carry new life with them into other contexts. So learn all you can from good and bad experiences, and don't give up. If you persevere stubbornly, some of the groups you start will become healthy, independent, multiplying house churches. What could be more rewarding!

"One purpose of this retreat is to get to know each other better. After dinner, Inne will facilitate a prayer time. Then we will play some games, and have time to meet one another. In Al Masih we are one big family," Dr. Hasan said with a laugh as he touched his belly, "and hopefully a happy one most of the time."

* * *

The next morning began with worship and an inspiring devotional by Eka, who shared how God had healed her wounded heart. She then introduced Umar.

"Assalam wa'alikum," Umar said.

"Wa alikum salam," the group answered in unison.

"Before we start our next session, get in your groups and list the three most important things you learned yesterday."

Umar debriefed the sharing from these group discussions, then introduced Aysha.

"Assalam wa'alikum," Aysha said.

"Wa alikum salam," the group answered in unison.

"In the opening session, Faisal explained that church-planting movements are really leadership development movements. A third aspect of leadership is pastoral care. The people we lead must know that we truly care for them, that they are more than a project to us, and that we care about what is important to them.

"I'm here today because someone cared about me." Aysha smiled at Nur, who returned the smile.

"Please return to your groups, discuss these verses, and write down everything you learn about pastoral care."

Afterward a musician again stood and began singing to let the groups know it was time to gather in the meeting room.

Aysha read what they had recorded on the whiteboard.

"Pastoral care means …

- investing lots of time.
- listening twice as much as we speak. (We have two ears and one mouth.)
- listening without teaching.
- setting aside your agenda to show you care about their concerns.
- crying with the other person.
- having your schedule interrupted because people have needs at inconvenient times.
- praying together.
- being vulnerable so others will be vulnerable with you.
- inviting people to trust their heavenly Father even with things they don't understand.
- learning to speak words that build up, not words that are judgmental or put people down.

"Now we are going to do a get-acquainted activity. We start our storying times with two questions: 'What are you thankful for?' and 'What are your struggles?' I want you to ask those questions to a person you don't know very well. Then after you have both shared, pray for one another."

* * *

"Assalam wa'alikum," Sharif said after the next break.

"Wa alikum salam," the group answered in unison.

"A fourth aspect of leadership is multiplication. Faisal introduced this retreat by saying church-planting movements are really leadership development movements. Let's discuss how Isa developed His disciples. I have listed several verses on the whiteboard. Please read these verses[171] in your groups, and talk about how they apply to us."

Again a song drew the groups back to the meeting room, and each group wrote their observations on the whiteboard.

"Isa's method of equipping His disciples can be summarized in four words: Model, Assist, Watch, and Leave, or MAWL for short. In other words, Isa gave His disciples a model to follow. Then He assisted them to understand what He wanted them to do. Next, He watched them as they did it. Finally He sent them out to do it by themselves. I want you to return to your groups and discuss how well you are following MAWL. Use our two evaluation questions: *What you are doing well?* and *How you could improve?*"

* * *

The three days flew by. Before Faisal knew it he was again in front of the group, this time closing the retreat. "I can't think of a better way to end this retreat than with the words of Isa. Please stand as I read the Great Commission:"

> And Isa came and said to them, "All authority in heaven and on earth has been given to me. Go therefore and make disciples of all nations, baptizing them in the name of the Father and of the Son and of the Holy Spirit, teaching them to observe all that I have commanded you. And behold, I am with you always, to the end of the age." [172]

---

[171] Matt. 4:18–25; 9:35; 10:1,7,8; 28:18–20; Mark 1:9; Luke 10:1,17; 11:1; John 4:1–2; 13:3–5, 12–15

[172] Matt. 28:18–20

Discuss and apply

1. How did you obey what you concluded God wanted you to do from the previous chapter?

2. Faisal said a church-planting movement is a leadership development movement. Do you agree? Why or why not?

3. Haji Ishmael said character is who you are when no one is looking. What do you think he meant?

4. What would you add to the list of essential character and leadership qualities?

5. How have you seen vision unify teams you have served on?

6. What is your vision statement? How can you make better use of it within your movement?

7. Dr. Hasan said to "Count what counts." What did he mean?

8. What is diagramming? If you have used diagramming, how has it helped your ministry?

9. In your own words, why is pastoral care important?

10. What pastoral care does your ministry give, and how could it improve? What would you add to the list in this chapter?

11. What does MAWL stand for? In terms of MAWL, what do you do well, and how could you improve?

12. Many trainers will review the previous day by putting people in small groups and asking them to identify the three most important insights from the previous day, and then share these with the whole group. Why is this beneficial?

13. Share what you believe God wants you to do in the next 24–48 hours from what you learned in this chapter.

14. Pray together for the leaders you are working with to grow—in character, ability to cast vision, pastoral care skills, and effectiveness in equipping new leaders.

37

Contextualizing Jesus' Resurrection and the Lord's Supper

*New believers testify to being transformed
through Jesus' resurrection power*

It was still dark as Faisal and Fatima prepared their food. As they rode to the meeting place, Faisal shivered in the cool night air. As he parked their motorcycle, he could see flashlights on the beach below. Clearly others had arrived ahead of them.

Faisal and his team had invited all the fellowships to share a sunrise service together to celebrate Isa's resurrection. As each family arrived they placed their food together for sharing, then spread woven grass mats on the sand and sat down.

Yusuf stood and welcomed everyone. Then the group sang a worship song softly, so as to not attract unwanted attention.

As the first rays of dawn cast a golden glow across the horizon, Faisal faced the group. "God created man in own His image, for fellowship with Himself, but man chose to rebel and go his own way. Our sins separated us from God.

"How could we be cleansed from our sin? Only by a blood sacrifice. The Scriptures say 'without the shedding of blood there is no forgiveness of sins.' But not just any sacrifice was adequate. A holy God demanded a holy sacrifice, so only God could provide this sacrifice.

"So God sent Isa Al Masih, who lived a sinless life. At the end of His life, Isa Al Masih shed His blood on a wooden cross as 'the Lamb of God who takes away the sins of the world.'

"Let me read from Romans 5:8–10:"

But God shows His love for us in that while we were still sinners, Al Masih died for us. Since, therefore, we have now been justified by His blood, much more shall we be saved by Him from the wrath of God. For if while we were enemies we were reconciled to God by the death of His Son, much more, now that we are reconciled, shall we be saved by His life.

"These verses describe you and me; we are sinners, but God demonstrated His incredible, undeserved love for us when Al Masih died a cruel and painful death for us on a rugged wooden cross. Because we are justified by Al Masih's blood, we will be saved from God's wrath toward sin.

"Let's continue in Romans 6:4:

We were buried therefore with Him by baptism into death, in order that, just as Christ was raised from the dead by the glory of the Father, we too might walk in newness of life.

"Why do we celebrate Isa's resurrection? At the moment we decided to follow Isa, our fleshly 'old man' was crucified with Al Masih and buried with Him. When He was raised to life, we too were raised to life. We are new!" Faisal lifted his hands to emphasize this last point.

"We celebrate Isa's resurrection because of the hope it gives us. All our past failures, our pain, and our heartaches can be transformed by Isa. As this verse says, 'We can walk in newness of life.'

"The word gospel literally means 'good news.' Isn't this good news? We can be healed! We can be transformed! We can be victorious!" Faisal's voice grew louder with each sentence.

"Isa's resurrection brings us tremendous hope, but it also brings us a challenge. Because we are new, we cannot live as if we are still old. What does it mean for you to live as a new creation? Think about your family. Think how you treat your husband or your wife, and how you treat your children. Are you living as a new creation? Are you establishing new patterns of communication with each other?

"Think about where you live. Are you living as a new creation in your neighborhood? What is God asking you to do to serve your community?

"Think about where you work. Does your life demonstrate that you are new? Do you work hard? Are you honest? Do you keep your promises?

"Ephesians 2:10 has a wonderful promise:

> For we are His workmanship, created in Al Masih Isa for good works, which God prepared beforehand, that we should walk in them.

"The Greek word for 'workmanship' literally means 'masterpiece.' God created you as a masterpiece, a beautiful painting, an elegant sculpture, an expert handicraft." As he spoke, Faisal made motions of painting and chiseling a piece of word.

"Notice further that this verse says we were 'created in Isa Al Masih for good works!' We aren't created as a masterpiece to be looked at and admired. We are created to work. This isn't boring or dull work. God prepared specific works for each of us to do, uniquely planned and crafted for *us*. No one else can do the good works God prepared for you. Only *you* can do them."

Faisal glanced at the faces before him. Each one was tracking with him, thinking about what it means to walk in newness of life.

"Let me conclude with this. We celebrate Isa's resurrection because Isa was raised to life again. The message of Isa's resurrection is one of hope and challenge. Because of His resurrection we can be free from our past and we can be new in every area of our lives."

After closing in prayer, Faisal invited people to share testimonies of how they were walking in newness of life.

- A mother had stopped calling her children "dogs."
- A husband was taking time daily to listen to his wife.
- A businessman had stopped cheating his customers.

- A woman was teaching her neighbors to read.
- A father had asked his children's forgiveness for his outbursts of anger.
- A man had donated his extra tiles to a poor neighbor whose roof leaked.
- A couple had paid off their debts, and decided not to borrow any more.
- A woman confessed her tendency to be easily offended, and determined to start seeing the other's viewpoint.
- A man had stopped smoking, drinking, and gambling.
- A family was turning off the TV and eating together.
- A woman confessed she had lied so often she sometimes forgot what the truth was; she determined to speak only the truth.
- A woman had decided she would not circumcise her daughters.

Haji Ishmael walked to the front.

"Assalam wa'alikum wa rahmatullahi wa barakatuh."

"Wa alikum salam rahmatullahi wa barakatuh," the crowd replied in unison.

"We are now going to celebrate the Lord's Supper together. There are three aspects of the Lord's Supper:

- Past: We remember Isa's death on a cross and His shed blood which cleanses us from sin.
- Present: We celebrate our fellowship as members of the Body of Al Masih.
- Future: We will one day celebrate Communion in heaven with the Lord Himself.

"1 Corinthians 11:27–30 says:

Whoever, therefore, eats the bread or drinks the cup of the Lord in an unworthy manner will be guilty concerning the body and blood of the Lord. Let a person examine himself, then, and so eat of the bread and drink of the cup. For anyone who eats and drinks without discerning the body eats and drinks judgment on himself. That is why many of you are weak and ill, and some have died.

"Apparently some members of the church at Corinth were sick, and some had even died because they had taken the Lord's Supper without repenting of their sins. This is a grave warning to us too that the Lord's Supper is a sacred time. Only those who have been baptized and confessed their sins should participate. Please close your eyes and ask the Holy Spirit if there are sins you haven't confessed, and then confess them in your heart."

A guitarist strummed softly as everyone prayed silently.

"If the Holy Spirit has revealed that you need forgiveness from someone, or you need to make restitution for something, make a commitment to take care of that as soon as possible.

"1 John 1:9 states:

"'If we confess our sins, He is faithful and just to forgive us our sins and to cleanse us from all unrighteousness.'

"If you have sincerely confessed your sins, this verse says God has forgiven you."

Haji Ishmael asked several teenagers to come forward. With an Injil in one hand and a plate holding a piece of bread and a cup of juice in the other, he read from 1 Corinthians 11:23–26:"

For I received from the Lord what I also delivered to you, that the Lord Isa on the night when He was betrayed took bread, and when He had given thanks, He broke it and said, "This is My body which is for you. Do this in remembrance of Me." In the same way also He took the cup, after supper, saying, "This cup is the new covenant in My blood. Do this, as often as you drink it, in remembrance of Me." For as often as you eat this bread and drink the cup, you proclaim the Lord's death until He comes.

Haji Ishmael prayed, then motioned for the teenagers to distribute the bread and juice. When everyone had partaken, he offered a prayer of thanksgiving. "Let us stand and declare our *confession of faith*.[173]

---

[173] Our movement uses a modernized version of the Apostles' Creed, like this.

I believe in God, the Father almighty, creator of heaven and earth.

I believe in Isa Al Masih, His only Son, our Lord, who was conceived by the Holy Spirit, born of the Virgin Mary, suffered under Pontius Pilate, was crucified, died, and was buried; He descended to the dead. On the third day He rose again; He ascended into heaven, He is seated at the right hand of the Father, and He will come to judge the living and the dead.

I believe in the Holy Spirit, the holy Christian Church, the communion of saints, the forgiveness of sins, the resurrection of the body, and the life everlasting. Amen.

Inne instructed everyone to sit in small groups. "We are going to pray in small groups for specific needs. As you know, our brother Abdullah was killed because of his faith in Isa, and his wife Titin was married off to a Muslim man. She wanted to be here with us today, but she couldn't. Please pray for her. Also, pray for Nasrudin, who is still in jail, and his wife Amina. Pray that God will sustain Nasrudin as a faithful witness, and give Amina strength to be both father and mother to her children. Now share additional prayer concerns in your groups, and pray for one another."

As the prayers subsided, Dr. Hasan spoke, "Let's close by reciting the prayer Isa taught, as shared by Isa's disciples worldwide:

"Our Father in heaven, hallowed be Your name. Your kingdom come, Your will be done, on earth as it is in heaven. Give us this day our daily bread, and forgive us our sins, as we also have forgiven those who have sinned against us. And lead us not into temptation, but deliver us from evil. For Yours is the kingdom and the power and the glory, forever. Amen.[174]

Dr. Hasan patted his large belly and smiled broadly. "Let's eat!" The women arranged the food on a mat so everyone could fill

---

[174] Our movement uses a modernized version of the Lord's prayer, like this one.

their own plate. The children ate as fast as they could, then stripped their clothes off to swim in the ocean. One of the younger men climbed a nearby coconut tree and knocked coconuts to the ground. Someone hacked them open with a machete and passed them around to whoever wanted to drink the sweet milk. A couple of men brought out fishing poles and went to the beach to fish. Everywhere people gathered into groups, talking, and laughing.

Faisal and Fatima were engaged in separate conversations, but when their eyes met they both smiled. Despite many setbacks and obstacles, they had learned to love God and to love people. Because they had stubbornly persevered, God had used them to birth a small movement. Those who had gathered to celebrate Isa's resurrection had been changed and were enjoying one another. Faisal thought, *I wonder what our next celebration of Isa's resurrection will be like?*

Faisal turned and headed toward the shore, praying silently, "Now to Him who is able to do immeasurably more than all we ask or imagine, according to His power that is at work within us, to Him be glory in the church and in Al Masih Isa throughout all generations, forever and ever! Amen." [175]

---

[175] Eph. 3:20–21

Discuss and apply

1. How did you obey what you concluded God wanted you to do from the previous chapter?

2. Summarize Faisal's message on the meaning of Isa's Resurrection in your own words.

3. What did you find new in the way Haji Ishmael led the Lord's Supper? What did you like, or not like?

4. Do you celebrate the Lord's Supper in your churches? Why or why not?

5. Do you recite the Apostle's Creed or another statement of faith? How about the Lord's Prayer? Why or why not?

6. In this chapter, people gave testimony of how they were living as new creations. Look at the list. How does God want you to become more like Jesus?

7. Review the Critical Elements of CPM listed in Appendix A. What examples of these principles do you observe in this chapter?

8. Share what you believe God wants you to do in the next 24–48 hours from what you learned in this chapter.

9. Pray together for each of your team members' ministries.

APPENDICES

Appendix A: CRITICAL ELEMENTS OF CPM

**GOD has a VISION for our People…
so we pursue PRAYER and EVANGELISM…
for reproducing DISCIPLES, CHURCHES, and LEADERS…
until there is NO PLACE LEFT where Christ is NOT preached!**

God

1. CPMs are God's work for His Glory (Hab 2:14, Eph 3:20–21).
   The Holy Spirit is the One who authors and empowers CPMs (Acts 1:8).
   God gives a person or team a **vision** to reach a UPG/city/tribe (Acts 19:10).
   Our responsibility is to
   * **Seek** the mind and heart of God, and join in His work of reaching a UPG/city/tribe/nation.
   * **Pray** and **share** this vision toward seeing God raise up co-laborers.
   (This continuing process often starts with outsiders but always moves to insiders.)

2. God's Word must be the foundation for all belief and practice (2 Tim 3:16–17).
   (Put aside tradition.)

Prayer

1. Prayer, relationship with God, and intercession for others are the starting point for all ministry (Mt 22:37). Prayer and fasting are foundational (Lk 10:2).

2. Spiritual Warfare is common and necessary, especially where the Gospel is newly being presented (Eph 6:12).

Reproduction of intercessors is key.

Evangelism

1. Pursue interaction with individual unbelievers to find Persons of Peace who welcome you (and then the gospel) into their family or social network (Mt 10, Lk 9-10).

2. Employ culturally appropriate anyone, anywhere, any time evangelism that disciples people while they are still lost (1 Cor 9:19–23).

3. Aim to impact whole oikos (households, families, non-related people living together, relational networks, etc.), inviting them to discuss God's Word. Seek God to lead them into loving and following Him (Lk 10:5–8).

4. Present truth with God's power—heal the sick, and say "God's Kingdom is near you" (Lk 10:9).

5. Seek God's guidance in developing *Access Business* and *Access Ministry* (see table below) to multiply spiritual conversations with the lost in order to find Persons of Peace (Lk 10:9, Mt 10, Lk 9–10).

Help new believers to begin reproducing immediately.

Definitions	
Access Businesses	Businesses which open doors to a large number of new non-believers; usually mobile (e.g. selling door to door), whereas traditional businesses are usually in one location (e.g. a store).
Access Ministries	Access ministries address felt needs (e.g. health, sanitation, nutrition, literacy, agriculture, micro-loans, human trafficking) in ways that open doors for personal interaction with many new lost people. Both access and traditional ministry serve felt needs, but traditional ministries are often localized and involve a large financial investment, whereas access ministries are generally more mobile and require less investment.

Ministry Examples	
Traditional	**Access**
Library	Mobile library
School	Mobile classes (e.g. teaching literacy, English, etc)
Medical Clinic	Mobile teams sent out to check high blood pressure, give immunizations, etc.
Agriculture plot	Mobile teams that take soil samples and give advice about crops, pests, fertilizers, marketing, etc.

Discipleship

1. Disciple lost individuals and their oikos to follow Jesus. Aim immediately for them to hear and learn directly from the Father (Jn 6:43–45).
2. Teach them to love Jesus and obey Scripture (Dt 6:4–9, Jn 14:15)—especially the Great Commission (Mt 28:20) and the Great Commandment (Mt 22:37–40, Mk 12:29–31)—rather than human doctrines and tradition.
3. Model group discussion that relies on God's Word and the Holy Spirit rather than your presence (Acts 2:42–47).
4. Train new believers to expect persecution and suffering as normal for those who follow Christ (Jn 15:20, Lk 21:12–19).

Help those becoming disciples to begin reproducing immediately.

Churches

1. Churches are discipled oikos that becomes obedient *ekklesia*, often meeting in homes (Phlm 1:2), and transforming individuals, families and communities.
2. Scripture and the Holy Spirit are sufficient (Acts 2:42, 1 Cor 14:26) to lead groups in replicating disciples, leaders, discovery groups, and churches.
3. Healthy churches discern how to redeem local culture by embracing all they biblically can and pursuing obedience to God's word to transform and redeem the rest (Rom 14).
4. Obedience to the Great Commission (Mt 28:20) and the Great Commandment (Mt 22:37–40, Mk 12:29–31) motivates healthy churches to reach out to all segments of their own culture, as well as beyond their own ethnic group.

Help these new house churches to begin reproducing immediately.

Leaders

1. Leaders from outside the culture or household model practices reproducible by inside leaders (Jn 13:3–15), using the MAWL pattern: Model, Assist, Watch, Leave (with continued support from the background).
2. Outside leaders de-contextualize God's word from their own background to introduce new concepts/patterns for reproducible contextualization by inside leaders (2 Tm 2:2).
3. Aim for everything to be led from the start by self-supporting inside leaders (2 Thes 3:7–9) with on the job training (Phil 4:9).

A CPM is a movement for developing reproducing leaders.

Planning and Evaluation

- Seek God for a detailed, written vision for "What God will Do" until there is no place left where the gospel is not proclaimed (Romans 15:18–23). Continue refining this in interaction with others.
- Research and continue learning about the people God is calling you to reach.
- Plan specifically regarding prayer, Scripture discussion, evangelism (including *access business* and *access ministry*), and church formation.
- Candidly evaluate both strengths and weaknesses of your current team and efforts, and make necessary changes.
- Remain humble, available and accountable to God and to each other.

Appendix B: OVERVIEW DIAGRAMS

Our Harvest Cycle Adaptation of *Four Fields*
based on Nathan and Kari Shank's Four Fields[176]

Empty: How do we enter a new field?
Seeded: What do we say? To whom?
Growing: How do we make disciples?
Harvest: How do we form churches?

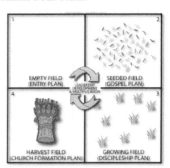

Our adaptation:

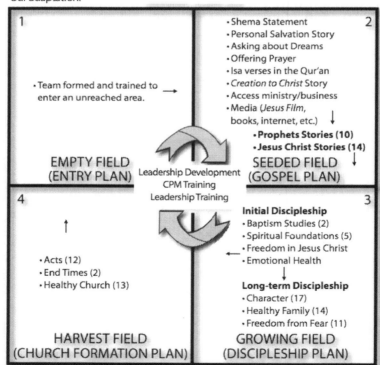

- **1** — EMPTY FIELD (ENTRY PLAN)
  - Team formed and trained to enter an unreached area.

- **2** — SEEDED FIELD (GOSPEL PLAN)
  - Shema Statement
  - Personal Salvation Story
  - Asking about Dreams
  - Offering Prayer
  - Isa verses in the Qur'an
  - *Creation to Christ* Story
  - Access ministry/business
  - Media (*Jesus Film*, books, internet, etc.)
  - **Prophets Stories (10)**
  - **Jesus Christ Stories (14)**

Leadership Development
CPM Training
Leadership Training

- **4** — HARVEST FIELD (CHURCH FORMATION PLAN)
  - Acts (12)
  - End Times (2)
  - Healthy Church (13)

- **3** — GROWING FIELD (DISCIPLESHIP PLAN)
  - **Initial Discipleship**
    - Baptism Studies (2)
    - Spiritual Foundations (5)
    - Freedom in Jesus Christ
    - Emotional Health
  - **Long-term Discipleship**
    - Character (17)
    - Healthy Family (14)
    - Freedom from Fear (11)

[176] Movements.net/4_Fields_nathan_shank

Our Implementation of CPM Principles

Disciple of Jesus → Looks for a POP → Person of Peace
(Lk 10:1)　　　　　(Lk 10:3)　　　　　　(Lk 10:6)

- Shema Statement
- Personal Salvation Story
- Asking about Dreams
- Offering Prayer
- Isa verses in the Qur'an
- Access ministry/business
- Media (Jesus Film, books, internet, etc)

Study CPM

New believers equipped to reproduce

POP introduces oikos to the message/messenger

Chronological stories
- Prophets (10)
- Jesus Christ (14)

New Believer studies
- Baptism (2)
- Spiritual Foundations (5)

Church studies
- Acts (12)
- End Times (2)
- Healthy Church Studies (13)

Freedom and Healing studies
- Steps to Freedom in Jesus Christ
- Steps Toward Emotional Health

Discipleship studies
- Character (17)
- Healthy Family (14)
- Freedom from Fear (11)

After the Jesus stories, men and women may meet separately through some or all of the *New Believer* and *Freedom and Healing* studies.

The oikos then resumes as a house church for *Acts* and further studies.

As others are later drawn into the church, or come to Christ without going through the prophet stories, they should be mentored privately through any studies they have missed.

Additional story and theme-based lessons for ongoing spiritual growth and maturity

Appendix C: CHRONOLOGICAL STORIES[177]

Most individuals and oikos start their study with the first Prophet story. Those eager to know about Jesus can skip ahead to the ninth (sacrifice) study and proceed from there, picking up prophet stories one to eight before proceeding to the Church studies. In our approach, those led to follow Christ through a *Creation to Christ* invitation proceed through all the prophet and Jesus stories before the Church studies.

See *Three Paths from Three Starting Points* at the end of this appendix.

Prophets story list

Story	Topic	Verses
1	Adam: Rebellion in God's creation	Gn 2:4–5,7–8,15–18, 21–22,25; 3:1–21
2	Noah and his family saved	Gn 6:5–8,13–14; 7:1–5, 17,19,23; 8:1–3,15–21
3	God calls Abraham and delivers Lot	Gn 12:1–5; 17:9–11; 18:1, 17–20; 19:1–17,24–26,29
4	Ishmael and Isaac born, and promise to Ishmael	Gn 16:1–11,13,15; 21:1–4,8–21
5	Burnt offerings: Abraham and Job	Job 1:1–5; Gn 22:1–18
6	Moses' commissioning, Passover and Bronze Serpent	Ex 3:1–8,10; 11:1,4–6; 12:21–23,28–33; Nm 21:4–9; Dt 6:1,4–5,13–15
7	David: King, warrior, and author of Psalms	1 Chr 21:1–2,5,7–19, 21–27; Ps 51:3–17
8	Jonah: Prophet who fled from God	Jnh 1:1–3:3
9 (start here for those interested in Jesus)	**Survey of the prophets: The importance of sacrifice**	**Job 25:2–6; Heb 9:22; Lev 17:11; 4:29–31; Gn 3:21; 8:18–20; 22:10–14; Job 1:4–5; Ex 12:21–23,28–30; 1 Chr 21:26; 2 Chr 7:4–5**
10	Prophecies about Jesus: the prophet born of a virgin	Isa 7:14; 49:6; 52:13–53:12; 61:1–2; Dt 18:17–19

---

[177] A Discovery study is facilitated using open-ended, general questions, and looks to the Holy Spirit for teaching rather than to a trained leader.

Jesus story list

Story	Topic	Verses
1	Birth of Jesus Christ	Lk 1:26–31,38; Mt 1:18–25; Lk 2:1–22
2	Power of Jesus over nature	Mk 4:35–41; 6:30–52
3	Power of Jesus over evil spirits	Mk 9:17–29; Lk 4:31–37
4	Power of Jesus over illness	Mk 5:21–42; Jn 4:46–53; Mt 15:29–31
5	Power of Jesus to forgive sins	Lk 5:18–26; Jn 8:2–12
6	Power of Jesus to help the poor and defend the weak	Mk 12:41–44; Mt 8:20; 23:23–28; Mk 11:15–18; 12:28–34; Mt 9:36; 14:14; 20:34; Mk 1:40–42
7	Ministry of Jesus Christ: give life	Jn 11:11–15,17, 20–26,38–44
8	Ministry of Jesus Christ: teach truth	Mk 7:14–23; Lk 15:11–24; Mt 5:43–46; 6:5–7; 7:24–29
9	Ministry of Jesus Christ: identified by His names	Mt 11:28–30; Lk 2:10–14; 7:11–16; Jn 1:29; 3:2; 6:35; 10:9–11; 12:46–48; 15:14; 16:33; Acts 4:12; Jn 18:36–37; 2 Thes 1:6–10
10	Death of Jesus Christ	Lk 22:47–54,63–65; Mt 27:1–2,11–14,22–25, 27–31; Lk 23:32–34,39–47; Mt 27:57–66
11	Resurrection and Ascension of Jesus Christ	Mt 28:1–8; Lk 24:13–35; Jn 20:24–31; Acts 1:3,8–11
12	Blood of Jesus Christ cleanses man from sin	Heb 9:22; Lev 17:11; Heb 5:1–3; 2:17; 4:15; 7:26–27; Mt 26:28; Heb 9:26; 10:10; 1 Pt 3:18; Heb 13:12; 2:9; Rom 6:23; Heb 2:14; 5:9; 7:25; 10:29–31
13	Jesus Christ as the mediator	1 Tm 2:4–6; Eph 1:7; Rom 3:23–26; 5:1,6,8–11; 2 Cor 5:18–21; 1 Jn 2:2; Col 1:20; Rv 1:5; Acts 17:30–31; Heb 9:27–28; Jn 14:3–6
14	Three responses to Jesus Christ	Jn 9:1–7,17–34; Heb 9:22; Lev 17:11; Jn 1:29; Heb 7:26; 10:10; Acts 17:30–31; Heb 9:28; Rom 5:8–9; Acts 4:12; Rom 10:9–10

Creation to Christ (C2C)

An *oral* version of *C2C* is useful in testing spiritual openness, as in Chapter 20.

When an oikos is *ready* to follow Christ immediately, perhaps after witnessing a healing or deliverance in Jesus' name, or someone starts attending a house church who doesn't yet know Jesus, a *written C2C* presentation may lead them to Christ.

Our written variation of *C2C* combines the ninth prophet story (about the importance of blood sacrifice) with a life of Christ gospel presentation summarized from these passages:

Matt. 1:18–21, Mark 1:21–27, 1:40–42, 6:45–51, Matt. 9:2–8, John 1:29, 1 Cor. 15:2–6, 2 Tim. 4:1, Heb. 4:15, 5:9, 7:25–27, 9:22, 9:27–28.

New believers are encouraged toward baptism and work through the *Baptism Studies* before proceeding through the Prophet and Jesus stories.

Three Paths from Three Starting Points

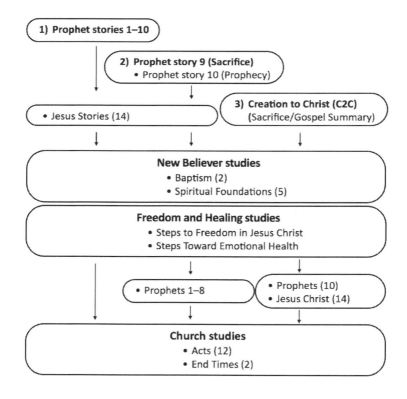

Appendix D:
NEW BELIEVER STUDIES[178]

Baptism studies

Study	Topic	Verses
1	Personal Testimony & Preparation for Suffering	Jn 4:25–30, 39-42; 9:1-7, 13-24, Acts 26:4–23, Jn 15:18-21, 2 Tim 3:12, 1 Pt 4:12-19, 5:8-9.
2	Meaning of Baptism	Mk 1:4–5, 9–11, Acts 2:36–38, 8:12, 8:26–38, 16:30–33, 18:8, 22:16, Rom 6:3–4, 1 Cor 12:12–13, Eph 4:4–6

Spiritual Foundations studies

Study	Topic	Verses
1	Discovery Study	Mt 13:10–17
	Role of Suffering	Jn 10:27–28, Rom 5:8–11, 8:1, 35–39, Eph 2:8–10, 1 Pt 1:3–6, 1 Jn 5:11–12, Jn 14:15, 15:18–21
2	The Great Commandment and the Great Commission	Mt 22:36–40, 28:18–20, Lk 8:38–39
	When we sin	Eph 1:7, Jas 1:13–15, 1 Jn 1:9, 2:2, Acts 19:17–20
3	Being Filled with the Holy Spirit	Jn 10:10, 14:12–13, Acts 1:8, Mt 12:28, Lk 1:35, 4:1, Jn 14:26, 16:7–13, Acts 4:31, Rom 5:5, 8:11, 1 Cor 2:12, Eph 1:13–14, Jn 16:14, Acts 2:38, 1 Cor 6:19, Eph 1:13, Jn 15:4–10, Gal 5:22–23, Rom 12:1, Eph 5:18
4	Hearing God's Voice	Ps 25:14, 27:13–14, 46:10, 118:1, 119:105, 139:23, Eph 5:15–21, Jas 4:7–10, I Jn 1:9, Eph 6:16, 1 Jn 4:1, Heb 13:17
5	Child in God's Kingdom	Jn 1:12, 8:1–11, 14:21,15:14; Rom 8:29; 1 Cor 6:19–20, 2 Cor 5:17, Eph 2:10, 4: 22–31; 1 Pt 2:9–10, 1 Jn 3:16–18

---

[178] These studies come immediately after the oikos decides to follow Christ.

Appendix E:
FREEDOM AND HEALING STUDIES

A Simple Guide to Emotional Health

We find emotional and spiritual health essential for the kind of personal transformation which multiplies and demonstrates the power of the gospel.

If you have been wounded, abandoned, neglected, or rejected, or you have experienced any other trauma, God wants to heal you and set you free.[179]

To experience the freedom Christ died to give you, you must be as thorough, open, and honest as you can, with both yourself and the Holy Spirit. You may find it helpful to write everything out in a notebook to focus your thoughts and create a memorial to what the Lord is doing in you. When you are done you may burn this as an offering to the Lord if you sense His leading to do so.

This author recommends involving a spiritual mentor in this process, as demonstrated by Fatima's presence in Chapter 30.

In preparation for this ministry:

1. Reread Chapter 30: *Discovering Freedom in Jesus Christ.*

2. Reread Chapter 31: *Moving Toward Emotional Health.*

Then with a spiritual mentor:

3. Work through *Steps to Freedom in Christ* in this appendix.

4. Work through *Steps Toward Emotional Health* in this appendix.

---

[179] 2 Sam. 22:49, Ps. 146:7, Isa. 45:13, 58:6, Luke 4:18, John 8:23,36, Acts 13:39, Rom. 6:7,18,22, 8:2, Gal. 5:1, Heb. 8:15

Steps to Freedom in Christ[180]

In war, you may use a sword. In spiritual warfare, our sword is the Word of God. Our enemy, Satan, is a liar and a deceiver. To fight him effectively, we must use the truth of God's Word.

1. Write out John 8:31–32,36 in your own words. Then write out and complete this sentence: "What sets me free is … ."

2. Read each of the following verses, restate them aloud in your own words, and place them under the appropriate heading (*What Christ accomplished or Who you are now*): Matt. 10:1, 16:19, 28:18, Rom. 8:16–17, 2 Cor. 5:17, Eph. 1:3–8, 1:13–14, 1:20–22; 2:4–6, 2:10, Col. 2:9–10, 2:15, Heb. 2:14, James 4:7–8, 1 Pet. 2:9, 1 John 3:8, 4:4, 5:18.

What did Christ Jesus accomplish?	Who are you now in Jesus Christ?

3. Write your own brief summary of Isa's authority to defeat Satan, and your authority in Christ.

Rats and Garbage

Rats look for garbage to eat. We can shoo them away, but they will return as long as the garbage remains. To get rid of rats, we must get rid of the garbage. No garbage means no rats!

Rats and garbage illustrate how evil spirits gain access to attack us, and what we can do about it. Evil spirits look for sin in our lives just as rats look for garbage, because sin opens a door for evil spirits to afflict us. We can cast out evil spirits, but they will return as long as we harbor sin in our lives. To end the supposed "right" of evil spirits in our lives we must "throw out the garbage."

There are at least seven categories of sins through which evil spirits can gain access to afflict you. Think of your life as a house, and these seven categories as doors into your house. After you cast out the evil spirits, you must also shut and lock the door if you want authority to keep the spirits out.

Praying in Preparation

1. Read 1 John 1:9. Write out this verse in your own words.

---

[180] This material has been adapted, with permission, from *Steps to Freedom in Christ* by Dr. Neil Anderson (ficm.org).

2. Write out this prayer to focus your mind on each point, then pray it aloud in your own words:

God, most merciful and gracious, I believe that Jesus Christ possesses all authority in heaven and on earth. I believe that when I abide in Him, I have delegated authority to bind and cast out evil spirits. In the name and authority of Jesus Christ, I bind every evil spirit which is in my presence now so that they may not manifest themselves during this study. I bind every evil spirit which would try to confuse or interfere in any way with this study. I cover myself now with the blood of Jesus Christ to protect me as I complete these assignments. In the name which is above every name, the name of Jesus Christ, My Savior and Lord, I pray. Amen.

Closing Seven Doors of Entry

Door #1 Involvement with the Occult

Explanation: Visiting shaman, prayer at sacred places, possessing talisman, speaking with the dead, making offerings to deities, using white or black magic, curses, etc.

1. Write out these verses in your own words: Acts 19:17–19.

2. Ask the Lord to reveal every involvement you have had with the occult. Make a list of everything He brings to mind, even if it was passive involvement (e.g. attending a ceremony).

3. Burn or throw away every talisman or other item related to your involvement in the occult.

4. Write out this prayer, confessing every involvement the Lord has revealed to you. Then pray it aloud in your own words:

God, most gracious and most merciful, I confess that I was involved with
  (occult activity) . Please forgive me.
In the name of Jesus Christ I now sever all relationship with
  (occult activity) , and cast it off completely. Amen.

Door #2 Deception

Explanation: You may believe things about yourself which aren't true. For example, you may believe you are more or less important, spiritual, intellectual, athletic, or wealthy, etc. than you really are. You may also believe something happened which never happened.

Or you may blame situations or others so you don't have to acknowledge and take responsibility for your own weaknesses or failures. To avoid appearing responsible, you may resort to excuses, rationalization, half-truths, or exaggerating your accomplishments while downplaying your weaknesses or misrepresenting situations. You may explode in anger so others will retreat or give in. You may think only of how you will benefit, without thinking about how your actions will impact others. You may harden your heart (shut down your emotions) so you won't be hurt again.

1. Write out these verses in your own words: Eph. 4:25, Phil. 2:3–4.

2. Ask God how you deceive yourself and write down everything God reveals.

3. Write out this prayer, confessing every deception the Lord has revealed to you. Then pray it aloud in your own words:

   God, most gracious and most merciful, I confess that I deceive myself by   (deception) .

   Thank you for your forgiveness. Renew my mind so my patterns of thinking and acting, and all my thoughts and actions, are based on who I am in Christ. Amen.

Door #3 Unforgiveness

Explanation: You may feel hatred, bitterness, or anger toward those who have hurt, frustrated, or disappointed you. You may even want revenge. Unforgiveness leads to anger, which opens a door for Satan to have a foothold in your life.[181] You must forgive those who hurt you, not because they are deserving of forgiveness, but so you can be freed from your pain and bitterness. (Trust God to punish the person who hurt you with perfect justice.)

1. Read each of the following verses, restate them aloud in your own words, then write a summary: Matt. 6:14–15, Rom. 12:19, 2 Cor. 2:10–11, Eph. 4:26–27, 4:31–32.

2. Ask God to reveal every person you haven't forgiven. Make a list of each person and circumstance which God reveals.

3. Write out this prayer, listing every person and offense the Lord has revealed to you. Then pray it aloud in your own words:

   God, I forgive   (name)   for   (offense) . Amen.

Door #4 Rebellion

Explanation: God has set the authorities of our world in place[182] (e.g. governmental leaders, parents, employers, older family members, religious leaders and teachers). Rebellion against authority opens a door for Satan to enter. However we must also listen to God ourselves, and obey Him even when the authorities over us disapprove.

---

[181] Eph 4:26–27

[182] Rom 13:1

1. Read each of these verses, restate them aloud in your own words, and write a summary: Eph. 5:21, 6:1–3; Col. 3:23; Heb. 13:17 1 Pet. 2:13, 3:1–6.

2. Ask God to reveal any rebellion you are harboring against the authorities He has placed over you. Write down each form of rebellion God reveals.

3. Write out this prayer, listing every rebellion the Lord has revealed to you. Then pray it aloud in your own words:

    O Lord, I confess my rebellion against ___(authority)___. Please forgive me.
    I choose to obey every authority you have instituted. Above all, I choose to obey you, the ultimate authority. In Jesus' name. Amen.

Door #5 Arrogance

Explanation: Our talents, abilities, experiences, and opportunities are gifts from God. We receive everything from God, and use everything to glorify Him. There are many symptoms of underlying pride: self-reliance, wanting praise, doing things to be noticed by others, thinking we are always right, putting others down, boasting of our accomplishments, being easily offended, or ordering others around.

1. Read each of the following verses, restate them aloud in your own words, and write a summary: Acts 12:21–23, 1 Cor. 4:7, Phil. 2:3–8, 3:4–8; James 1:17.

2. Ask God to reveal times and places in which you have exhibited pride. Make a list of every instance God reveals.

3. Write out this prayer, listing every evidence of pride the Lord has revealed to you. Then pray it aloud in your own words:

    God, most gracious and most merciful, I confess I was prideful when I ___(evidence of pride)___. Please forgive my arrogance. I choose to humble myself, and to base my self-worth on who I am in Christ. Amen.

Door #6 Sins of the Flesh

Explanation: There are many sins of the flesh (old nature), including drunkenness, pornography, gluttony, attempting suicide, or having an abortion. The more we give in to sins of the flesh the wider we open the door for evil spirits to come in.

1. Read each of the following verses, restate them aloud in your own words, and write a summary: John 8:34, Rom. 6:11–13, 13:14, 1 Cor. 6:19–20, Gal. 5:19–21, James 4:1, 1 Pet. 2:11.

2. Ask God to reveal your sins of the flesh. Make a list of each sin God reveals.

3. Write out this prayer, listing every sin of the flesh the Lord has revealed to you. Then pray it aloud in your own words:

Father, I confess __(sin of the flesh)__. I acknowledge that when I succumb to sin I become a slave to sin. Please forgive me. Strengthen me to live a holy life and always see the door of escape you provide. Train me to be constantly led by the Holy Spirit. In the name of Jesus. Amen.

Door #7 Curses and Generational Sins

Explanation: Evil spirits can enter our ancestors through their sins, then be passed down from generation to generation. Evil spirits also can enter through curses cast by others. Even if we had no involvement with the sins of our ancestors or curses cast by others, Satan can still take advantage of these "doors."

1. Read each of the following verses, restate them aloud in your own words, and write a summary: Gen. 12:3, 27:29, Num. 22:12, Deut. 23:5, Josh. 24:9–10, Pss. 25:15, 27:1, 109:28, Prov. 26:2, Luke 6:28, John 8:36, Rom. 8:11, Gal. 3:13, Rev. 22:3.

2. Ask God to reveal anything He wants you to consider regarding the sins of your ancestors and curses against you or your family. Make a list of anything that comes to mind.

3. Write out this prayer, then pray it aloud in your own words:

I reject and cancel all relationship with __(sins of ancestors)__, and any other sins of my ancestors. As someone who has been redeemed and moved from the kingdom of darkness to the Kingdom of Light (Col. 1:13), I sever all work of Satan that has been passed down through my family.

As someone who has been crucified, buried, and resurrected with Christ, and now sits with Christ in the heavens, I cancel and destroy __(curses)__, and every other curse and attack of the evil one against myself, my family, and my ministry.

I declare to Satan and all his angels that Christ became a curse for me (Gal. 3:13) when he died on the cross for my sins. I declare that I am a child of God, a new creation, and I have been sealed by the Holy Spirit.

I surrender myself to my Savior and Lord, Jesus Christ. In my authority as a child of God, I command every evil spirit to flee from my presence.

I commit myself to doing only your will, O God. In the name of Jesus. Amen.

Guarding Your Freedom

Daily Prayer

This prayer assumes you have already spent time in worship and confessing sin. It can be used to pray for yourself, your family, or others. Rewrite this prayer in your own words, incorporating, and adapting it as the Lord leads for use in your daily prayers:

> Heavenly Father I approach Your throne this morning not on my own merits, but on the basis of what Christ has done for me.
>
> Jesus, I thank and praise You that You paid for my sin on the cross. Through Your death and resurrection, You broke the power of the evil one. When You ascended as the victorious warrior, You publicly humiliated all rulers and authorities. You are now seated at the Father's right hand, with all rule, authority, power, and dominion in subjection under Your feet. I praise You that You have absolute power and victory over all the forces of darkness. You affirmed Your authority before Your ascension, when You declared, "All authority on heaven and earth has been given to Me."
>
> Father, I thank and praise You that I have been crucified, buried, and raised with Christ, and am right now seated with Him in the heavenly realm. Thank You for giving us the wonderful privilege of interceding for our loved ones and standing in the gap on their behalf. Today as I pray, I apply the victory which the Lord Jesus Christ has already secured to our lives. I do so in faith.
>
> In the name of the Lord Jesus Christ, I smash every plan and every scheme the evil one has made against me and __(those you are led to pray for)__ . I break every curse and every spell the evil one has cast against us. I render every plan, scheme, curse, and spell powerless today by faith in the name and authority of Jesus Christ.
>
> In the name of the Lord Jesus Christ, I declare God's presence and power in the present Kingdom of God, breaking forth in our community today to heal and deliver. I tear down every stronghold and foothold the evil one has in our lives and our community. I take back any ground that any of us, knowingly or unknowingly, have surrendered to Satan. Believing in Christ's teaching that what we loose on earth shall be loosed in heaven, I loose each one of us in any way we have been held captive, deceived, influenced, or confused by the evil one.
>
> By the same authority of the Lord Jesus Christ, I bind Satan in any way he would try to harm, tempt, deceive, accuse, kill, steal, or destroy us, or keep lost people from turning to Christ. I bind every evil spirit sent to hinder

God's Kingdom, or to bring accident, illness, terrorist attack, or criminal act against God's people. I bind Satan in any way he would try to disguise himself as an angel of light, or to interfere with, hinder, distort, hurt, or counterfeit the Holy Spirit's work in our lives and community today.

I submit each of us to You, Jesus, as our Lord and Master, for indeed You alone are worthy. I resist the evil one in any way he would try to work his evil plans in our lives. Submitting myself to God, in Jesus name I command Satan to flee from each of us. I cover each of us in the blood of the Lord Jesus Christ.

I invite You, Holy Spirit, to work in our community and in each of our lives today, perfecting what the Father has begun in and through us, conforming us to the image of Christ, leading us into all Truth, convicting us of sin, righteousness, and judgment, and using us to bring forth Your kingdom here on earth as it is in heaven. Fill and empower us. I give You free reign in our lives today, to work in us and through us for the Father's good pleasure.

Lord God, You are our Heavenly Father. As Your child I ask You boldly to encamp around each of us, and be a hedge of protection around us. Protect us from all evil, keep our soul, and guard our going out and coming in. Charge Your angels to be a shield around each of us. Assign Your angels to thwart every scheme, frustrate every plan, defeat every attack, and drive back and utterly humiliate every evil spirit sent against us today. Assign Your angels to remove every roadblock, hurdle, obstacle, diversion, and distraction the evil one will throw our way to keep us from obeying You today.

I put on the full armor of God around each of us, that we may stand firm against the evil one.

Lead us not into temptation, but deliver us from evil. For Yours is the kingdom, and the power, and the glory forever and ever. Amen.

Discovering Your Identity

Meditate often on these verses about your new identity in Jesus:

I am *Accepted*	
I am a child of God.	Jn 1:12
I am a friend of Christ.	Jn 15:15
I have been justified.	Rom 5:1
I am united with God and one spirit with Him.	1 Cor 6:17
I have been purchased and belong to God.	1 Cor 6:19,20
I am a member of the body of Christ.	1 Cor 12:27
I am a saint.	Eph 1:1
I have been lifted up as a child of God.	Eph 1:5
I have access to the Father through the Holy Spirit.	Eph 2:18
I have been redeemed and forgiven of my sins.	Col 1:14
I am in Christ.	Col 2:10

I have *Meaning*	
I am the light of the world.	Mt 5:14,15
I have been chosen to bear fruit.	Jn 15:16
I am a witness for Christ to the world.	Acts 1:8
I am a worker of God.	1 Cor 3:9
I am a temple of God.	1 Cor 3:16
I am an ambassador for God.	2 Cor 5:17
I sit with Christ in the heavens.	Eph 2:6
I am God's workmanship.	Eph 2:10
I can freely come before God.	Eph 3:12
I can do all things through Christ who strengthens me.	Phil 4:13

I am *Safe*	
I am free from condemnation.	Rom 8:1,2
I believe God will work all things for my good as I love Him.	Rom 8:28
I know God is for me.	Rom 8:31,32
I cannot be separated from God's love.	Rom 8:35–39
I have been sealed by God	2 Cor 1:21,22
I have been hidden with Christ in God.	Col 3:3
I believe God is working to complete His good work in me.	Phil 1:6
I am a citizen of heaven.	Phil 3:20
I was not given the spirit of fear but of love and a sound mind.	2 Tm 1:7
I can receive grace and mercy in a time of need.	Heb 4:16
I am born of God and the evil one cannot touch me.	1 Jn 5:18

Steps Toward Emotional Health

Make a list of your "sorrows" and "thankfulnesses," then follow this pattern:

Recall

- Remember the event in detail.
- Name the feelings, then and now.

Repent

- Forgive the people who wronged you.
- Repent of your own wrong thoughts, attitudes, and actions.
- Apologize to people you have wronged when appropriate.

Renew the mind

- Renounce the lies.
- Replace with truth.

Receive God's touch and respond to Him

- Verses or images.
- Thank and worship Him.

Appendix F: CHURCH STUDIES

Acts Studies[183]

Story	Worship/Thanksgiving	Acts
1	Ps 29:1–2	1:1–11
2	Ps 66:1–5	2:1–17,21–24,29–41
3	Ps 8:1–10	2:42–47; 3:1–26
4	Ps 3	4:1–22,29–31
5	Ps 9:2–3,8–11,17	4:32–5:11
6	Ps 16:5–11	5:14–42
7	Ps 18:2–6	6:3,8–12; 7:1–3; 7:51–8:4
8	Ps 18:31–37	9:1–31
9	Ps 22:23–31	11:19–30; 13:1–5; 14:19–23
10	Ps 23	16:13–40
11	Ps 4:1–8	19:8–41
12	Ps 29	20:16–38; 28:30–31

End Times Studies

Story	Worship/Thanksgiving	Topic	Verses	Memory Verse
1	Ps 31:2–8, 15–22	Signs of the End Times	Mt 24:1–14; 2 Tm 3:1–5	Mt 24:14
2	Ps 33:12–22	Second Coming of Christ	2 Thes 1:3–12; Rv 19:11–16; 20:11–15; Acts 10:38–43	Mt 24:14

---

[183] Starting in the Acts Study, the oikos learns to function as a house church by adapting New Testament practices. Appendix H presents a simple pattern for worship together as a church.

Healthy Church Studies

Churches become stronger when several oikos combine.

Lesson 1: Essential Church Ingredients

Verses: Jn 4:19–24, Acts 1:8, 2:37–47, 4:29–37, 6:4, 8:4–6, 8:12, 8:36–38, 11:27–30, 14:23, 18:13, 1 Cor 11:23–26, 16:2, Gal 6:2, Heb 10:24–25

Lesson 2: Mission of a Church

Worship/Thanksgiving: Psalm 73:23–28

Verses: Mt 5:13–17; 24:14; 28:18–20; Acts 1:8; 20:18–24; 2 Cor 5:18–21; Rv 2:10–11

Lesson 3: Evangelism

Worship/Thanksgiving: Psalm 107:1–9

Verses: Lk 19:10, Jn 14:6, Acts 4:12, 5:42, 16:5, 17:17, 19:10, 26:19–21, 1 Cor 9:19–23, Eph 6:19–20, Col 4:5

Lesson 4: Blessed to be a Blessing

Worship/Thanksgiving: Psalm 77:12–16

Verses: Mt 25:14–30 (A "talent" can be anything God has blessed us with. It can be a skill or opportunity, or your education, knowledge, possessions, and time. It is also good to consider this parable literally in terms of stewarding wisely what God has entrusted us so we will be able to offer Him more.)

Mk 10:45; Lk 12:42–48; Acts 20:35; Eph 2:10; Col 3:17

Bless your community

Every believer has been blessed by the Lord. Our most important blessing is the forgiveness of our sins, our assurance of salvation, the Holy Spirit, the love of God, and the Word of God. As we have seen from the verses above, those who are blessed are called upon to bless others. In other words, the blessed become a channel of blessing.

There are many practical ways you can bless your community. For example, you can volunteer at a local maternity clinic, repair roads, go to the market for someone who is sick. Decide as a group what God is leading you to do.

Lesson 5: Prayer and Fasting

Worship/Thanksgiving: Psalm 84:2–5

Verses: Acts 6:4; Mt 6:5–11; Lk 11:1–13; Jas 1:19–20; 4:1–3; 1 Jn 5: 14–15

A pattern for times of intercession:
- Honor God as our Father.
- Plead for His Kingdom to come in our lives and others
  (that is, God's will done in every situation):
  - Break strongholds to create openness among non-believers
  - Pray for
    - civic leaders,
    - church needs, and
    - those with whom you are and will be sharing the gospel.
- Remind God of your personal and family needs.
- Confess our sins and ask Him to forgive us as we forgive others.
- Seek His protection from the enemy's temptations.
- Honor God again for who He is.

Practice this method and memorize the Lord's Prayer together.

Fasting:
- The early Church often fasted and prayed to seek God's will.
- Many churches around the world fast once a week.
- There are many ways to fast. A fast can be 8, 12, 24 hours, or longer. You can fast from eating and drinking (most people still drink water), or fast from food while drinking fruit juices.
- Each person is free to fast according to their own convictions. Not everyone should fast. Those who are sick, pregnant, or nursing shouldn't fast.
- The goal of fasting is to pray more effectively, so plan extra time for prayer.
- Remember that fasting does not earn merit with God.
- Often, after members of a church have been fasting, they will meet together to pray, and then break their fast together.

When will we have our first fasting day?

Lesson 6: Word

Worship/Thanksgiving: Psalm 86:5–12,15

Verses: Acts 13:1–3; 14:23; Mt 6:16–18; 2 Tm 3:16

Practice the basic discussion pattern together.

Also, review and pray the Lord's Prayer together.

Lesson 7: Worship

Worship/Thanksgiving: Psalm 89:2–19

Verses: Ps 139:1–4; Isa 5:16; 30:18; 40:25–26; Jer 23:23–24;
2 Tm 2:13; 1 Jn 4:8–10

How can we bless our community?

Lesson 8: Offerings

Worship/Thanksgiving: Psalm 2:10–12

Verses: Dt 16:17; Ps 37:21; Prv 3:9–10; Mal 3:8–11;
Lk 21:1–4; 2 Cor 8:1–5,9,14; 9:6–7

Offerings:

1. Most people give 10 percent of their income at each weekly worship gathering, but people are often moved by the Lord to give more.
2. Our offerings can be money, rice, fruit, vegetables, or other things.
3. Our house church leadership will use our offerings as follows:
   i. 10 percent toward training of our church network leadership,
   ii. the rest for our ministries
      a) to help the poor,
      b) for celebrating Isa's birth and resurrection, and cultural life-cycle ceremonies like weddings and funerals, etc.,
      c) for transportation to our places of ministry,
      d) for people with financial needs such as medical expenses, funeral expenses, school fees, and
      e) for other needs.
4. The accounting and use of our offerings must be transparent.

Lesson 9: "One another" commands

Worship/Thanksgiving: Psalm 92:2–6

Verses: Acts 2:42; Jn 13:34–35; 1 Cor 12:25–27; Gal 6:2; Eph 4:32; Phil 2:2–4;
Heb 10:24–25; 1 Pt 4:10

Lesson 10: Word pictures of Churches

Worship/Thanksgiving: Psalm 95:1–7

Family: Eph 2:19–22

Body of Christ: Rom 12:3–8; 1 Cor 12:14–22,25–27; Col 1:18

Temple of God: 1 Cor 3:16–17

Chosen Race: 1 Pt 2:9

Bride: Rv 19:7–9

Lesson 11: The Lord's Supper

Worship/Thanksgiving: Psalm 96:1–13

Verses: Acts 2:42; Mt 26:17–30; Ex 12:1–13; 1 Cor 11:23–30; Eph 4:4–6

Application

Celebrate the Lord's Supper. All who have been baptized are invited to participate. (There is no "correct" method of celebrating the Lord's Supper. What follows is one outline which can be used.)

Introduction: Explain three aspects of Communion

1. Past: We remember Jesus' death on a cross, and His shed blood which cleanses us from sin.
2. Present: We celebrate our fellowship as members together of the Body of Christ.
3. Future: We will one day celebrate Communion in heaven with the Lord Himself.

Preparation: Invite each person to confess the sins in his or her own heart, and genuinely repent. The consequences of not being sincere in our repentance are great (1 Cor. 11:27–30). Suggest that any necessary apology or restitution be made after observing the Lord's Supper.

Celebration: Read aloud 1 Cor. 11:23–26, then pass the bread and juice. (Since these are just symbols,use what is readily available as basic elements of the local diet.)

Prayer of Thanksgiving

Have a printed or memorized Confession of Faith ready to recite together[184]

I believe in God, the Father almighty, creator of heaven and earth.

I believe in Jesus Christ, His only Son, our Lord, who was conceived by the Holy Spirit, born of the Virgin Mary, suffered under Pontius Pilate, was crucified, died, and was buried; He descended to the dead. On the third day He rose again; He ascended into heaven, He is seated at the right hand of the Father, and He will come to judge the living and the dead.

I believe in the Holy Spirit, the holy Christian Church, the communion of saints, the forgiveness of sins, the resurrection of the body, and the life everlasting. Amen.

---

[184] Our movement uses a modernized version of the Apostles' Creed, like this.

Lesson 12: Leadership

Worship/Thanksgiving: Psalm 97:1–6

Verses: Acts 14:23

Shepherd: Ez 34:1–6; Jn 10:1–14; 1 Pt 5:1–4

Servant: Mk 10:42–45; 2 Tm 2:24–26

Example: 1 Cor 4:14–17; 1 Tm 3:1–7

How will we bless our community?

Lesson 13: Discipline in the Churches

Worship/Thanksgiving: Psalm 98:1–9

Verses: Acts 5:1–11; Mt 18:15–17; 1 Cor 5:1–13; 2 Cor 2:5–11; Eph 5:1–12;
1 Tm 5:20; 2 Tm 2:21

Explanation

Follow these steps for church discipline:

1. Purify your motives. Why do you want to address this issue with this person at this time?
2. Ask clarifying questions of all involved, in an attempt to understand the situation fully and correctly.
3. Approach the person needing discipline with humility and, gently but clearly, point out where you believe he or she has erred according to the Word of God.
4. If the person is unwilling to repent yet you are convinced he or she is in sin, take along a second person and repeat the previous step.
5. If you are still convinced the person is in sin, and he or she is still unwilling to forsake the sin, bring the matter before the church.
6. If the person remains unwilling to repent, ask them not to attend weekly gatherings or other fellowship-related activities until they have repented.

Appendix G: DISCIPLESHIP STUDIES

Character Studies[185]

	Worship/ Thanksgiving	Topic	Verses
1	Ps 36:6–11	How great is **God's love**	Lk 15:3–7; 15:11–24; Jn 15:15; Rom 5:8; 8:31–39; Eph 2:4–5; 1 Jn 3:1 **Memory Verse: Jn 14:21**
2	Ps 40:1–6, 9–12	Who am I **in Christ**	Jn 1:12; 15:15–16; 1 Cor 6:19–20; 2 Cor 5:17; Eph 1:3,5; 2:6,19; 1 Pt 2:9–10 **Memory Verse: Jn 14:21**
3	Ps 46:1–4, 11–12	**Loving God**	Mt 22:37–40; Lk 9:23; Jn 14:21; 1 Cor 6:20; Col 3:23; Dn 13:9–28 **Memory Verse: Jn 14:21**
4	Ps 47	**Loving** others	1 Jn 4:20–21; Jn 13:34–35; 1 Cor 13:4–8; Lk 6:27–38; 10:3–37 **Memory Verse: Rom 12:18**
5	Ps 50:1–6, 10–12	**Serving** others	Lk 10:29–37; Mk 10:42–45; Jn 13:3–5,12–15; Gal 6:9–10 **Memory Verse: Rom 12:18**
6	Ps 56:9–14	**Humility**	Prv 12:15; Mt 6:1–4; 11:28–30; Lk 14:7–11; 1 Cor 4:7; Phil 2:3–4; 1 Pt 5:5–6; Dn 4:18–37 **Memory Verse: Rom 12:18**
7	Ps 65	Control your **tongue**	Mt 7:1–5; 12:36–37; Lk 6:43–45; Eph 4:29; Col 3:8; 1 Thes 5:18; Jas 3:2–12; Nm 16:1–3,28–33 **Memory Verse: Rom 12:18**
8	Ps 66	Control your **anger**	Jas 1:19–20; Prv 14:29; 15:1; 16:32; 19:11; Nm 22:20–35; Gal 5:19–23 **Memory Verse: Ps 66:18**
9	Ps 67	Attitude toward **possessions**	Dt 8:10–14; Prv 3:9–10; 11:25; Ecc 5:10; Mt 6:24–33; Lk 12:15–21; Rom 13:8; Phil 4:11–13; 1 Tm 6:7–10,17–19 **Memory Verse: Ps 66:18**

---

[185] These topics were chosen based on a worldview study of our target people.

10	Ps 68	Overcoming jealousy	Gn 37:2–4,12–36; Ex 20:17; Prv 27:4; Mt 20:1–16; Jas 3:14–17 **Memory Verse: Ps 66:18**
11	Ps 71:3–8	God's view of appearance	1 Sm 16:4–13; Ecc 5:15; Hag 1:2–14; Mt 23:5–7,25–28; Lk 12:15,22–34; 1 Pt 3:3–4 **Memory Verse: Ps 66:18**
12	Ps 34	Overcoming feeling offended	Prv 24:29; Mt 5:23–24; Mk 11:25–26; 1 Cor 13:4–8; Phil 2:2–5; Jas 4:1; 5:9; 1 Pt 3:9; 2 Sm 25:2–38 **Memory Verse: Ps 66:18**
13	Ps 71:14–24	Overcoming lust	Mt 5:27–28; 1 Cor 6:9–10; 6:13–20; 1 Thes 4:3–7; Heb 13:4; 2 Sm 11:1–17,26–27; 12:1–14 **Memory Verse: Phil 4:6–7**
14	Ps 51:1–13	**Gratefulness**	Lk 17:11–19; Eph 5:20; Col 1:12; 4:2; Ph 4:6–7,11–13; 1 Thes 5:16–18; Job 1:12–22 **Memory Verse: Phil 4:6–7**
15	Ps 27:1–5, 13–14	**Restitution/ Reconciliation**	Mt 5:23–24; 7:12; Lk 19:1–10; Rom 12:18–21; 1 Thes 5:15; Gn 50:15–21; Ex 22:5–6,14; Lev 19:11–18 **Memory Verse: Phil 4:6–7**
16	Ps 30:2–8, 11–13	Experiencing joy and peace	Mt 7:9–11; Rom 8:28,32–39; 2 Cor 12:9; Rv 1:4; 1 Jn 1:9; Rom 5:3–5; Jer 29:11–13; Ps 16 **Memory Verse: Phil 4:6–7**
17	Rv 5:9–13; 15:3–4; 19:1–10	Facing **persecution**	Mt 10:21–22; Lk 6:22–23; Acts 5:40–42; Rom 5:3–5; Phil 1:12–14,29; 2 Thes 1:6–7; Heb 12:1–3; 1 Pt 4:12 **Memory Verse: Phil 4:6–7**

Healthy Family Studies

	Worship/ Thanksgiving	Topic	Verses
1	Ps 99:1–9	Responsibilities of husband and wife toward each other	Jn 13:3–5,12–15; Rom 15:5–7; 1 Cor 13:4–8; Eph 5:21; 1 Thes 5:14–15; 1 Pt 4:8; 1 Sm 1:1–8 **Memory Verse: 1 Pt 4:8**
2	Ps 100	Specific Responsibilities of a husband and wife	Ps 23:4; 1 Pt 3:1–7; 5:1–3; Prv 31:10–12,20,25–30; Ti 2:4–5 **Memory Verse: 1 Pt 4:8.**
3	Ps 103:1–14	Conflict Resolution	Jas 3:14,16; 4:1–3; Prv 15:1; Mt 7:1–5; 5:23–24; 6:14–15; Eph 4:26–27; Gn 50:15–21 **Memory Verse: 1 Pt 4:8**
4	Ps 104:1–18	Communication (I)	Eph 4:15,25–27,29; 1 Pt 3:10; Prv 18:13; 19:20; Jas 1:19; Josh 22:10–31 **Memory Verse: 1 Pt 4:8**
5	Ps 111:1–10	Communication (II)	Prv 10:19,32; 11:13; 13:3; 15:23,28; Col 4:6; Jas 1:26 **Memory Verse: Eph 4:29**
6	Ps 113:1–4	Family of faith	Eph 5:22–6:4; Col 3:18–21; 1 Thes 2:5–12 **Memory Verse: Eph 4:29**
7	Ps 116:1–9	God's plan for marriage	Gn 2:18–25; Prv 5:18; 1 Cor 7:2–5; Mt 19:3–9 **Memory Verse: Eph 4:29**
8	Ps 135:1–7	Tongues: edifying or destroying	Prv 16:24,28; 18:21; Mt 12:36; Jas 1:26; 3:9–12; 1 Pt 3:10; Eph 4:29 **Memory Verse: Eph 4:29**
9	Ps 136:1–9	Forgiveness	Mt 6:14–15; 18:21–35; Rom 12:19; 2 Cor 2:10–11; 5:21; Eph 4:32 **Memory Verse: Eph 4:29**
10	Ps 138:2–6	Children: God's gift	Gn 1:28; 1 Sm 1:1–20,24–28; Ps 127:3–5; 113:9 **Memory Verse: Eph 4:32**

11	Rv 5:6–14	Imitating your Heavenly Father	Dt 26:16–18; Pss 32:8; 56:9; 68:20; Isa 12:1; 49:15–16; Jn 15:9; 2 Cor 1:3–5; He 12:5–11 **Memory Verse: Eph 4:32**
12	Rv 15:3–4	Purpose of parenting: children who glorify God	Dt 6:4–7,13; 11:26–28; 1 Chr 28:9; Ps 115:1 **Memory Verse: Eph 4:32**
13	Isa 40:12–26	Duty of parents: teach children to respect others	Gn 18:18–19; Dt 5:16; 1 Sm 2:12,22–25; 3:11–14; 4:14–17; Col 3:20–21; 1 Tm 3:4 **Memory Verse: Eph 4:32**
14	1 Chr 29:10–17	Commands for parents	Gn 37:3–4; Prv 3:12; 4:1–4; 6:20–23; 22:6; 29:17; 2 Cor 12:14 **Memory Verse: Eph 4:32**

Freedom From Fear Studies

	Worship/ Thanksgiving	Freedom from ...	Verses
1	Ps 139:1–18, 23–24	fear of **evil spirits**	Mt 10:1–8; 28:18; Mk 1:21–39; Eph 1:19–22; Col 1:13–14; 1 Jn 4:4; 5:18 **Memory Verse: 1 Jn 4:4**
2	Ps 144:1–4	fear of **death**	Pss 18:5–7; 23:4; 33:18–22; 116:15; Mt 10:28; Jn 14:1–6; Rom 8:37–39; 1 Cor 15:24–26 **Memory Verse: 1 Jn 4:4**
3	Ps 33:1–11	fear of **final judgment**	Lk 23:39–43; Jn 5:24; 14:1–6; 1 Thes 4:12–18; 1 Pt 3:18; Rv 3:5 **Memory Verse: 1 Jn 4:4**
4	Ps 145	fear of **the future**	1 Kgs 17:8–24; Jer 29:11; Prv 24:13–14; Mt 6:25–34; Heb 13:5–6 **Memory Verse: 1 Jn 4:4**
5	Ps 146	**depression**	Ps 13:1–6; 34:1–8,19; 40:1–4; Mt 5:4; 2 Cor 1:3–11 **Memory Verse: 1 Jn 4:4**
6	Ps 147	**worry**	Ps 55:23,61; Mt 11:28–30; Lk 10:38–42; Phil 4:4–7; 1 Pt 5:6–7 **Memory Verse: Rom 8:28**
7	Ps 148	**hopelessness**	Ps 46; Rom 8:28; 2 Cor 4:7–18; 2 Cor 12:9–10; Phil 4:13; Heb 4:14–16; Jas 1:2–5 **Memory Verse: Rom 8:28**
8	Ps 149	fear of **rejection**	Ps 103; Isa 41:8–10; Jn 1:12; Rom 8:1–2,31–39; 15:7; Eph 1:5,11; 1 Pt 2:9 **Memory Verse: Rom 8:28**
9	Ps 150	**loneliness**	Gn 28:15; Dt 31:6; Jo 1:9; Isa 43:1–3; Jn 14:26–27; Heb 13:5–6 **Memory Verse: Rom 8:28**
10	Lam 3:19–40	feelings of **meaninglessness**	Isa 12:2–3; 41:8–10; 2 Cor 5:17; Ti 2:11–14; 1 Pt 1:3–5; Rv 21:1–4 **Memory Verse: Rom 8:28**
11	Isa 40:12–31	fear the Lord only	Dn 6:6–28, Mt 10:28–33, Acts 5:1–11, Ecc 12:13–14, Pss 31:19, 33:8–9, 103:10–14, 147:11 **Memory Verse: Rom 8:28**

Appendix H:
WORSHIP PATTERNS FOR CHURCHES

Worship (Do one or more of the following.)

- Sing
- Worship through Psalms
- Offer thanksgiving
- Worship God for His various attributes
- Give an offering

Sharing

- Personal Sharing
  - What are you thankful for?
  - What are your struggles?
- Ministry Sharing
  - Share about looking for POPs and the groups you are mentoring
- Variations for Personal Sharing
  - How has God answered prayer for you?
  - What are you trying to apply from God's Word?
  - How is God changing you?
  - How has He helped you this week?
  - What blessings have you received in praying and reading God's Word?
  - What has been your experience in trying to share with others?
  - What practical ways are you trying to serve others?

Prayer

- Praises/Thanksgiving
- Prayer Requests

Word

- Prepare a simple introduction to interest your group in the topic, such as:
  - A story,
  - A personal experience,
  - An example from the community, or
  - A rhetorical question.
- Ask each one how they applied the previous study. (Accountability)
- Read the passage twice. (Practice)
- Have each person retell the passage in their own words. (Practice)
- Act out part of the story, especially if children are present.
- Application
  a. What do you learn about _____ (the current week's topic)?
  b. How can you apply this story to your personal life?
  c. How can you apply this story to help someone else? (Commissioning)
- Ask the Holy Spirit to guide and empower you in obeying this material.

Appendix I:
HEALTHY STANDARDS FOR KINGDOM LIVING

Guided by God's Word, and empowered through the Holy Spirt, CPMs can transform individuals, families, and communities. Yet the physical needs of those among whom we minister can be overwhelming. To address such needs we found it helpful, in collaboration with local partners, to identify inexpensive and reproducible ways to improve the quality of life of those in our movement.

We encourage you to work with the local leaders of your movement to develop similarly reproducible, holistic ways to transform individuals, families, and communities in your own context.

Education
- All my children will finish 12th grade.
- All adults in my household can read.

Nutrition
- We eat balanced meals each day.
- We eat fruit rather than other snacks.

Sanitation
- We wash our hands before eating and cooking, and after using the bathroom.
- We take baths with soap every day.
- We don't eat or drink from the same cups or plates as others.
- We each have our own toothbrush, and use only that one.
- We clean the kitchen every day.
- We clean the bathroom every day.
- We change the water in the bathroom every day.

Healthy Activities
- We do not smoke.
- All my children have their immunizations.

Daily
Each day we each drink eight glasses of water which has been filtered, or boiled for 10 minutes! Tea and coffee don't count, as they draw water from the body rather than replenishing it. (Many headaches are caused by not drinking enough water.)

Weekly
We exercise three or more times per week.

Yearly
We take worm medication once every year.

Insects and Animals:

- We keep all animals, including dogs, cats, and chickens, outside the house. (Animals spread many diseases.)
- We don't let dogs or cats eat off our plates and pans.
- We store food so rats and insects can't reach it.
- We keep flies off our food.
- We keep our toothbrushes covered.
- We avoid animal feces.

Family emotional health

Daily

- Each person gives thanks for one thing.
- We pray together as a family each day.
- We turn off the television at meal times.

Weekly

- We eat a special meal together with just our family.

Monthly

- We go to a place we enjoy as a family

Utilize the yard

- We plant vegetables in our yard, or plants used for traditional medicines.
- We keep our yard clean, putting a fence around our yard if necessary.
- We make our house more beautiful by planting flowers.

Manage your money wisely

- We give 10 percent to God first.
- We next put 10 percent aside for savings and investing.
- We pay our obligations as soon as possible (electric bill, water bill, school fees, motorcycle payment, etc).
- We make a list of what we need at the market/store, and take only enough money to buy those items.
- We don't waste money on gambling, smoking, alcohol, or other drugs.

Appendix J: MUSLIM APOLOGETICS

Muslims believe the Qur'an is inspired. While believers in Jesus would not agree, some find the Qur'an a helpful starting point for countering objections that hinder Muslims from even discussing the Bible.

This appendix equips believers with responses *from the Qur'an* to common Muslim objections (e.g. the death of Jesus on a cross).

While the Qur'an is not inspired, as with any other book we can acknowledge that some of its statements are true without validating the entire book.

When preparing to discuss a verse from the Qur'an with a Muslim, read the verse several times along with the surrounding context so that you are confident of what *you* think it says, then ask questions to determine what they think it means.

In discussion with a Muslim you may find it helpful to introduce verses from the Qur'an with the phrase "Your book says...."

1. Have the Old and New Testament been corrupted?

يَٰٓأَيُّهَا ٱلَّذِينَ ءَامَنُوٓاْ ءَامِنُواْ بِٱللَّهِ وَرَسُولِهِۦ وَٱلۡكِتَٰبِ ٱلَّذِى نَزَّلَ عَلَىٰ رَسُولِهِۦ وَٱلۡكِتَٰبِ ٱلَّذِىٓ أَنزَلَ مِن قَبۡلُ وَمَن يَكۡفُرۡ بِٱللَّهِ وَمَلَٰٓئِكَتِهِۦ وَكُتُبِهِۦ وَرُسُلِهِۦ وَٱلۡيَوۡمِ ٱلۡءَاخِرِ فَقَدۡ ضَلَّ ضَلَٰلَۢا بَعِيدًا ﴿١٣٦﴾

Qur'an 4:136 O you who have believed, believe in Allah and His Messenger and the Book that He sent down upon His Messenger and the Scripture which He sent down before. And whoever disbelieves in Allah, His angels, His books, His messengers, and the Last Day has certainly gone far astray.

The Qur'an says true believers believe in God, His angels, the previous Holy Books, His prophets, and the final judgment. The one who denies these truths is lost, and far from God. This verse says "Believe in the previous books." If they had been changed, this verse would say "Don't believe in the previous books."

وَتَمَّتْ كَلِمَتُ رَبِّكَ صِدْقًا وَعَدْلًا لَّا مُبَدِّلَ لِكَلِمَٰتِهِۦ وَهُوَ ٱلسَّمِيعُ ٱلْعَلِيمُ ﴿١١٥﴾

Qur'an 6:115 And the word of your Lord has been fulfilled in truth and in justice. None can alter His words, and He is the Hearing, the Knowing.[186]

The Qur'an declares that it is impossible for man to change the Words of God. If someone says the Old and New Testament have been corrupted, what they are really saying is "God does not have the power to protect His Word from error." Does it make sense that God would give the Old and New Testament to mankind, and then let man change or corrupt them? God is all powerful, and He gave us the Holy Books to read and obey. He will severely punish the person who tries to change His Words.

وَقَفَّيْنَا عَلَىٰٓ ءَاثَٰرِهِم بِعِيسَى ٱبْنِ مَرْيَمَ مُصَدِّقًا لِّمَا بَيْنَ يَدَيْهِ مِنَ ٱلتَّوْرَىٰةِ وَءَاتَيْنَٰهُ ٱلْإِنجِيلَ فِيهِ هُدًى وَنُورٌ وَمُصَدِّقًا لِّمَا بَيْنَ يَدَيْهِ مِنَ ٱلتَّوْرَىٰةِ وَهُدًى وَمَوْعِظَةً لِّلْمُتَّقِينَ ﴿٤٦﴾

Qur'an 5:46 And We sent, following in their footsteps, Isa, the son of Mary, confirming that which came before him in the Torah; and We gave him the Gospel, in which was guidance and light and confirming that which preceded it of the Torah as guidance and instruction for the righteous.

This verse says 1) Jesus confirmed the Old Testament, 2) He was given the New Testament, and 3) The New Testament is guidance and light for the righteous.

---

[186] Qur'an 6:34 and 10:64.

وَأَنزَلْنَا إِلَيْكَ ٱلْكِتَٰبَ بِٱلْحَقِّ مُصَدِّقًا لِّمَا بَيْنَ يَدَيْهِ مِنَ

ٱلْكِتَٰبِ وَمُهَيْمِنًا عَلَيْهِ فَٱحْكُم بَيْنَهُم بِمَا أَنزَلَ ٱللَّهُ وَلَا

تَتَّبِعْ أَهْوَآءَهُمْ عَمَّا جَآءَكَ مِنَ ٱلْحَقِّ لِكُلٍّ جَعَلْنَا مِنكُمْ شِرْعَةً

وَمِنْهَاجًا وَلَوْ شَآءَ ٱللَّهُ لَجَعَلَكُمْ أُمَّةً وَٰحِدَةً وَلَٰكِن لِّيَبْلُوَكُمْ فِى

مَآ ءَاتَىٰكُمْ فَٱسْتَبِقُوا۟ ٱلْخَيْرَٰتِ إِلَى ٱللَّهِ مَرْجِعُكُمْ جَمِيعًا

فَيُنَبِّئُكُم بِمَا كُنتُمْ فِيهِ تَخْتَلِفُونَ ﴿٤٨﴾

Qur'an 5:48 And We have revealed to you, [O Muhammad], the Book in truth, confirming that which preceded it of the Scripture and as a criterion over it. So judge between them by what Allah has revealed and do not follow their inclinations away from what has come to you of the truth. To each of you We prescribed a law and a method. Had Allah willed, He would have made you one nation [united in religion], but [He intended] to test you in what He has given you; so race to [all that is] good. To Allah is your return all together, and He will [then] inform you concerning that over which you used to differ.

وَهَٰذَا كِتَٰبٌ أَنزَلْنَٰهُ مُبَارَكٌ مُّصَدِّقُ ٱلَّذِى بَيْنَ يَدَيْهِ وَلِتُنذِرَ أُمَّ ٱلْقُرَىٰ

وَمَنْ حَوْلَهَا وَٱلَّذِينَ يُؤْمِنُونَ بِٱلْءَاخِرَةِ يُؤْمِنُونَ بِهِۦ وَهُمْ عَلَىٰ صَلَاتِهِمْ

يُحَافِظُونَ ﴿٩٢﴾

Qur'an 6:92 And this is a Book which We have sent down, blessed and confirming what was before it, that you may warn the Mother of Cities and those around it. Those who believe in the Hereafter believe in it, and they are maintaining their prayers.[187]

Observe that these two verses teach that the Qur'an was given to Muhammad to confirm the Old and New Testament.

---

[187] Qur'an 2:136.

وَإِذَا قِيلَ لَهُمُ ٱتَّبِعُوا مَآ أَنزَلَ ٱللَّهُ قَالُوا بَلْ نَتَّبِعُ مَآ أَلْفَيْنَا عَلَيْهِ ءَابَآءَنَآ
أَوَلَوْ كَانَ ءَابَآؤُهُمْ لَا يَعْقِلُونَ شَيْـًٔا وَلَا يَهْتَدُونَ ﴿١٧٠﴾

Qur'an 2:170 And when it is said to them, "Follow what Allah has revealed," they say, "Rather, we will follow that which we found our fathers doing." Even though their fathers understood nothing, nor were they guided?

Notice that this verse says to follow what God already has revealed. What had God already revealed? The Old and New Testament!

فَإِن كُنتَ فِى شَكٍّ مِّمَّآ أَنزَلْنَآ إِلَيْكَ فَسْـَٔلِ ٱلَّذِينَ يَقْرَءُونَ
ٱلْكِتَٰبَ مِن قَبْلِكَ لَقَدْ جَآءَكَ ٱلْحَقُّ مِن رَّبِّكَ فَلَا تَكُونَنَّ مِنَ
ٱلْمُمْتَرِينَ ﴿٩٤﴾

Qur'an 10:94 So if you are in doubt, [O Muhammad], about that which We have revealed to you, then ask those who have been reading the Scripture before you. The truth has certainly come to you from your Lord, so never be among the doubters.

According to this verse, if Muhammad doubted the revelation given to him, he was to ask the people who had been reading the previous Scripture (the Taurat, Zabur, and Injil). If these books had been corrupted, would it make sense for God to tell Muhammad to ask experts in the Taurat, Zabur, and Injil? If Muhammad had doubts about his calling, then reading books that had been corrupted would have only added to his confusion, not dispelled it.[188]

۞ وَلَا تُجَٰدِلُوٓا أَهْلَ ٱلْكِتَٰبِ إِلَّا بِٱلَّتِى هِىَ أَحْسَنُ إِلَّا ٱلَّذِينَ
ظَلَمُوا مِنْهُمْ وَقُولُوٓا ءَامَنَّا بِٱلَّذِىٓ أُنزِلَ إِلَيْنَا وَأُنزِلَ إِلَيْكُمْ
وَإِلَٰهُنَا وَإِلَٰهُكُمْ وَٰحِدٌ وَنَحْنُ لَهُۥ مُسْلِمُونَ ﴿٤٦﴾

---

[188] This may be the most useful verse to memorize in bridging from the Qur'an to the Bible. If a Muslim disagrees with your interpretation of the Qur'an you can say, "It sounds like there is some doubt or confusion about this. 10:94 says we should look at the 'Before Books' to solve this disagreement. Could we do that together?"

Qur'an 29:46 And do not argue with the People of the Scripture except in a way that is best, except for those who commit injustice among them, and say, "We believe in that which has been revealed to us and revealed to you. And our Allah and your Allah is one; and we are Muslims [in submission] to Him."

Speaking to Jews and Christians, Muhammad said, "Our God and your God are one. We believe in the Scriptures revealed to you, the Old and New Testament, and the Scriptures revealed to us." Why would Muhammad say he believed in the previous Scriptures if they had been corrupted?

Some Muslims claim all the truth of the Old and New Testament has been incorporated into the Qur'an, and that one only needs to read the Qur'an. However, Qur'an 3:50 says to obey Jesus, but not all of Jesus' commands are recorded in the Qur'an. For example, in the New Testament Jesus taught his followers, "But I say to you, Love your enemies and pray for those who persecute you" (Matt. 5:44). This command is not found in the Qur'an. How can we obey Jesus if we don't know His commands? And how will we know His commands unless we read the New Testament?

Furthermore, if the previous Holy Books have been corrupted, then why does the Quran instruct Muhammad and his followers to read them? (See 3:3–4, 18:27, 2:136,170, 3:84, 4:163, 5:43–48,68, 10:94, 17:55, 29:46, 32:23, 42:15.)

Let's summarize the testimony of the Qur'an:

1. The Qur'an instructs Muslims to believe in the previous books, and says those who deny the previous Scriptures have strayed far from God.

2. Man is unable to change the words of God because God is all powerful and guards the integrity of His Word.

3. The Qur'an confirms the previous Scriptures.

4. Muhammad believed in the previous Scriptures.

5. The Qur'an says to obey Jesus.

2. What did Muhammad teach about man's sin?

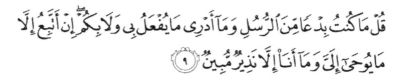

Qur'an 46:9 Say, "I am not something original among the messengers, nor do I know what will be done with me or with you. I only follow that which is revealed to me, and I am not but a clear warner."

What did Muhammad warn people about?

1. Adam and Eve committed sin (Qur'an 7:23; 20:121).

2. Every person who has ever lived has also committed sin (Qur'an 14:34; 29:40; 22:66; 10:44; 16:61; 80:17; 33:72; 12:53).

3. The prophets committed sin
   - Noah (Qur'an 11:47; 71:28),
   - Abraham (Qur'an 26:82; 14:41),
   - Moses (Qur'an 28:15–16),
   - Aaron (Qur'an 20:93),
   - Moses and Aaron (Qur'an 7:151; 26:51),
   - David (Qur'an 38:24),
   - Solomon (Qur'an 38:32,35), and
   - Jonah (Qur'an 21:87; 37:142).

4. Even Muhammad committed sin:

لِيَغْفِرَ لَكَ ٱللَّهُ مَا تَقَدَّمَ مِن ذَنۢبِكَ وَمَا تَأَخَّرَ وَيُتِمَّ نِعْمَتَهُۥ عَلَيۡكَ وَيَهۡدِيَكَ صِرَٰطًا مُّسۡتَقِيمًا ﴿٢﴾

Qur'an 48:2 That Allah may forgive for you what preceded of your sin and what will follow and complete His favor upon you and guide you to a straight path.

فَٱعۡلَمۡ أَنَّهُۥ لَآ إِلَٰهَ إِلَّا ٱللَّهُ وَٱسۡتَغۡفِرۡ لِذَنۢبِكَ وَلِلۡمُؤۡمِنِينَ وَٱلۡمُؤۡمِنَٰتِ وَٱللَّهُ يَعۡلَمُ مُتَقَلَّبَكُمۡ وَمَثۡوَىٰكُمۡ ﴿١٩﴾

Qur'an 47:19 So know, [O Muhammad], that there is no deity except Allah and ask forgiveness for your sin and for the believing men and believing women. And Allah knows of your movement and your resting place.

5. Man must ask forgiveness from God (Qur'an 4:106; 7:23; 14:41; 23:118; 40:55; 47:19; 48:2; 71:28; 110:3).

3. What is the Straight Path?

Qur'an 1 (Al Fatihah) is prayed 17 times every day by devout Muslims.

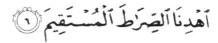

Qur'an 1:6 Guide us to the straight path

And according to Zukhruf 61, Jesus knows and guides in the Straight Path:

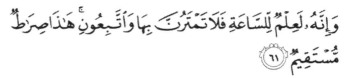

Qur'an 43:61 And indeed, Jesus will be [a sign for] knowledge of the Hour, so be not in doubt of it, and follow Me. This is a straight path.

In fact, the New Testament calls Him the Way.

4. How is the Qur'an consistent with teaching in the Old and New Testament regarding Jesus?

Qur'an 3:42–55:
- Jesus is the foremost in this world, and the next (v 45).
- Jesus was born of a virgin (v 47)
- Jesus has power to perform miracles (v 49).
- We must obey Jesus (v 50).
- Jesus knows the way to heaven (v 55).

5. Why is heeding the signs so important in the Qur'an?

God gave signs to guide mankind to the truth (Qur'an 20:133). Those who disregard the signs will be friends in hell (Qur'an 7:36), and will not go to heaven (Qur'an 7:40). Jesus Christ is a sign from God (Qur'an 3:49); therefore, we must learn from Him.

6. Who is Jesus Christ according to the Qur'an and Bible?

Jesus...	Quran	Bible
... is the Christ (meaning "Messiah" or "Savior")	3:45; 4:157, 171	Lk 2:11
... is a servant of God	4:172; 19:30, 43:59	Mk 10:45
... is a great prophet	19:30	Lk 7:16
... is sent from God	4:157, 171; 5:75	Jn 20:21
... is blessed by God	2:87, 253, 19:31	Mk 11:9
... is guided by the Holy Spirit	3:47; 19:20–21	Mt 4:1
... taught mankind the truth	3:49	Jn 14:6
... is born of a virgin	3:47; 19:20–21	Is 7:14; Lk 1:27
... is called the Word of God	3:45; 4:171, 19:34	Jn 1:1
... is a sign to mankind	19:21; 21:91	Is 49:6; Acts 4:12
... is the mercy of God	3:45, 19:21	Lk 17:13; Rom 6:23
... is foremost in this life and the next	3:45, 3:46; 6:85	Rv 1:8
... never sinned	3:46; 19:19	2 Cor 5:21, Heb 4:15; 7:26
... healed the sick	3:49	Mk 5:21–42
... raised the dead	3:49, 5:110	Jn 11:11–44
... cast out demons	2:253 ("performed signs")	Mk 9:17–27
... rose to heaven after dying, and was raised back to life	3:55, 5:117, 19:33	Acts 1:9–11
... is the Straight Way	1:6, 43:61, 63	Jn 14:6
... forgave sins		Lk 5:20–25; Jn 8:1–12
... will return as the final judge/Imam Mahdi	4:159, 172, 43:61, 63	Acts 17:30–31, Heb 9:28
... must be obeyed; those who don't will be destroyed	3:50; 3:55; 43:63	Dt 18:19; 2 Thes 1:6–10; Heb 10:29–31
... His followers are called Muslims	3:52; 3:55; 5:111	
... takes those who follow Him to heaven when they die		1 Pt 3:18
... is alive and presently in heaven	Surah 3:45, 55, 19:33	Mt 28:1–7, Acts 1:9–11, 1 Cor 15:3–4

7. How in the Qur'an is Jesus different than all other prophets?

a. Only Jesus Christ was born of a virgin.

قَالَتْ رَبِّ أَنَّىٰ يَكُونُ لِى وَلَدٌ وَلَمْ يَمْسَسْنِى بَشَرٌ قَالَ كَذَٰلِكِ ٱللَّهُ يَخْلُقُ مَا يَشَآءُ إِذَا قَضَىٰٓ أَمْرًا فَإِنَّمَا يَقُولُ لَهُۥ كُن فَيَكُونُ ﴿٤٧﴾

Qur'an 3:47 She said, "My Lord, how will I have a child when no man has touched me?" [The angel] said, "Such is Allah; He creates what He wills. When He decrees a matter, He only says to it, 'Be,' and it is.

قَالَتْ أَنَّىٰ يَكُونُ لِى غُلَٰمٌ وَلَمْ يَمْسَسْنِى بَشَرٌ وَلَمْ أَكُ بَغِيًّا ﴿٢٠﴾

قَالَ كَذَٰلِكِ قَالَ رَبُّكِ هُوَ عَلَىَّ هَيِّنٌ وَلِنَجْعَلَهُۥٓ ءَايَةً لِّلنَّاسِ وَرَحْمَةً مِّنَّا وَكَانَ أَمْرًا مَّقْضِيًّا ﴿٢١﴾

۞ فَحَمَلَتْهُ فَٱنتَبَذَتْ بِهِۦ مَكَانًا قَصِيًّا ﴿٢٢﴾

Qur'an 19:20–22 She said, "How can I have a boy while no man has touched me and I have not been unchaste?" He said, "Thus [it will be]; your Lord says, 'It is easy for Me, and We will make him a sign to the people and a mercy from Us. And it is a matter [already] decreed.'" So she conceived him, and she withdrew with him to a remote place.

b. Only Jesus is the Word of God, distinguished both in this world and in the next.

إِذْ قَالَتِ ٱلْمَلَٰٓئِكَةُ يَٰمَرْيَمُ إِنَّ ٱللَّهَ يُبَشِّرُكِ بِكَلِمَةٍ مِّنْهُ ٱسْمُهُ ٱلْمَسِيحُ عِيسَى ٱبْنُ مَرْيَمَ وَجِيهًا فِى ٱلدُّنْيَا وَٱلْءَاخِرَةِ وَمِنَ ٱلْمُقَرَّبِينَ ﴿٤٥﴾

Qur'an 3:45 [And mention] when the angels said, "O Mary, indeed Allah gives you good tidings of a word from Him, whose name will be the Messiah, Isa, the son of Mary — distinguished in this world and the Hereafter and among those brought near [to Allah].

c. Only Jesus was taken up to heaven by God.

$$
\text{إِذْ قَالَ اللَّهُ يَعِيسَىٰ إِنِّي مُتَوَفِّيكَ وَرَافِعُكَ إِلَيَّ وَمُطَهِّرُكَ مِنَ}
$$

$$
\text{الَّذِينَ كَفَرُوا وَجَاعِلُ الَّذِينَ اتَّبَعُوكَ فَوْقَ الَّذِينَ كَفَرُوا إِلَىٰ يَوْمِ}
$$

$$
\text{الْقِيَامَةِ ثُمَّ إِلَيَّ مَرْجِعُكُمْ فَأَحْكُمُ بَيْنَكُمْ فِيمَا كُنتُمْ فِيهِ}
$$

$$
\text{تَخْتَلِفُونَ ﴿٥٥﴾}
$$

Qur'an 3:55 [Mention] when Allah said, "O Jesus, indeed I will take you and raise you to Myself …"

$$
\text{وَالسَّلَامُ عَلَيَّ يَوْمَ وُلِدتُّ وَيَوْمَ أَمُوتُ وَيَوْمَ أُبْعَثُ حَيًّا ﴿٣٣﴾}
$$

Qur'an 19:33 And peace is on me the day I was born and the day I will die and the day I am raised alive.

8. Why do Muslims celebrate Id Al-Adha?

$$
\text{فَلَمَّا بَلَغَ مَعَهُ السَّعْيَ قَالَ يَبُنَيَّ إِنِّي أَرَىٰ فِي الْمَنَامِ أَنِّي أَذْبَحُكَ}
$$

$$
\text{فَانظُرْ مَاذَا تَرَىٰ قَالَ يَأَبَتِ افْعَلْ مَا تُؤْمَرُ سَتَجِدُنِي إِن شَاءَ اللَّهُ}
$$

$$
\text{مِنَ الصَّابِرِينَ ﴿١٠٢﴾}
$$

$$
\text{فَلَمَّا أَسْلَمَا وَتَلَّهُ لِلْجَبِينِ ﴿١٠٣﴾}
$$

$$
\text{وَنَادَيْنَاهُ أَن يَا إِبْرَاهِيمُ ﴿١٠٤﴾}
$$

$$
\text{قَدْ صَدَّقْتَ الرُّؤْيَا إِنَّا كَذَٰلِكَ نَجْزِي الْمُحْسِنِينَ ﴿١٠٥﴾}
$$

$$
\text{إِنَّ هَٰذَا لَهُوَ الْبَلَاءُ الْمُبِينُ ﴿١٠٦﴾}
$$

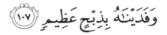

Qur'an 37:102–107 And when he reached with him [the age of] exertion, he said, "O my son, indeed I have seen in a dream that I [must] sacrifice you, so see what you think." He said, "O my father, do as you are commanded. You will find me, if Allah wills, of the steadfast." And when they had both submitted and he put him down upon his forehead, We called to him, "O Abraham, You have fulfilled the vision." Indeed, We thus reward the doers of good. Indeed, this was the clear trial. And We ransomed him with a great sacrifice.

Why did Abraham have to make an offering? According to the Qur'an it was because he was sinful. (Note other prophets who made offerings: Qur'an 14:34; 29:40; 22:66; 10:44; 16:61; 80:17; 33:72; 12:53.)

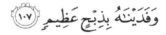

Qur'an 14:41 Our Lord, forgive me and my parents and the believers the Day the account is established.

Why did God demand an offering? Because without the shedding of blood there is no forgiveness of sins (Qur'an 5:27, Heb 9:22). Observe that God Himself provided the sacrifice.

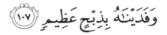

Qur'an 37:107 And We ransomed him with a great sacrifice.

Note that God ransomed Abraham's son with a substitute sacrifice. Where was this place? Abraham was directed to a mountain where present day Jerusalem is located. Many hundreds of years after Abraham, John the Baptist said of Jesus Christ, "Behold, the Lamb of God, who takes away the sin of the world!" (John 1:29). God provided another offering, the person of Jesus Christ, to ransom mankind from their sins. Where did Jesus Christ die? On a mountain where present day Jerusalem is located. It is no coincidence that the place where God ransomed Abraham's son, and the place where God ransomed mankind, are located in the same part of the world.

9. Did someone else die in place of Jesus Christ?

This is a very important question. Let's examine the evidence from the Qur'an.

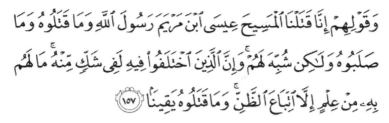

Qur'an 4:157 And [for] their saying, "Indeed, we have killed the Messiah, Isa, the son of Mary, the messenger of Allah." And they did not kill him, nor did they crucify him; but [another] was made to resemble him to them. And indeed, those who differ over it are in doubt about it. They have no knowledge of it except the following of assumption. And they did not kill him, for certain.

This verse has two interpretations:

A. Jesus was not killed but someone resembling him was killed, or

B. Jesus was not killed by the Jews, but by the Romans.

So which interpretation is correct?

Many Islamic scholars disagree with the first interpretation, including Dr. Mahmud Shaltut, a former president of Al-Azhar University: "[It] is entitled in this verse to bear the meaning of ordinary death … there is no way to interpret 'death' as occurring after his [Jesus] return from heaven … because the verse very clearly limits the connection of Jesus … to his own people of his own day and the connection is not with the people living at the time when he returns." [189]

Consider carefully what Dr. Shaltut said. This verse cannot be interpreted to mean Jesus will die upon his return; therefore, Jesus died at the end of his time on earth.

So why do people say someone else died instead of Jesus?

Look again at the Qur'an.

Qur'an 4:157 And [for] their saying, "Indeed, we have killed the Messiah, Isa, the son of Mary, the messenger of Allah." And they did not kill him, nor did they crucify him; but [another] was made to resemble him to them. And indeed, those who differ over it are in

---

[189] *Muslim World*, xxxiv, pp. 214 ff.; as quoted by Parrinder. Geoffery, in *Jesus in the Qur'an*, pp.115–116 (Sheldon Press, London, 1965).

doubt about it. They have no knowledge of it except the following of assumption. And they did not kill him, for certain.

Notice that those who claimed to have killed Jesus were filled with doubts. They didn't know who was killed.

This verse is very difficult to interpret. Even the best Islamic scholars don't agree, as Qur'anic translator Abdullah Yusuf Ali acknowledges: "There is difference of opinion as to the exact interpretation of this verse." [190] However, there are many other verses in the Qur'an which are clear. Consider the following verses:

1. *God killed Jesus Christ.*

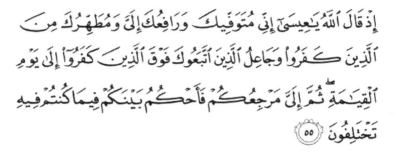

Qur'an 3:55 Thus, Allah said "O Isa, I am terminating your life, raising you to Me and ridding you of the disbelievers ...." [191]

Some translators ignore the clear statement of the Qur'an that Isa died and instead translate common beliefs. However in 4:157 the Qur'an tells us the Jews did not kill Isa. So who did? Here in 3:55 the Qur'an uses the Arabic word *mutawaffeeka* to say clearly that Allah killed Isa. This Arabic word means "terminating your life," and comes from the root word *tawaffa*, meaning "to cause to die." Forms of this verb occur 25 times in the Qur'an in various forms. Twice (here and 5:117) it refers to Isa and is often mistranslated to reflect common beliefs. However everywhere else in the Qur'an it is translated properly as indicating death. [192] Even today, variants of *tawaffa* are used

---

[190] *The meaning of the holy Qur'an,* translated by Abdullah Yusuf Ali, footnote 664 (Kazi Publications (October 1995).

[191] *Qur'an: The Final Testament* translated by Rashad Khalifa (Tucson, AZ; Universal Unity; 3rd edition, January 2001).

[192] 2:234,240, 3:193, 4:15,97, 6:60,61, 7:37,126, 8:50, 10:46,104, 12:101, 13:40, 16:28,32,70, 22:5, 32:11, 39:42, 40:67,77, 47:27

euphemistically to mean "to pass away," and the Arabic word for "obituaries" is from the same root.[193]

2. If John the Baptist died, then Jesus Christ also died.

According to the Qur'an, John the Baptist died:

$$وَسَلَـٰمٌ عَلَيْهِ يَوْمَ وُلِدَ وَيَوْمَ يَمُوتُ وَيَوْمَ يُبْعَثُ حَيًّا ﴿١٥﴾$$

Qur'an 19:15 And peace be upon him the day he was born and the day he dies and the day he is raised alive.

The exact same expression describes Jesus Christ's death.

$$وَالسَّلَـٰمُ عَلَيَّ يَوْمَ وُلِدتُّ وَيَوْمَ أَمُوتُ وَيَوْمَ أُبْعَثُ حَيًّا ﴿٣٣﴾$$

Qur'an 19:33 And peace is on me the day I was born and the day I will die and the day I am raised alive.

There is no difference in the Arabic in these two verses except the pronouns ("he" and "I"). Commenting on these two verses, noted Muslim scholar A. H. Obaray writes, "No Muslim will shift the death of John to the future. All know that John died .... Since no one can now shift the death of John to the future, therefore no one can shift the death of Jesus to the future. In fact, there is not one single passage throughout the Qur'an showing that Jesus will return to die. The parallel statement with regard to John, who died, clearly shows that Jesus also died." [194]

If John died (Qur'an 19:15) then Jesus also died (Qur'an 19:33).

---

[193] Kevin Greesan—author of *The Camel: How Muslims Are Coming to Faith in Christ!* (WIGTake Resources, 2007)—reports, "Maulana Wahiduddin Khan's first edition in 2010 of his widely used English translation of the Qur'an translated *mutawaffeeka*, 'cause to die.' In his second edition, also in 2010, he changed the translation to 'take.' When I asked him in person 'Why did you make this change?' his reply was, 'I was pressured to do so.' When I asked him, 'Which is correct?' he replied, 'The first edition is correct.'" *Mutawaffeeka* is also translated "cause to die" by Palmer, Rodwell, Saleh, and ReferenceQuran.com

[194] *Miraculous Conception, Death, Resurrection, and Ascension of Jesus in the Qur'an* by A.H. Obaray, p. 45 (Kimberley, South Africa; published by the author, 1962).

3. We know from the word order in Qur'an 19:33 that Jesus died.

$$\text{وَٱلسَّلَـٰمُ عَلَيَّ يَوْمَ وُلِدتُّ وَيَوْمَ أَمُوتُ وَيَوْمَ أُبْعَثُ حَيًّا ۝}$$

Qur'an 19:33 And peace is on me the day I was born and the day I will die and the day I am raised alive.

All Muslims know Jesus was born and was raised to heaven by God. If Jesus hasn't died yet, why does the Qur'an say Jesus was born, died, and raised? The order of these words is very important. If Jesus were to die after being raised, the order would be: was born, was raised, and will die. But the order in this verse is: was born, died, and was raised. Since we know Jesus was born and was raised, the word order proves Jesus died.

The Qur'an itself says in the next verse that the words ascribed to Jesus in 19:33 are true:[195]

$$\text{ذَٰلِكَ عِيسَى ٱبْنُ مَرْيَمَ قَوْلَ ٱلْحَقِّ ٱلَّذِى فِيهِ يَمْتَرُونَ ۝}$$

Qur'an 19:34 That is Isa, the son of Mary — the word of truth about which they are in dispute.

4. The Jews killed the prophets.

Prophets were sent by God to warn mankind concerning their sins. These prophets were frequently persecuted by those who rejected their message. Some of these prophets were even killed.

$$\text{لَّقَدْ سَمِعَ ٱللَّهُ قَوْلَ ٱلَّذِينَ قَالُوٓا۟ إِنَّ ٱللَّهَ فَقِيرٌ وَنَحْنُ أَغْنِيَآءُ}$$

$$\text{سَنَكْتُبُ مَا قَالُوا۟ وَقَتْلَهُمُ ٱلْأَنۢبِيَآءَ بِغَيْرِ حَقٍّ وَنَقُولُ ذُوقُوا۟}$$

$$\text{عَذَابَ ٱلْحَرِيقِ ۝}$$

$$\text{ذَٰلِكَ بِمَا قَدَّمَتْ أَيْدِيكُمْ وَأَنَّ ٱللَّهَ لَيْسَ بِظَلَّامٍ لِّلْعَبِيدِ ۝}$$

---

[195] While we don't ascribe or want to imply inspiration in the Quran, we can let the Qur'an point the Muslim who doesn't yet believe in Jesus toward the Bible.

$$\text{ٱلَّذِينَ قَالُوٓاْ إِنَّ ٱللَّهَ عَهِدَ إِلَيْنَآ أَلَّا نُؤْمِنَ لِرَسُولٍ حَتَّىٰ}$$

$$\text{يَأْتِيَنَا بِقُرْبَانٍ تَأْكُلُهُ ٱلنَّارُ قُلْ قَدْ جَآءَكُمْ رُسُلٌ مِّن قَبْلِي}$$

$$\text{بِٱلْبَيِّنَٰتِ وَبِٱلَّذِي قُلْتُمْ فَلِمَ قَتَلْتُمُوهُمْ إِن كُنتُمْ}$$

$$\text{صَٰدِقِينَ ﴿١٨٣﴾}$$

Qur'an 3:181–183 Allah has certainly heard the statement of those [Jews] who said, "Indeed, Allah is poor, while we are rich." We will record what they said and their killing of the prophets without right and will say, "Taste the punishment of the Burning Fire. That is for what your hands have put forth and because Allah is not ever unjust to [His] servants. [They are] those who said, "Indeed, Allah has taken our promise not to believe any messenger until he brings us an offering which fire [from heaven] will consume." Say, "There have already come to you messengers before me with clear proofs and [even] that of which you speak. So why did you kill them, if you should be truthful?[196]

$$\text{فَبِمَا نَقْضِهِم مِّيثَٰقَهُمْ وَكُفْرِهِم بِـَٔايَٰتِ ٱللَّهِ وَقَتْلِهِمُ ٱلْأَنۢبِيَآءَ بِغَيْرِ حَقٍّ}$$

$$\text{وَقَوْلِهِمْ قُلُوبُنَا غُلْفٌۢ بَلْ طَبَعَ ٱللَّهُ عَلَيْهَا بِكُفْرِهِمْ فَلَا يُؤْمِنُونَ إِلَّا}$$

$$\text{قَلِيلًا ﴿١٥٥﴾}$$

Qur'an 4:155 And [We cursed them] for their breaking of the covenant and their disbelief in the signs of Allah and their killing of the prophets without right and their saying, "Our hearts are wrapped." Rather, Allah has sealed them because of their disbelief, so they believe not, except for a few.

Muhammad himself was persecuted by the people of Mecca who rejected his message. Jesus was similarly persecuted, and even killed, by those who rejected his message. These verses prove God permits His prophets to be killed. In the case of Jesus, he was arrested by the Jews, then given to the Romans to be killed.

---

[196] Qur'an 2:61, 2:87, 2:91, 3:21, 3:112, 3:181, 3:183,5:70, 8:17.

5. Jesus was commanded to give zakat as long as he remained alive.

وَجَعَلَنِي مُبَارَكًا أَيْنَ مَا كُنتُ وَأَوْصَنِي بِالصَّلَوٰةِ وَالزَّكَوٰةِ مَا دُمْتُ حَيًّا ﴿٣١﴾

Qur'an 19:31 And He has made me blessed wherever I am and has enjoined upon me prayer and zakah[197] as long as I remain alive.

If Jesus didn't die, he remains alive in heaven. Abdullah Yusuf Ali writes, "One school holds that Jesus did not die the usual human death but still lives in the body in heaven which is the generally accepted Muslim view." [198] If he is alive, he is in heaven and still giving zakat. But who is he giving zakat to since there are no poor people in heaven? This verse only makes sense if Jesus died.

6. Id Al-Adha commemorates God ransoming the son of Abraham.

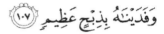

وَفَدَيْنَٰهُ بِذِبْحٍ عَظِيمٍ ﴿١٠٧﴾

Qur'an 37:107 And We ransomed him with a great sacrifice.

God ransomed the son of Abraham with a great sacrifice. God also ransomed mankind with a great sacrifice. In the same area where God provided a sacrifice for Abraham's son, God provided the perfect sacrifice for man's sins, the person of Jesus Christ.

In conclusion, one verse of the Qur'an (Qur'an 4:157) seems to imply Jesus didn't die; however Islamic scholars don't agree in interpreting this verse. On the other hand, at least six passages in the Qur'an support the death of Jesus.

Let's review these:

1. God killed Jesus Christ (Qur'an 3:55, 5:117).

2. Qur'an 19:15 and Qur'an 19:33 state that John and Jesus died.

3. We know Jesus Christ died because of the word order in Qur'an 19:33. He was born, died, and was raised.

---

[197] Alternate spelling for *zakat.*

[198] *The Holy Qur'an: English Translation and Commentary,* translated by Abdullah Yusuf Ali, footnote 664 (Kazi Publications, October 1995).

4. Many prophets were persecuted, including Muhammad, and some were even killed (Qur'an 2:87,91; 3:112,181–183).

5. Jesus was commanded to give zakat as long as he lived (Qur'an 19:31). If he didn't die he would still be giving zakat in heaven.

6. According to Qur'an 37:102–107, God ransomed Abraham's son. God ransomed mankind through the sacrifice of Jesus Christ in the same place.

10. Is there additional evidence Jesus Christ died?

Yes:

1. Proof from historical evidence.

There is strong historical evidence Jesus was put to death by the Romans.

2. Proof from the New Testament.

Many verses in Matthew, Mark, Luke, and John teach that Jesus Christ was crucified by the Romans, and the New Testament can be trusted because no one can change God's Word (Qur'an 3:3–4; 4:136; 6:115).

3. Further proof from the Qur'an.

The Qur'an says the disciples asked for a sign from God that what Jesus taught was true, and God provided this sign by giving a table from heaven.

قَالَ عِيسَى ٱبْنُ مَرْيَمَ ٱللَّهُمَّ رَبَّنَا أَنزِلْ عَلَيْنَا مَآئِدَةً مِّنَ ٱلسَّمَآءِ تَكُونُ لَنَا عِيدًا لِّأَوَّلِنَا وَءَاخِرِنَا وَءَايَةً مِّنكَ وَٱرْزُقْنَا وَأَنتَ خَيْرُ ٱلرَّزِقِينَ ۝

قَالَ ٱللَّهُ إِنِّي مُنَزِّلُهَا عَلَيْكُمْ فَمَن يَكْفُرْ بَعْدُ مِنكُمْ فَإِنِّي أُعَذِّبُهُۥ عَذَابًا لَّآ أُعَذِّبُهُۥٓ أَحَدًا مِّنَ ٱلْعَٰلَمِينَ ۝

Qur'an 5:114–115 Said Isa, the son of Mary, "O Allah, our Lord, send down to us a table [spread with food] from the heaven to be for us a festival for the first of us and the last of us and a sign from You. And provide for us, and You are the best of providers." Allah said, "Indeed, I will send it down to you, but whoever disbelieves afterwards from among you

— then indeed will I punish him with a punishment by which I have not punished anyone among the worlds."

The New Testament says that on the day before He died, Jesus ate a special meal with his disciples[199] to commemorate His death.[200] The Qur'an calls this meal a "sign," and tells us those who disbelieve this sign will be punished with a punishment greater than any other punishment. The table commemorates Jesus's death. Why would God send the table down if Jesus didn't die?

Throughout history Jesus' followers have commemorated His death by participating in this table, which the New Testament calls the Lord's Supper. A terrifying punishment awaits those who reject this sign from God.

4. Proof from blood

The New Testament states, "… without the shedding of blood there is no forgiveness of sins" (Heb. 9:22). Cultures all over the world have historically made offerings by shedding animal blood. This widespread practice reflects widespread awareness of the biblical truth that blood must be shed for mankind to receive forgiveness of sins.

Every year Muslims offer a sacrifice called Id Al-Adha, in which they commemorate Abraham's willingness to offer his son before God provided a ram for the sacrifice. This animal's blood was shed, and not Abraham's son's.

All of the prophets made offerings except one. Jesus Christ never made an offering because He Himself was the offering. He lived a holy life; He never committed a single sin. Of every person who ever lived only His blood is holy, therefore only He could become the sacrifice for mankind's sin. He shed His blood so that we might receive forgiveness of our sins. If Jesus didn't die on the cross, there is no sacrifice for sins. But He did die, therefore He alone can forgive sins, because He alone shed His blood after living a sinless life.

Let's summarize all the evidence:

1. Proof from strong historical evidence that the Romans killed Jesus.

2. Proof from the many verses in the New Testament.

3. Proof from at least six passages in the Qur'an.

4. Proof from ceremonies involving blood:
   - Heb. 9:22, "… without the shedding of blood there is no forgiveness of sins."
   - Muslims shed animal blood every year for Id Al-Adha.
   - Only Jesus' blood is holy, so only Jesus could shed His blood for mankind's sin.

---

[199] Matt. 26–29, Mark 14:22–25, Luke 22:17–20

[200] 1 Cor. 11:23–26

- If Jesus didn't die, His blood was not shed. And if His blood was not shed, there is no forgiveness of sins.

These four proofs speak with one voice, all affirming that Jesus Christ died.

11. Jesus' followers are called Muslims

فَلَمَّآ أَحَسَّ عِيسَىٰ مِنْهُمُ ٱلْكُفْرَ قَالَ مَنْ أَنصَارِىٓ إِلَى ٱللَّهِ ۖ قَالَ ٱلْحَوَارِيُّونَ نَحْنُ أَنصَارُ ٱللَّهِ ءَامَنَّا بِٱللَّهِ وَٱشْهَدْ بِأَنَّا مُسْلِمُونَ ٥٢

Qur'an 3:52 But when Jesus felt [persistence in] disbelief from them, he said, "Who are my supporters for [the cause of] Allah?" The disciples said, "We are supporters for Allah. We have believed in Allah and testify that we are Muslims [submitting to Him]."

إِذْ قَالَ ٱللَّهُ يَٰعِيسَىٰٓ إِنِّى مُتَوَفِّيكَ وَرَافِعُكَ إِلَىَّ وَمُطَهِّرُكَ مِنَ ٱلَّذِينَ كَفَرُوا۟ وَجَاعِلُ ٱلَّذِينَ ٱتَّبَعُوكَ فَوْقَ ٱلَّذِينَ كَفَرُوٓا۟ إِلَىٰ يَوْمِ ٱلْقِيَٰمَةِ ۖ ثُمَّ إِلَىَّ مَرْجِعُكُمْ فَأَحْكُمُ بَيْنَكُمْ فِيمَا كُنتُمْ فِيهِ تَخْتَلِفُونَ ٥٥

Qur'an 3:55 [Mention] when Allah said, "O Jesus, indeed I will take you and raise you to Myself and purify you from those who disbelieve and make those who follow you [in submission to Allah alone] superior to those who disbelieve until the Day of Resurrection. Then to Me is your return, and I will judge between you concerning that in which you used to differ."

وَإِذْ أَوْحَيْتُ إِلَى ٱلْحَوَارِيِّـۧنَ أَنْ ءَامِنُوا۟ بِى وَبِرَسُولِى قَالُوٓا۟ ءَامَنَّا وَٱشْهَدْ بِأَنَّنَا مُسْلِمُونَ ١١١

Qur'an 5:111 And [remember] when I inspired to the disciples, "Believe in Me and in My messenger Jesus." They said, "We have believed, so bear witness that indeed we are Muslims [in submission to Allah]."

GLOSSARY

Access Business
Any business that multiplies personal interaction with non-believers, such as through door-to-door sales

Access Ministry
Any ministry that addresses community needs through personal contact with many lost people

al hamdulilah
Arabic: "Praise be to God"

Allah
Arabic: "God" (All Muslims call the creator of heaven and earth by this name; from before Muhammad's birth to this very day, Arabic-speaking Christians have used this name for God)

Allahu akbar
Arabic: "God is great"

arisan
Indonesian: monthly neighborhood meeting

assalam wa'alikum
Arabic: "peace be unto you"

assalam wa'alikum wa rahmatullahi wa barakatuh
Arabic: "peace be unto you, with the mercy of Allah and His blessings"

bismillahi
Arabic: "in the name of Allah"

bismillahi arrahmani arrahim
Arabic: "in the name of Allah, the most gracious and most merciful" (This first verse of the Qur'an is repeated frequently in the Qur'an, and in Muslim daily prayers)

Camel Method
Uses Qur'an 3:40–55 as a bridge to talk about Isa Al Masih. See *The Camel: How Muslims Are Coming to Faith in Christ!* by Kevin Greeson (WIGTake Resources, 2007)

chronological Bible stories
Stories discussed in chronological order to increase depth of understanding and retention

church-planting movement (CPM)
A rapidly reproducing movement of disciples making new disciples, leaders equipping new leaders, and churches planting new indigenous churches, which transforms individuals, families, and communities by the power of the Holy Spirit within a population group — a people group, city, province, or nation

church-planting *Kingdom* movement
A CPM which integrates a more comprehensive emphasis on transforming individuals, families, and their communities

Creation to Christ
A brief overview of the Bible story, presenting the gospel along with the context for Christ's sacrificial death and resurrection. Many variants are in wide use by CPM practitioners

DBS
Discovery Bible Study is an inductive approach in which the Holy Spirit helps participants discover Truth as a facilitator leads them to consider questions regarding the text, with no one "teaching"

Discovery group
A gathering of non-believers to discuss chronological Bible stories. See DBS

Ekklesia
Greek: any gathering of believers seeking to follow Jesus

Hadith
Traditional commentaries on the Qur'an

haji
Muslim title of respect for a man who has made the pilgrimage to Mecca

hajja
Muslim title of respect for a woman who has made the pilgrimage to Mecca

house church/fellowship
An oikos which fulfills the functions of *ekklesia* found in the New Testament: covenanting together to study and obey God's Word, especially in baptism, worship, fellowship, prayer, communion, giving, and witness/ministry

Idul Fitri
Arabic: two-day holiday following Ramadan

imam
Islamic leader or teacher

Injil
Qur'anic: Gospels or New Testament (Gospel of Jesus)

Isa Al Masih
Arabic: Jesus Christ

jinn
Qur'anic: Identified in the Qur'an as spirit beings with free will, different from humans, angels, and demons

Kaaba
Arabic: the holiest site in Islam

Kalimatullah
Arabic for a word (or the Word) of God

keris
Indonesian: A sword believed to have power to protect the family

Kholdi
Qur'anic name for the tree of the knowledge of good and evil

magrib
Arabic for the fourth daily prayer of Muslims, around sunset

mosque
Muslim place of worship

oikos
Greek: "household" — a family or group of close friends

oikos leader
A leader raised up from within the household

pbuh
Devout Muslims generally say "peace be upon him" after mentioning Muhammad. In writing this is sometimes abbreviated "pbuh" or "SAW"

peci
traditional Indonesian hat

people group
A group with a shared sense of identity, in which a CPM could spread

person of peace
A person who receives the gospel messenger, and opens his household or community to this messenger. In other words, the person of peace opens a door to an oikos. This person is not necessarily a peaceful person, but is looking for peace (Mt 10:11, Lk 10:6)

personal salvation story
a) Your life before coming to Christ (your felt needs and prior misconceptions about God),
b) Your process of committing your life to Christ (what convinced you to follow Christ), and
c) Your life after coming to Christ (your joys and difficulties)

Qur'an
Arabic: "recitation" (Muslims are taught that the Qur'an has existed unchanged throughout eternity, and was revealed to Muhammad who faithfully recited it)

Ramadan
Holy month of daily community fasting from dawn to sunset

sarong
Indonesian: a one-piece cloth worn around the waist

SAW
Abbreviation used in translating the Qur'an for the Arabic version of "pbuh": "salle alaa hu alaihi wa sallim"

Sayang
"Beloved" in Indonesian; a fictional Indonesian Muslim unreached people group

shema statements
Spiritual comments made intentionally and naturally in conversation

Syawal
An extra six days of fasting after Ramadan, observed by especially devoted Muslims

Taurat
Qur'anic: Torah or Old Testament (Books of Moses)

tawaffa
Arabic: "to die"

unreached people group
A people group without a well established CPM. Alternately: a people group with less than 2% believers (considered inadequate to evangelize the rest of their group)

wa alikum salam
Arabic: "and peace be unto you", (the normal response to assalam wa'alikum)

Wa alikum salam rahmatullahi wa barakatuh
Arabic: "and peace be unto you, with the mercy of Allah and His blessings"

wajeeh
Arabic for distinguished, as Moses was in this world, and only Isa is in the next world

Zabur
Qur'anic: Psalms (Books of David)

Zakiy
Arabic for sinless, applied in the Qur'an only to Isa

For Further Training

For coaching in applying the principles in this book to pursue God for a church-planting kingdom movement in your own context:
- visit beyond.org/events
- email training@beyond.org or
- call 469–814–8222.

Women seeking to apply these principles will value these resources compiled by my wife, R. Nyman:
- WomenInChurchPlantingMovements.blogspot.com
- the Jan/Feb 2016 issue of *Mission Frontiers*

Extensive additional resources are available
- in the appendices, and
- at StubbornPerseverance.com

James Nyman

Since the early 1990s my wife and I have been seeking to reach Muslim Unreached People Groups (UPGs) in Indonesia. In the beginning we used a strategy of evangelism, discipleship, small groups, and leadership development we learned in college through our involvement with Campus Crusade for Christ (CCC).

In 1999, we read and incorporated David Garrison's booklet *Church Planting Movements*. That same year, we began using chronological Bible stories.

In 2002, we attended a CPM workshop lead by David Watson. We began using his discovery questions with his chronological Bible stories. Working with twenty-five Indonesian colleagues from 1997–2008, we saw about twenty people come to the Lord and start a few churches in their homes, but we weren't seeing the new believers start additional groups or raise up local leaders.

In 2004, we attended a second CPM training by David Watson.

In 2008, as part of my D.Min. studies through Trinity Evangelical Divinity School, I studied twenty-two forms of Chronological Bible Storying (CBS), the vast majority of which were CPM-oriented, including several versions of Training for Trainers (T4T). Variants studied included the "textbook" version, "storying T4T" and T4RT (Training for Rural Trainers). I was pleased to find our college experience with CCC had already guided us to incorporate most of T4T's underlying principles from the start of our ministry. One thing I gained from this study was a conviction that chronological Bible stories studied in a discovery format could be effective in launching CPMs among UPGs.

As part of my 2008 studies, I also conducted a worldview study of our target people and then developed a chronological Bible story series with the goal of facilitating a CPM among them. I field tested this story set for two years through interviews and written reports from field workers.

In 2009, we took Stan Parks' three week CPM course. Then as part of our field research, we held a retreat for our twenty-five Indonesian colleagues in which we re-taught CPM principles. We challenged them to form discovery groups (DGs) to study chronological Bible stories. Five of our leaders dropped out, but each of the remaining twenty eventually started at least one DG.

DGs either become house churches or disband. Several of these first DGs did not continue beyond the end of 2010. But at the end of 2012, we had sixteen DGs.

At the end of 2013, we had thirty-four DGs and fourteen house churches, including two second-generation house churches, a third-generation house church, and a fourth-generation DG.

At the end of 2014, we had thirty-three DGs, and two new house fellowships to replace two that had disbanded, for a total of fourteen churches meeting in homes.

As of this writing, my wife and I are formally or informally coaching eleven missionary teams. We have trained over 600 workers in the United States and internationally.

Robby Butler

In late 1979 Robby was preparing to become a "tentmaker" behind the Iron Curtain, studying Russian and computer programming. Then he realized the missionary task could be completed in his lifetime, and God used this discovery to lead him into mission strategy and mobilization.

In 1980 Robby joined the U.S. Center for World Mission (USCWM, now Frontier Ventures), and graduated from the California Institute of Technology (Caltech) just a few months later. In his twenty-four years with the USCWM he served in the computer department, as personal assistant to Ralph Winter, and as personnel director. He also assisted a wide range of ministries including the Lausanne and AD2000 movements, *Mission Frontiers*, and Perspectives.

While at the USCWM, Robby developed relationships with pioneering leaders around the globe from whom he continues to learn and distill strategic insights.

Since 2004 Robby has served the mission community through *Mission Network*, a service agency to link Christ's body with proven insights for multiplied effectiveness in advancing God's Kingdom. He has continued serving the Perspectives network in various ways, and also played a key role in refining and publishing Steve Smith's *No Place Left* saga. Since 2010 Robby has volunteered significantly with *Mission Frontiers*, supporting its emphasis on movements.

Robby's vision is to accelerate the shift God is bringing about in sending-base churches—from primarily ministering *to* their members to *equipping* their members to seek God for movements at home (thereby preparing laborers with skills and experience for greater fruitfulness among the unreached and unengaged).

Robby and his wife Jackie live in Mount Vernon, WA with their three children J, D and W.

Forthcoming Editions

This *Study Edition* includes chapter discussion questions, extended appendices, and the Arabic for most references to the Qur'an.

If there is sufficient interest, we anticipate also producing a shorter *Story Edition* of this book, removing the Arabic images and moving the discussion questions and longer appendices into a companion *Study Guide*.

Also anticipated are a series of shorter booklets:

1. *Starting a CPM* (Faisal builds a team)
2. *Beginning with Friends/Family* (Ahmad and Hasan)
3. *Engaging Muslims* (Haji Ishmael, Sharif, Abdullah)
4. *Thorough Transformation* (Inne, Eka, Aysha, Wati)
5. *Developing Church Leaders* (Faisal and the team)

Sign up for promotional discounts and new release information at

eepurl.com/beXiv9

Extensive additional resources are available at

StubbornPerseverance.com

James Nyman and his wife serve with Act Beyond

BEYOND

Vision:

All Unreached People Groups (ethnê) reached.
Jesus' Command to make disciples of all nations (ethnê) fulfilled.
(Hab 2:14; Lk 4:18–19; Mt 24.14, 28.19–20; Rv 5:9, 7:9)

Mission:

We start Church-Planting Movements to transform unreached people groups — where obedient disciples make obedient disciples and reproducing churches start reproducing churches — which make Jesus known while transforming lives, relationships, and communities.

Made in the USA
San Bernardino, CA
26 February 2016